White-winged Dove and Gila Woodpecker
quarreling over the ripe fruit of a saguaro cactus
near Tucson, Arizona

National Geographic Guide to

Birdwatching
Sites

Western U.S.

By Mel White

NATIONAL
GEOGRAPHIC
WASHINGTON D.C.

Preceding pages: American White Pelicans cruising the Snake River in Grand Teton National Park, Wyoming
Above: Western Tanager
Right: Temperate rain forest in Olympic National Park, Washington

Contents

Your Guide to the Guide

Curiosity may have killed the cat, but it's given many a casual feeder-watcher a whole new life as an avid birder. "What's that yellow-and-black bird with the big bill eating my sunflower seeds?" you wonder. Or, "What kind of bird is that little brown thing I saw climbing a tree like a miniature woodpecker?"

So there's a trip to the bookstore, and a first field guide. The mystery bird gets a name, and for some that's enough; the guide goes on the shelf, neglected until the next stranger arrives in the backyard. Others, though, will find more questions in those colorful pages of previously unheard-of species. Who knew there were so many kinds of sparrows? You mean there are gulls that nest in the prairies? Where can I see some of these pretty little birds called warblers?

Then comes a phone call to a bird-watching friend and an early morning walk in a nearby park. At the end of the day, you've seen 50 or 60 species—more than you would have thought possible when your identifications went no further than hawk, gull, or finch. "This is nothing," your friend says. "If we put some effort into it, we could find a hundred species in a day around here, easy."

A few experiences like this and you realize that there are lots of birds to be seen in the right places. And now you'd better be careful. Next thing you know, you'll be planning your vacations around spring migration at Texas' Big Bend National Park, or fall at Point Reyes National Seashore in California.

How This Guide Works In this book you'll find more than 350 of the right places to go bird-watching in the western contiguous United States, from the Hill Country of Texas to North Dakota, from San Diego to Washington's San Juan Islands. (This

volume doesn't cover Hawaii or Alaska because of the unique and disparate bird life of the former and the logistical complications of travel in the latter; see the bibliography for suggested references for these states.) In consultation with local birders, we've chosen some of the top sites in each state: city and state parks, national wildlife refuges, national forests, nature preserves, lakes and marshes, and in some cases something as unstructured as a particularly productive stretch of beach or road.

The text presents a short description of each area and a list of a few of the most typical or notable species found there. It's the nature of books like this that only the highlights can be covered: Many regionally common birds—

A flock of shorebirds including Short-billed Dowitchers and Dunlins on the California coast

say, Song Sparrow or Bewick's Wren, or Western Gull along the coast—will go unremarked, while rarities and locally scarce species receive disproportionate coverage. After all, it's the chance to find an unusual species, or one you've never seen before (a "life bird"), that entices birders to visit new places.

If you're new to this business of traveling to see birds, remember that birds travel, too. Some sites are rewarding year-round, while others are at their best only in nesting season or winter, or in spring and fall migration.

States are grouped into chapters by region, with sites throughout each state arranged in a logical flow. Site numbers are keyed to the map at the beginning of each chapter, to aid you in finding your way from one site to the next (sites near one another occasionally share the same number). Throughout the book sidebars feature species of regional interest, as well as ideas for the traveling birder.

At the end of each chapter we've included information

about the sites that can help you plan your trip. First, you'll find telephone numbers of rare bird alerts. These are recorded messages, updated frequently, that list unusual species seen in a state or locality, often with directions to sites or numbers to call for more information. When you arrive in Tucson, for instance, to begin your birding tour of southeastern Arizona, you should call the hot line there to learn about any rarities in the area. In fact, many birders start calling the hot line for their destination several days before a visit to aid in trip planning. (It goes without saying that you should call your home rare bird alert regularly to keep up with what's being seen locally.) This section also includes mailing addresses and telephone numbers of the sites or their administrative offices, so you can call or write ahead for additional information. Symbols indicate facilities available at each site, although be advised that these can be seasonal or limited.

At the end of the guide, we've included a bibliography of some of the many excellent state and local bird-finding guides now available. As you become more experienced and serious about birding, these guides can take you to more sites in your own region and in the places you visit. Many parts of the United States are covered by these guides, and their number is growing each year.

A Few Other Ideas

New birders should first of all join their local National Audubon Society chapter or birding club. On field trips, and with advice from experienced birders, you'll begin to learn the species in your area and the best places to find them. The study of migration patterns, habitats, and abundance provides endless opportunity for discovery no matter where you live, and amateurs can contribute to ornithological knowledge with conscientious observation and record keeping. You'll soon discover the fun and challenge of spring "big days" and Christmas bird counts, wherein birding becomes a bit more structured and even competitive (even if only with yourself).

The leading national organization for bird-watchers is the American Birding Association, or ABA (800-850-2473), with headquarters in Colorado Springs, Colorado. The ABA publishes a bimonthly magazine, Birding, and a

Adult Bald Eagle perched on irrigation equipment at Lower Klamath National Wildlife Refuge in northern California

monthly newsletter, *Winging It*, with articles on many aspects of birding, from identification to destinations. Many ABA members are involved in the sporting side of birding, in which the object is to see as many species as possible in a defined geographic area, or in a given period of time. This is certainly not a requirement, though, and many other members watch birds just for fun.

One of the benefits of ABA is its membership guide, published annually, which lists thousands of birders all over the country who are willing to provide advice to travelers, and in many cases even to guide visitors to good birding sites in their home regions. If you join ABA, don't be shy about asking for help either by telephone or letter. Birders are by and large a friendly bunch who enjoy talking about their favorite places, and one inquiry to the right person could save you hours of driving or hiking in search of that elusive species you're determined to find.

The Internet increasingly offers another source of birding information. All around the country, bird clubs and ornithological societies are setting up web sites, many of which offer guides to birding spots, lists of local contacts,

and schedules of field trips. One place to start your search is the National Audubon Society *(www.audubon.org)*; check here for local chapters in the area you'll be visiting. Chapter sites will often have links to other regional birding web sites, which will have links to other sites. . .and so forth. Or you can use a search engine, inquiring about something as specific as "Bosque del Apache National Wildlife Refuge" (many parks and refuges now have maps and bird lists on-line) or as general as "birding+Kansas."

If you're a beginner, or even if you're not, consider attending one of the many birding festivals held annually around the country. Most feature programs and field trips led by experts, often concentrating on regional specialties. As more local tourism groups wake up to the economic impact of traveling birders, more of these festivals are springing up, especially in well-known birding destinations. A few of the most popular festivals in the West: the Morro Bay Winter Bird Festival, in January at Morro Bay, California; the Klamath Basin Bald Eagle Conference, in February at Klamath Falls, Oregon; the Salton Sea International Bird Festival, in February at Imperial, California; Wings Over the Platte, in March in south-central Nebraska; the Grays Harbor Shorebird Festival, in April on the Washington coast; the American Falls Shorebird Festival, in August at American Falls, Idaho; the Southwest Wings Birding Festival, in August at Sierra Vista, Arizona; and the Festival of the Cranes, in November at Socorro, New Mexico. Call the National Fish and Wildlife Foundation (202-857-0166) for a directory listing many more festivals.

Beyond Your List Birding is fun and rewarding even if you approach it only on the level of a sport or hobby, like golf or coin-collecting. It's exciting to spot the frustratingly elusive Three-toed Woodpecker in a burned Colorado forest after you've spent countless hours searching for it. It's satisfying to look over the list of birds you've seen and remember your first trip to Texas' Big Bend National Park or your first pelagic trip out of Monterey, California.

After they've been at it awhile, though, most birders become conservationists. Learning where to look for birds and understanding a bit about ecosystems and habitat requirements leads to some inescapable conclusions. Sprague's Pipits need naturally managed prairie; if all our grasslands are plowed or overgrazed, there won't be any more Sprague's Pipits. Spotted Owls need old-growth forests; if all the woods are clear-cut before they reach maturity, this species will disappear.

Nestling Spotted Owl, an endangered species of western forests

Increasingly, birders are realizing that their interest in, even love for, birds doesn't exempt them from responsibility. Playing a tape of a bird's song or call is often an effective way to bring it in close, and sometimes avoids habitat damage caused by trying to get near a bird. But for some vulnerable species, or in heavily birded places, the tape recorder should be left in the car. Wanting, even really wanting, to see a Yellow Rail doesn't give you an excuse to go thrashing about in a marsh to flush one up, especially where the species is nesting. Parks and refuges occasionally close areas where a sensitive species—Bald Eagle or Peregrine Falcon, for example—is nesting; ethical birders obey such regulations, realizing that the birds' welfare comes before the desire to put a checkmark on a list.

Get Started

It's no wonder that birding ranks among the fastest growing outdoor pursuits in the country. All it takes to get started is a pair of binoculars, a field guide, and a notebook; you can watch birds alone or, if you prefer, you can share the adventure with friends. You're observing some of the earth's most colorful and interesting creatures; you'll be traveling, in many cases, to beautifully scenic wild places that you might otherwise never have discovered; and the challenges will last a lifetime, for no one will ever see all the different kind of birds there are.

MAP KEY and ABBREVIATIONS

National Conservation Area ...... NAT. CONS. AREA
National Monument .... NAT. MON.
National Park .... N.P.
National Recreation Area ... NAT. REC. AREA, N.R.A.
National Seashore

National Forest .... NAT. FOR., N.F.
National Grassland

National Wildlife Refuge .... N.W.R.

State Park .... S.P.

ADDITIONAL ABBREVIATIONS

County .... CO.
Memorial .... MEM.
National .... NAT.
National Historical Park .... N.H.P.
Preserve .... PRES.
Recreation Area .... R.A.
State Beach .... S.B.
State Historic Park .... S.H.P.
State Recreation Area .... S.R.A.
State Scenic Viewpoint .... S.S.V.
State Wildlife Management Area .... S.W.M.A.
Wilderness .... WILD.
Wildlife Area .... W.A.
Wildlife Habitat Management Unit .... W.H.M.U.
Wildlife Management Area .... W.M.A.

POPULATION

- **San Francisco**   500,000 and over
- Tucson   50,000 to under 500,000
- Palm Springs   under 50,000

Interstate Highway
——(10)——

U.S. Federal Highway
(90)

State Road
(35)

County, Local, or Other Road
[74]

Trans-Canada Highway
(20)

Other Canadian Highway
(55)

Ferry
. . . .

State Boundary

National Boundary

National Forest Boundary

■1 Featured Area
• Point of Interest
✷ State or Provincial Capital
| Dam
+ Peak

Northwest

J ust as it does in many areas, water defines some of the best and most characteristic birding opportunities in the Northwest. The Pacific Ocean meets land in beautiful scenes of rock and sand along the Washington and Oregon coasts, encompassing some of America's finest sites for loons, cormorants, sea ducks, shorebirds, alcids, and other waterbirds. Water in the form of abundant rainfall fuels the lush greenery of Washington's Olympic National Park, a temperate rain forest where 12 feet or more of precipitation falls each year. Varied Thrushes sing here and American Dippers haunt rocky mountain streams. Spotted Owls still call in areas where dense old-growth forest remains, though clear-cutting of vast tracts of northwestern woodland had pushed this species to endangered status, and intense debate over timber management has, for better or worse, made it one of the most famous and controversial birds in the country.

Farther east, in the rain shadow of the Cascade Range, rainfall dwindles so much that semidesert conditions prevail in some areas. Arid-country species add appealing variety to regional birding, and where water does occur in the midst of desert terrain—as at Oregon's Malheur National Wildlife Refuge or along the Columbia

Preceding pages: Great Gray Owl at its nest with young *Above:* Trumpeter Swans

River in southeastern Washington—it can attract substantial numbers of breeders and migrants.

Lakes and marshes host great flocks of waterfowl at Montana's Freezout Lake Wildlife Management Area, Idaho's Camas National Wildlife Refuge, Washington's Ridgefield National Wildlife Refuge, and many other sites throughout the region. Where waterfowl gather, birders assemble to look for eagles and large falcons. The Skagit and Samish Flats area in northwestern Washington is famed for sightings of the powerful Gyrfalcon (among many other varieties of raptors), and the Klamath Basin, on the Oregon-California border, serves as winter home to hundreds of Bald Eagles.

This region stretches more than a thousand miles from

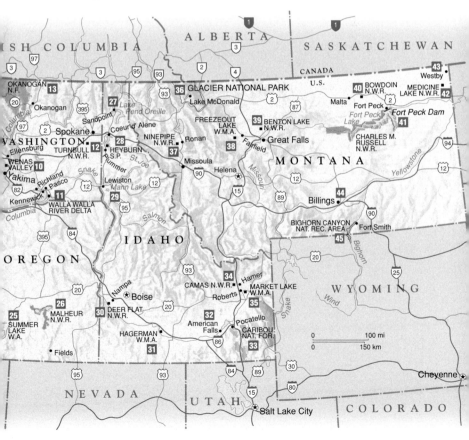

corner to corner. Within that span lie mountains rising above tree line, home to nesting American Pipits, and the short-grass prairie of eastern Montana, home to nesting Sprague's Pipits. Habitats include coniferous forest, riparian woodland, sagebrush shrub-steppe, oak chaparral, coastal salt marsh, and others providing good birding throughout the year. Sites range from Glacier National Park, famed for scenery and wildlife, to the small town of Westby,

Varied Thrush

Special Birds of the Northwest

Pacific Loon
Black-footed
    Albatross
Pink-footed
    Shearwater
Buller's Shearwater
Fork-tailed Storm-
    Petrel
Brandt's Cormorant
Pelagic Cormorant
Trumpeter Swan
Eurasian Wigeon
Harlequin Duck
Barrow's Goldeneye
Gyrfalcon
Spruce Grouse

White-tailed
    Ptarmigan
Blue Grouse
Pacific Golden-
    Plover
Black Oystercatcher
Black Turnstone
Surfbird
Sharp-tailed
    Sandpiper
Rock Sandpiper
Mew Gull
Thayer's Gull
Common Murre
Pigeon Guillemot
Marbled Murrelet

Ancient Murrelet
Cassin's Auklet
Rhinoceros Auklet
Tufted Puffin
Spotted Owl
Boreal Owl
Black Swift
Vaux's Swift
Rufous
    Hummingbird
Calliope
    Hummingbird
Red-breasted
    Sapsucker
White-headed
    Woodpecker
Three-toed
    Woodpecker

Black-backed
    Woodpecker
Pacific-slope
    Flycatcher
Cassin's Vireo
Northwestern Crow
Sky Lark
Chestnut-backed
    Chickadee
Boreal Chickadee
Varied Thrush
Wrentit
Sage Thrasher
Sprague's Pipit
Townsend's Warbler
Hermit Warbler
Sage Sparrow
Baird's Sparrow

in extreme eastern Montana, known to birders as a regional hot spot for eastern species straying west on migration. Whether your idea of fun is scanning for rare seabirds on a pelagic trip, hiking up rugged mountains to tundra in search of White-tailed Ptarmigan, or driving through a wildlife refuge to marvel at masses of geese, you'll find the Northwest full of possibilities for discovery.

This chapter begins in northwestern Washington near the shore of Samish Bay and continues south to Oregon and east to Idaho. Crossing the snowy peaks of the Rockies, it finishes on the Great Plains, in the Big Sky Country of eastern Montana. ∎

WASHINGTON

1 One of the most famous birding areas in northwestern Washington is referred to by locals as the "Skagit." An area of agricultural fields, wetlands, and bay shore near the mouths of the Skagit and Samish Rivers, it's also called the **Skagit and Samish Flats.** The area's fame derives from its large wintering flocks of waterfowl, including both Trumpeter and Tundra Swans and great numbers of Snow Geese, as well as excellent viewing of raptors. Among the latter group, the star is Gyrfalcon, a rare and prized sighting anywhere south of Canada but seen regularly here in winter, though usually only one or two birds at a time. Bald Eagle, Red-tailed and Rough-legged Hawks, Peregrine Falcon, and Short-eared Owl also frequent this area in winter.

From I-5 about 25 miles south of Bellingham, take the exit for Josh Wilson Road and follow it to the water. Turn right, drive through Edison, and then go west on the Bayview-Edison Road. Where this road turns south in 1.5 miles, continue west about a mile, checking nearby fields before returning to Bayview-Edison and driving south. Anywhere in this area can turn up wintering Rough-legged Hawk, Gyrfalcon, and Peregrine Falcon among the common Northern Harriers and Red-tailed Hawks. You might find a Short-eared Owl hunting at dusk (and on overcast days), or a Sharp-shinned or Cooper's Hawk flashing by. Snowy Owl is seen occasionally.

Continue south on Bayview-Edison Road to **Padilla Bay National Estuarine Research Reserve** and **Bayview State Park,** where you can scan the bay for wintering Brant, scoters, and other waterfowl. Huge flocks of Dunlin, sometimes numbering well over 10,000, winter in the vicinity.

Where Bayview-Edison Road meets Wash. 20, turn east, drive 0.9 mile, and turn south on Best Road. In 3.5 miles,

- Waterfowl and raptors at Skagit Flats
- Shorebirds and seabirds at Ocean Shores
- Diverse nesting birds in the Wenas Valley area

Information section p. 57

continue south on Chilberg Road and then Fir Island Road; where Fir Island Road turns east, follow it 1.8 miles and turn south to the headquarters of **Skagit Wildlife Management Area.** Large flocks of Snow Geese winter here, along with lesser numbers of Trumpeter and Tundra Swans, Greater White-fronted Goose, and assorted dabbling ducks. Bald Eagle and other raptors can turn up anywhere in the area. Hunting is allowed here, so use discretion in season.

Swift's Bay, Lopez Island, in the San Juan Islands of northwestern Washington

2 The beautiful San Juan Islands are among Washington's most popular destinations. The **San Juan Ferry,** which makes stops in the islands as it travels from Anacortes, Washington, to Sidney, British Columbia, serves as an easily accessible seabird trip. You might see four species of wintering loons (including possible, though rare, Yellow-billed); grebes; Double-crested and Pelagic Cormorants; ducks; Bonaparte's, Heermann's, Mew, Thayer's, Glaucous-winged, and other gulls; and alcids including Common Murre, Pigeon Guillemot, Marbled and Ancient Murrelets, and Rhinoceros Auklet. Bald Eagles nest in the islands and can be seen anytime of year. You can ride the ferry as a pedestrian quite inexpensively; if you take a car,

you can drive to the American Camp area at the southern end of **San Juan Island** to look for Sky Lark—a Eurasian bird that spread here from Vancouver Island, where it was introduced around 1901. Sky Lark is found in extensive grassy areas and is easier to find when singing in spring. Watch also for Golden Eagle, seen regularly in the islands, and in fall for Pacific Golden-Plover in the grassy areas where Sky Lark is found.

3 The northern entrance to **Olympic National Park** provides easy access to high-country birds. A well-marked road leads south from US 101 in Port Angeles past the main park visitor center, winding up to the Hurricane Ridge Visitor Center, a mile above sea level. If possible, make this trip early in the morning for more bird activity and less traffic. Along the way, you'll have terrific views of forested slopes and rugged, glacier-sculptured peaks. Watch for Blue Grouse, Northern Pygmy-Owl (seldom seen, but listen for small birds "scolding" if they've found an owl perched in daylight), Vaux's Swift, Red-breasted Sapsucker, Olive-sided and Pacific-slope Flycatchers, Cassin's (uncommon) and Hutton's Vireos, Gray and Steller's Jays, Common Raven, Chestnut-backed Chickadee, Winter Wren, Townsend's Solitaire, Hermit and Varied Thrushes, Yellow-rumped and Townsend's Warblers, Western Tanager, Dark-eyed Junco, Pine Grosbeak, and Red Crossbill. Walk the **Hurricane Hill Nature Trail,** and check open areas for nesting Horned Lark and American Pipit. If it's open, drive the dirt road to **Obstruction Peak** for more birding and fabulous vistas.

Gyrfalcon

A breeding bird of the Arctic, the Gyrfalcon sometimes travels south to the northern U.S. in winter, where a sighting of this majestic raptor is always an exhilarating moment. Large and powerful enough to capture ptarmigans and even geese, the Gyr is irregular in its wanderings in search of prey. Probably the best spot to look for this rare bird is near the mouths of the Skagit and Samish Rivers in northwestern Washington, where one or more Gyrfalcons usually spend part of the winter feeding on waterfowl in farmlands and wetlands.

4 **Dungeness National Wildlife Refuge** (*N from US 101 on Kitchen-Dick Rd., 5 miles W of Sequim*) is a long sandspit reaching out into the Strait of Juan de Fuca, creating a bay where waterfowl gather from fall through

Near the Hoh River in Olympic National Park

spring. From the parking lot a half-mile trail leads to the spit. Some birders walk the 5 miles to the lighthouse to find waterbirds and shorebirds, but much can be seen closer in. **Marina Drive,** on the bay's south shore west of Dungeness, also offers some good places to see loons, Brant, ducks, gulls, and terns (one of the best viewpoints is from the locally famous Three Crabs restaurant).

5 Washington birders consider the **Ocean Shores** area *(Chamber of Commerce 360-289-2451)* among the state's top birding sites. This seaside town occupies a peninsula at the north entrance to Grays Harbor, where beaches, marshes, and jetties attract a variety of seabirds and shorebirds. Follow Ocean Shores Boulevard south along the west side of the peninsula; side roads lead to a long Pacific Ocean beach where shorebirds and gulls can always be seen. At the southwestern corner of the peninsula, check the jetty for "rocky shorebirds": Black Oystercatcher and, from late summer through spring, Black Turnstone, Surfbird, and Rock Sandpiper. Inshore waters will have loons, grebes, cormorants (including Brandt's), ducks (all three species of scoter), and alcids such as Common Murre and Rhinoceros Auklet. Brown Pelicans appear in summer and fall, when Sooty Shearwaters pass offshore in great numbers.

Blue Grouse, an elusive bird of western forests

Return north for 1.6 miles on Ocean Shore Boulevard and turn east on Marine View Drive. When this road turns north in about 1.7 miles, continue east on Damon Point Road. Walk southwest from the parking area for good shorebird habitat. From Whimbrel to Least Sandpiper, the diversity of species can be extensive. Watch for both American and Pacific Golden-Plovers, look-alike birds formerly considered races of the same species. Wherever there are concentrations of shorebirds, be alert for Peregrine Falcons hunting for a meal. Return to Marine View and drive north; check the marina for loons, grebes, and ducks, and stop at the nearby **Ocean Shores Environmental Interpretive Center.**

6 From late April through early May the opportunity to see hundreds of thousands of massed shorebirds attracts birders to **Grays Harbor National Wildlife Refuge,** just west of Hoquiam. To reach this area, drive west on Wash. 109 about 1.7 miles from US 101, turn south on Paulson Road and west on Airport Way. Park across from the airport café and walk west on the paved road leading to the refuge's **Sandpiper Trail.** The majority of spring migrants are Western Sandpipers; other common species include Black-bellied and Semipalmated Plovers, Ruddy Turnstone,

Red Knot, Least Sandpiper, Dunlin (large flocks winter here), and Short-billed and Long-billed Dowitchers. Fall migration doesn't see the same concentration of birds as spring, but the refuge is still worth a visit. Best viewing occurs within two hours of high tide.

On the south side of Grays Harbor, **Westport** is the embarkation point for popular commercial pelagic trips that cruise 40 miles or more offshore looking for seabirds. Trips

Rhinoceros Auklet, showing the yellow "horn" it acquires in breeding season

last from 9 to 13 hours *(call 360-733-8255 for a schedule)*. Expected on all trips are species including Black-footed Albatross, Northern Fulmar, Fork-tailed Storm-Petrel, Common Murre, Cassin's and Rhinoceros Auklets, and Tufted Puffin, while seasonal sightings include Laysan Albatross; Pink-footed, Buller's, and Short-tailed Shearwaters; South Polar Skua; all three species of jaeger; Sabine's Gull; Black-legged Kittiwake; and Arctic Tern.

7 Wash. 105 heads south from Westport, past Tokeland along the north side of **Willapa Bay** to the town of Raymond. Between Tokeland and Raymond you'll have many chances to pull off the road and scan the bay for waterbirds and shorebirds. At Raymond, take US 101 west and then south for about 9 miles, stopping at Bruceport Park for more bay views. After the highway crosses the mouth of the Naselle River, watch for the headquarters of **Willapa National Wildlife Refuge;** shorebird viewing can be good here. Ask about visiting the nearby **Lewis Unit** of the refuge, where winter waterfowl can be abundant.

Intrepid birders searching for rarities, and ready for a

hike, visit the **Leadbetter Point Unit** of Willapa refuge. At Seaview, take Wash. 103 north 20 miles along Long Beach Peninsula, with the Pacific on the west and Willapa Bay on the east, following signs for **Leadbetter Point State Park.** From a parking lot at the end of the road, trails lead north 2 miles or more to the tip of the peninsula. Snowy Plover breeds on the ocean side, but nesting areas are closed seasonally to protect the birds. Large numbers of shorebirds frequent this area in migration (mostly on the bay side), sometimes including rarities such as Pacific Golden-Plover, Sharp-tailed Sandpiper, and Ruff. There's always something to see, from Brown Pelican in summer to Sooty Shearwater in summer and fall to flocks of Brant in spring migration.

8 "Geese, geese, geese," is how one Washington birder describes winter at **Ridgefield National Wildlife Refuge,** just west of Ridgefield, about 20 miles north of Portland, Oregon. Swans and ducks might be added to that, along with Bald Eagle and other raptors and Sandhill Crane. Tens of thousands of waterfowl winter here, including Tundra Swan (with occasional Trumpeter), Snow and Canada Geese, American Wigeon (look for a few Eurasian Wigeon mixed in with Americans), Mallard, Northern Shoveler, Northern Pintail, Green-winged Teal, Common Merganser, and others. Off South Ninth Street, the refuge entrance road leads past several parking areas where you can scan wetlands and fields. North of town, off North Main Street, another refuge entrance offers access to a 1.9-mile loop nature trail; this area can be excellent for winter sparrows. Nesting birds at Ridgefield include Great Blue Heron, several species of duck, Bald Eagle, Virginia Rail, Sora, Willow and Pacific-slope Flycatchers, Western Scrub-Jay, Marsh Wren, Warbling Vireo, and Yellow Warbler.

9 At **Mount Rainier National Park,** look for birds of middle and high elevations on the slopes of this snow- and ice-capped volcano. All areas of the park are open from July through Labor Day, and most are accessible from Memorial Day into October; in spring and fall, call to check the status of roads and trails.

In the southeastern part of the park, trails along the

Glacier-topped Mount Rainier, in west-central Washington

Ohanapecosh River pass through old-growth forest of Douglas-fir and western red cedar. Along the short **Trail of the Patriarchs** or the longer **Eastside Trail** watch for Olive-sided Flycatcher, Gray and Steller's Jays, Chestnut-backed Chickadee, Townsend's Solitaire, Varied Thrush, Yellow-rumped and Townsend's Warblers, Western Tanager, and Pine Siskin. With luck you might see Blue Grouse, Hammond's Flycatcher, Cassin's Vireo, Hermit Warbler, Purple Finch, or Evening Grosbeak. Look for American Dipper along the river. To the north, the popular Sunrise Visitor Center provides access to trails leading above timberline, where White-tailed Ptarmigan and Gray-crowned Rosy-Finch breed. The **Wonderland Trail** near the White River entrance station is the park's best spot for Hermit Thrush.

In the southwest, Harlequin Duck frequents the Nisqually River at the **Sunshine Point Campground.** The **Trail of Shadows** at Longmire may have Band-tailed Pigeon and Red-breasted Sapsucker, as well as interesting migrants. As you're driving, look also for Vaux's Swift, Clark's Nutcracker, and Mountain Bluebird; Rufous Hummingbird is common in summer in wildflower-dotted meadows.

10 In nesting season, the **Wenas Valley,** northwest of Yakima, hosts a fine diversity of species. Washington birders converge here on Memorial Day weekend for a camp-out and field trips. From Naches on US 12, take the Naches-Wenas Road northeast to Longmire Road; continue north 2 miles to North Wenas Road and turn northwest up the Wenas Creek Valley. In about 2 miles, check **Wenas Lake** on the south for waterfowl; a walk upstream from the lake might provide Gray Catbird and Yellow-breasted Chat. Continue up the valley about 7 more miles and turn left on Audubon Road, which leads to a campground called the **Hazel Wolf Wenas Bird Sanctuary,** in honor of a long-time Washington environmental leader.

This route includes riparian areas with aspen groves, brushy hillsides, and open ponderosa pine forest. By searching these habitats, you may find such species as Blue Grouse; Vaux's Swift; Calliope Hummingbird; Red-naped Sapsucker; Least (rare in aspens), Gray, Dusky, and Pacific-slope (riparian) Flycatchers; Western and Mountain Bluebirds; Veery; Nashville Warbler; Black-headed Grosbeak; Lazuli Bunting; and Bullock's Oriole. Check in pines around the campground for White-headed Woodpecker (a specialty of this area), Mountain Chickadee, Pygmy Nuthatch, Western Tanager, and Cassin's Finch. By returning to North Wenas Road and following it north and east (it becomes Umtanum Road) to Ellensburg, you'll pass through arid sagebrush country where you may find Rock Wren, Sage Thrasher, and Brewer's Sparrow.

11 You'll find one of the region's best inland shorebird sites just southeast of the Tri-Cities area of Richland, Kennewick, and Pasco. The **Walla Walla River Delta,** at the confluence of the Walla Walla and Columbia Rivers, hosts an excellent assortment of fall migrants, with peak numbers between mid-August and mid-September. To reach the best viewing location, take US 12 to just north of the Walla Walla River Bridge, south of Wallula. Turn west on a gravel road opposite the entrance to the U.S. Army Corps of Engineers' Madame Dorian Park; cross the railroad tracks and go down to the water. A telescope is essential here, and some birders wade out on the mudflats to get better looks. Washington's only breeding American White Pelicans nest on an island nearby, along with Caspian Terns. Gulls can be common here (Glaucous winters in small numbers), and both Trumpeter (uncommon) and Tundra Swans appear in migration. In winter, the area hosts diving ducks, 15 to 20 Bald Eagles, and an occasional Merlin or Peregrine Falcon.

12 Less than 20 miles southwest of Spokane, **Turnbull National Wildlife Refuge** holds a variety of habitats, including ponderosa pine woodland, aspen groves, grassland, and dozens of lakes. Among the highly diverse set of nesting birds are Eared Grebe; Canada Goose; more than a dozen species of ducks including divers such as Canvasback, Redhead, Ring-necked Duck, and Lesser Scaup; Northern Harrier; California Quail (introduced here); Black Tern; Willow Flycatcher; Western (rare) and Eastern Kingbirds; Black-billed Magpie; Rock and Marsh Wrens; Western Bluebird; Veery; American Redstart (scarce); and Chipping, Vesper, Lark, Savannah, Grasshopper, and Song Sparrows. Impressive flocks of waterfowl, including Tundra Swans, gather here in migration. A

5-mile auto tour route provides good access to wildlife viewing (you may see elk here) and hiking trails.

13 In the **Okanogan National Forest,** northwest of Winthrop, the **Hart's Pass** area is known as an important raptor migration route and a productive spot for many high-elevation species. From Winthrop, take Wash. 20 northwest 7 miles and turn north onto Lost River Road, which runs along the east side of the Methow River (look for nesting Harlequin Duck). Golden Eagles soar most summer days on the updrafts along Goat Wall here; in spring and summer, Least Flycatcher, Red-eyed Vireo, and American Redstart can be found in riverside cottonwoods. The road then climbs through several life zones, arriving in 13 miles at 6,197-foot Hart's Pass, Washington's highest drivable point. Along the way look for Blue Grouse (both coastal and northern Rockies races), Black (scarce) and Vaux's Swifts, and four species of chickadee (Black-capped, Mountain, Chestnut-backed, and Boreal). Later in summer, both Red and White-winged Crossbills are possible. Open meadows at high elevations have Savannah, Fox, and White-crowned Sparrows, with Lincoln's in wet areas.

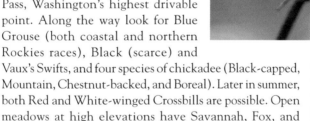

White-headed Woodpecker, a resident of western ponderosa and sugar pine forests

Late September is the best time for southbound raptors at the pass, including possible Northern Harrier, Cooper's Hawk, Northern Goshawk, Golden Eagle, Merlin, and Peregrine Falcon. A walk on the **Pacific Crest National Scenic Trail** here could turn up Gray Jay, Clark's Nutcracker, Mountain Bluebird, Hermit Thrush, American Pipit, Bohemian Waxwing, Pine Grosbeak, and Pine Siskin. Several woodpecker species are possible in this area, including Three-toed, Black-backed, and Pileated, and Williamson's and Red-naped Sapsuckers.

The road to Hart's Pass is narrow and steep and is closed to trailers. Be advised that the high-country season is short (mid-July to early October); be prepared for stormy weather any time.

OREGON

14 Conveniently located just minutes from Portland, **Sauvie Island** earns its considerable birding reputation as a home for wintering waterfowl, raptors, Sandhill Crane, gulls, and sparrows, as well as for migrant shorebirds. To reach it, take US 30 northwest from Portland 10 miles and turn east to cross the Sauvie Island Bridge. To reach the headquarters of **Sauvie Island Wildlife Area,** turn north and drive 2 miles on Sauvie Island Road; you can get advice and pick up a map and wildlife checklist here. The south half of the approximately 15-mile-long island is private, while most of the north is in the public wildlife area. Access to the wildlife area is restricted from October through mid-April, but much can still be seen from island roads and observation areas.

In fall and winter, tens of thousands of waterfowl congregate here, including Greater White-fronted, Snow, and Canada (abundant) Geese; Tundra Swan; and 15 or more species of ducks, the most common of which are Wood Duck, American Wigeon (look for Eurasian Wigeon as well), Mallard, Northern Shoveler, Northern Pintail, Green-winged Teal, Bufflehead, Common Merganser, and Ruddy Duck. Sandhill Crane is common in spring and fall migration, and has been increasing as a wintering bird. Bald Eagle may be the most publicized wintering raptor (as many as 20 or more may be present), but look also for Northern Harrier; Sharp-shinned, Cooper's, Red-tailed, and Rough-legged Hawks; and an occasional Peregrine Falcon, among other possibilities. In late summer, drive roads in the wildlife area looking for mudflats where shorebirds rest and feed. The Coon Island observation area is one good spot, and the Eastside Viewing Platform on Reeder Road is another.

On the southern part of the island, on Gillihan Road, a livestock feed plant attracts wintering gulls, always worth checking for rarities, or simply to practice your identification skills on plumages that vary with age for each species. This is one of the best places anywhere in the country to find Thayer's Gull.

Canada Geese at Sauvie Island Wildlife Area, near Portland

15 At the extreme northwestern corner of Oregon you'll find one of its finest birding sites. **Fort Stevens State Park** sits on the south bank where the Columbia River meets the Pacific Ocean, west of Astoria. Though seabirds and shorebirds are its claim to fame, it's also attracted many rare songbirds over the years, especially vagrants from the east that make a wrong turn in migration and are able to go no farther when they reach the sea. The favorite spot in the park is the **south jetty** of the Columbia River. To reach it, drive past the park's campground, enter the day-use area, and go to parking lot C, where a viewing platform is nearby. Around high tide in spring and, especially fall, shorebirds congregate below. The rare Sharp-tailed Sandpiper has been seen almost annually, though its habitat has deteriorated in recent years. Walking out on the jetty from fall through spring brings views of loons (Red-throated, Pacific, and Common, with Yellow-billed rare); grebes; Sooty Shearwater (summer and fall); Brown Pelican (summer and fall); Brandt's, Double-crested, and Pelagic Cormorants; sea ducks; gulls; terns; and alcids (members of the auk family such as Common Murre and Pigeon Guillemot). Pomarine and Parasitic Jaegers and Black-legged Kittiwake are sometimes spotted close to shore. After visiting the jetty, check **Trestle Bay,** reached by walking east from parking lot B or driving to parking lot D, where there's an observation bunker.

Marbled Murrelet

In the controversy over logging in the last remaining old-growth forests of the Pacific Northwest, the bird most often mentioned is the Spotted Owl, a large, nocturnal resident of these magnificent woodlands. Much less celebrated, the small seabird called the Marbled Murrelet also depends on this seriously threatened resource. A member of the alcid, or auk, family—all the rest of which nest on rocky islands or cliffs—the Marbled Murrelet nests high in mature redwoods, Douglas-firs, and other conifers along the Pacific coast as far south as central California. Mottled (or marbled) brown in breeding season, it molts to black and white plumage in winter. It can be found in small numbers just offshore throughout the year.

The park's beaches are Oregon's best location for both American and Pacific Golden-Plovers in migration. These are also among the best places to look for winter rarities such as Gyrfalcon, Snowy Owl, and Snow Bunting; Lapland Longspur can be found annually in winter. Nesting birds include Wood Duck, Osprey, Bald Eagle, Pacific-slope Flycatcher, Winter and Marsh Wrens, Wrentit, and Orange-crowned Warbler.

16 Excellent birding sites dot the length of the beautiful Oregon coastline, and as you travel US 101 you'll pass many state parks, recreations sites, and scenic viewpoints. All but one of the more than 1,400 rocks, reefs, and islands that you see out in the Pacific Ocean make up **Oregon Islands National Wildlife Refuge,** which protects breeding or resting areas for more than a million seabirds (among them Brandt's, Double-crested, and Pelagic Cormorants; Black Oystercatcher; Western and Glaucous-winged Gulls; Common Murre; Pigeon Guillemot; Rhinoceros Auklet; Leach's Storm Petrel; and Tufted Puffin), as well as harbor seal, Steller's sea lion, California sea lion, and northern elephant seal.

One of the best coastal sites is **Tillamook Bay,** just

northwest of the town of Tillamook. US 101 skirts the north and east sides of the bay. Visit the public marina in Garibaldi to scan for waterbirds of all sorts, and check the cove where the Miami River enters the bay just east of town for migrant shorebirds at low tide. In Tillamook, turn west on Third Street, and after 1.7 miles turn north on Bayocean Road toward Cape Meares; to the east will be good views of the bay. Where this road turns west in about 5 miles, continue north to **Bayocean Peninsula,** a spit of land separating Tillamook Bay from the Pacific. From the parking lot, walk east to the bay; shorebirding can be exciting here, especially around high tide in late summer and fall. The shrubs and coniferous woodland are productive for migrant songbirds, and Bald Eagle and Peregrine Falcon are often spotted.

Tufted Puffin, a colorful resident of northwestern seacoasts whose population has declined in recent years

Return to Bayocean Road and drive west to **Cape Meares National Wildlife Refuge** and **Cape Meares State Park.** From the lighthouse, scan for all manner of seabirds, from loons and ducks to an occasional Fork-tailed Storm-Petrel and, in August, great flocks of Sooty Shearwaters passing offshore. Cormorants, Common Murre, Pigeon Guillemot, and Tufted Puffin are among the nesting species on the cliffs and sea rocks below. Just south, the community of Oceanside and Oceanside Beach State Wayside provide views of **Three Arch Rocks National Wildlife Refuge,** a half mile offshore (you'll need a scope), home of the state's largest colony of Tufted Puffins and the largest Common Murre colony south of Alaska, with more than 200,000 birds some years.

17 Many Oregonians consider **Boiler Bay State Scenic Viewpoint,** 45 miles south of Cape Meares, the best seabird-watching site in the state. Birding is best from March through November when you might find species including loons, shearwaters, all three scoters, gulls (look for Black-legged Kittiwake in spring and fall), and alcids. Many rarities have been seen here, particularly after storms.

Common Murres, with Brandt's Cormorant and Western Gull, at Yaquina Head Outstanding Natural Area, near Newport, Oregon

Here, as at many places along the coast, the spring birder may also see large numbers of gray whales migrating north from Mexico to Alaska. On rocks below, you may find Black Oystercatcher and, from fall through spring, Black Turnstone, Surfbird, and Rock Sandpiper.

18 Continue south from Boiler Bay on US 101 for 10 miles to **Yaquina Head Outstanding Natural Area.** The area's rocky headland offers a 93-foot lighthouse dating from 1872, an interpretive center, and paths leading down to tide pools where you can study marine animals such as sea stars, sea anemones, and hermit crabs. Cliffs and offshore rocks here are home to nesting Brandt's and Pelagic Cormorants, Black Oystercatcher, gulls, Common Murre, Pigeon Guillemot, and Tufted Puffin. The lighthouse is a good place to scan for migrant and winter seabirds.

Just south of nearby Newport, Oregon State University's **Hatfield Marine Science Center** offers exhibits of sea life, and its nature trail leads to viewpoints of Yaquina Bay, where from fall through spring you'll find loons, grebes, Brant, ducks, shorebirds, and gulls. A nearby road following the south shore of the estuary outlet leads west to a jetty

that in winter often provides close looks at Harlequin Duck and Oldsquaw, among many other waterbirds.

19 US 101 crosses the Coquille River just north of Bandon. Less than a half mile south, turn west on Riverside Drive to reach **Bandon Marsh National Wildlife Refuge,** outstanding for migrant shorebirds. Look for a path leading west about 0.7 mile from US 101; just before and after high tide are the best birding times. In Bandon, First Street and Jetty Road will lead you toward the south jetty at the Coquille River mouth, another fine site for seabird- and shorebird-watching. Take Beach Loop on the west side of town to **Coquille Point** (part of Oregon Islands National Wildlife Refuge), at the west end of 11th Street, where you'll find Tufted Puffins and other nesting seabirds on strikingly beautiful offshore rocks.

20 In the Willamette Valley of west-central Oregon, **William L. Finley National Wildlife Refuge** is one of several areas set aside to provide wintering habitat for the large dusky race of Canada Goose, which breeds in a small area of southern Alaska. The refuge's fields, oak

Wizard Island rising from the water at Crater Lake National Park, where roads and trails provide easy access to highland birds

savanna, and woodland of bigleaf maples and Douglas-fir make it one of the state's finest birding destinations. Ten miles south of Corvallis off Ore. 99W, Finley offers excellent viewing of waterfowl and raptors (including an occasional Peregrine Falcon) from fall through spring. Greater White-fronted and Snow Geese, Tundra Swan, and many species of duck join the abundant Canada Geese (of several races) in cropland and wetlands. Diversity of habitat makes Finley excellent for all-around birding, including spring songbird migration and, depending on water levels, shorebird migration. Parts of the refuge are closed from November through April to minimize disturbance to waterfowl.

21 From Eugene, take Ore. 126 west 8 miles to **Fern Ridge Wildlife Area,** noted for a variety of waterbirds. Pied-billed Grebe, American Bittern, Wood Duck, Osprey, Acorn Woodpecker, Purple Martin, Yellow-breasted Chat, Yellow-headed Blackbird, and Lesser Goldfinch are just a few of the species nesting here. In recent years, this has been the only nesting site in western Oregon for Western Grebe and Black Tern, and Red-shouldered Hawk is an occasional visitor fall through spring. Stop at **Perkins Peninsula Park** just north of Ore. 126 to scan the lake, then continue less than a mile to a pull-off on the north with views of a marshy area. At Veneta, take Territorial Road north about 8 miles and turn east on Clear Lake Road to reach the dam area, a good place to scan for waders (including Great Egret), waterfowl, and gulls. Parks at each end of the dam offer viewing sites. In winter, low water in the reservoir exposes mudflats that attract migrant shorebirds.

22 The eastern slope of the Cascade Range is drier than the western; ponderosa pine dominates in upland forests. Nesting birds of the pine forest can be found at **Indian Ford Campground** in **Deschutes National Forest,** off US 20, 5.6 miles northwest of Sisters. Indian Ford Creek runs through this local favorite birding area, offering riparian species as well. Explore the creek vicinity and surrounding forest for Northern Pygmy-Owl; Calliope Hummingbird; Williamson's and Red-naped Sapsuckers; White-headed Woodpecker (this beautiful bird is a specialty here); Hammond's and Dusky Flycatchers; Cassin's (formerly a subspecies of Solitary Vireo) and Warbling Vireos; Mountain Chickadee; Pygmy Nuthatch; Townsend's Solitaire; Orange-crowned, Townsend's, and MacGillivray's Warblers; Green-tailed Towhee; Fox Sparrow; Cassin's Finch; and Red Crossbill.

23 **Crater Lake National Park** is one of the most beautiful, and certainly one of the most popular, recreational areas in Oregon. The blue lake set in the caldera of a dormant volcano creates a spectacular panorama from the park's Rim Road and its overlooks. Birders know it as a place offering easy access to mid- and high-elevation species of coniferous forest and alpine habitats. Some of these species—Olive-sided and Hammond's Flycatchers, Gray and Steller's Jays, Clark's Nutcracker, Mountain Chickadee, Townsend's Solitaire, and Hermit Thrush among them—are fairly easy to find. Others require searching or a bit of luck, including Blue Grouse, Great Gray and North-ern Saw-whet Owls, Three-toed and Black-backed Wood-peckers, and Gray-crowned Rosy-Finch. Driving Rim Road and hiking a few of the easier trails such as **Godfrey Glen** (an easy 1-mile loop through old-growth forest) can turn up a good number of these species. The strenuous 3.4-mile round-trip hike up **Garfield Peak** offers great views and a better chance at finding the rosy-finch.

24 A far different landscape awaits you at **Lower Table Rock,** a Nature Conservancy preserve and Bureau of Land Management Area of Critical Environmental Con-cern just north of Medford. To reach it, take the Medford exit off I-5, go east on Pine Street and Biddle Road 0.8 mile, and turn north on Table Rock Road. Drive about 7.5 miles and turn left on Wheeler Road, which, in less than a mile, leads to a trailhead on the west side of the road. The upper portions of Lower and nearby **Upper Table Rocks** are remnants of lava flows that occurred nearly 7 million years ago, rising 800 feet above the Rogue River Valley on flared bases of sandstone. The relatively dry habitats here include grassland; woodlands of oak, madrone, and pon-derosa pine; and shrub chaparral on the slopes. As you climb the rocky, but not overly steep, trail 1.75 miles to the top, look in spring and summer for Mountain Quail, Acorn Woodpecker, Loggerhead Shrike (rare), Hutton's Vireo, Western Scrub-Jay, Oak Titmouse (formerly a race of Plain Titmouse), Blue-gray Gnatcatcher, Wrentit, Western Blue-bird, California Towhee, and Lesser Goldfinch. If birding is slow here, wildflowers can provide a beautiful diversion.

25 Just south and east of the small town of Summer Lake in south-central Oregon, **Summer Lake Wildlife Area** offers wetlands in an arid landscape, and sea-sonally attracts waders, waterfowl, and shorebirds. Pick up a map of the area at the headquarters on Ore. 31, and then drive the 8.3-mile wildlife loop. (*Part of area closed for hunt-ing season, Oct.-Jan.*) During nesting season you can find Western and Clark's Grebes; American White Pelican; Double-crested Cormorant; Great and Snowy Egrets; Black-crowned Night-Heron; White-faced Ibis; Sandhill

Crane; Snowy Plover (look for this small shorebird on alkali flats); Black-necked Stilt; American Avocet; Willet; Wilson's Phalarope; and Caspian and Forster's Terns. In migration, Snow Geese arrive in numbers, along with Tundra Swan and 15 or more species of ducks. Watch here for Trumpeter Swans, some from the introduced population at nearby Malheur National Wildlife Refuge.

Part of the extensive wetlands of Malheur National Wildlife Refuge, southeastern Oregon

26 Similar to Summer Lake but on a grander scale, **Malheur National Wildlife Refuge** ranks with Oregon's finest and most popular birding sites. This 187,000-acre refuge hosts such large numbers of migrant birds (up to

300,000 Snow and Ross's Geese, hundreds of thousands of ducks, and thousands of Sandhill Cranes in spring and fall migration) that even nonbirders will be impressed.

In spring and fall, Malheur is great for migrants and serves as an excellent "vagrant trap," where out-of-range species are attracted to this oasis in the desert. In Oregon, Memorial Day weekend is called Malheur Day weekend, so many of the state's top birders make the trip here to look for eastern warblers and other rarities. For this sort of birding, check especially the headquarters area, Benson Pond, P-Ranch, and the Page Springs Campground. (The hamlet of **Fields,** 20 miles from the Nevada border on Ore. 205, is another classic migrant and vagrant trap.)

The spectacular courtship display of the Sage Grouse, at Malheur National Wildlife Refuge

The list of nesting species at this site is long, including five species of grebes; American White Pelican; American Bittern; Snowy Egret; White-faced Ibis; Trumpeter Swan; Swainson's and Ferruginous Hawks; Golden Eagle; Prairie Falcon; Chukar; Sandhill Crane; Snowy Plover; Long-billed Curlew; Franklin's Gull; Caspian, Forster's, and Black Terns; Burrowing and Short-eared Owls; Common Poorwill; Sage Thrasher; Black-throated (scarce) and Sage Sparrows; and Bobolink.

At dawn from March to May, male Sage Grouse perform their thrilling courtship "dance" at leks, or traditional courtship areas, near the refuge. Ask the refuge staff and other birders you meet about any significant sightings; ask also about a locally sponsored early-April birding festival that features tours of grouse leks, or for directions to viewing sites to see this spectacle on your own.

Mosquitoes can be bothersome at Malheur in summer, and birding is usually slow in winter (though Bald Eagle and Rough-legged Hawk are seen commonly); spring and fall are the best times to visit. Waterfowl numbers peak in late March and April, and migrant shorebirds can be plentiful in spring, late summer, and early fall.

IDAHO

27 Glacier-carved Lake Pend Oreille, Idaho's largest lake, winds among mountains covered in evergreen forest in the northern Panhandle. At 43 miles long and more than 1,100 feet deep, it offers plenty of room for a wide variety of waterbirds. Visit the **Sandpoint City Beach** (*in Sandpoint, take Bridge St. E from US 95*) to check the upper part of the lake. During the most productive period of fall through spring, you may find numbers of loons, grebes, and waterfowl here, and the beach area itself can host migrant shorebirds, gulls, and terns. Fewer birds are present in winter than at migration peaks, but interesting rarities can appear in that season, and Bald Eagles are usually here.

The **Pend Oreille Scenic Byway** follows Idaho 200 east from Sandpoint and then south to Clark Fork, 8 miles from the Montana border. All along the way you'll find lookouts to scan the lake for waterbirds, including such rare migrants as Greater Scaup, Oldsquaw (both possible in fall), and Barrow's Goldeneye. Western Grebe, Double-crested Cormorant, Osprey, and Bald Eagle nest on the lake. About 5 miles from Sandpoint, watch for the Sportsman Access sign at Sunnyside Road, leading southeast from Idaho 200; take this road for good lake views before continuing on the scenic byway.

28 **Heyburn State Park** encompasses 7,800 acres of woods, marshes, and lakes to the south of famed Coeur d'Alene Lake. From Plummer on US 95, drive east on Idaho 5 for 5.5 miles and turn north on Chatcolet Road toward park headquarters. At Plummer Creek, stop at a wildlife viewing area with interpretive displays and blinds overlooking a marsh, where you may see nesting Pied-billed and Red-necked Grebes, Wood Duck, Mallard, and Marsh

- Waterfowl and shorebirds at Deer Flat National Wildlife Refuge
- Winter waterbirds and Bald Eagles at American Falls
- Varied breeders and migrants at Camas National Wildlife Refuge

Information section p. 59

The rocky shoreline of Lake Pend Oreille, in Idaho's northern Panhandle

Wren. From here, the easy **Lake Shore Trail** runs east to Hawley's Landing Campground, with good marsh and lake views along the way. Continue to the Chatcolet Use Area, where the popular **Indian Cliff Trail** climbs from cedar-hemlock forest into woods of ponderosa pine and Douglas-fir. Here you'll find Northern Pygmy-Owl (scarce), Cassin's Vireo, Chestnut-backed Chickadee, Pygmy Nuthatch, Townsend's Solitaire, and Yellow-rumped and Townsend's Warblers. The trail has excellent views of the lakes below, including Osprey nests along the St. Joe River.

Return to Idaho 5 and drive east along **Chatcolet Lake.** Pull-offs along the road provide viewing opportunities for migrant waterfowl and wintering Bald Eagle. At shallow **Benewah Lake,** wild rice attracts waterfowl and other wildlife. Great Blue Herons nest in the vicinity, remaining throughout winter as long as there's open water.

29 **Mann Lake,** a small reservoir southeast of Lewiston, is northern Idaho's best shorebirding spot. To reach it from Lewiston, take 21st Street south from US 12, continue southeast when it becomes Thain Road (County Road P2). In 3.6 miles, turn east on Powers Avenue and drive 4.5 miles to the lake. In late summer and fall, look for regular migrants including Black-bellied and Semi-

palmated Plovers; American Avocet; Greater and Lesser
Yellowlegs; Spotted, Semipalmated, Western, Least, Baird's,
and Pectoral Sandpipers; and Long-billed Dowitcher.
Spring shorebirds aren't as common, but watch in this season and fall for other species such as Common Loon;
Horned, Red-necked, Eared, and Western Grebes (Clark's
is rare in fall); Tundra Swan; geese; ducks; gulls; and terns.

30 Easily accessible from Boise, **Deer Flat National
Wildlife Refuge** is known for large concentrations
of waterfowl in migration and winter, interesting nesting
birds, and shorebirds in migration. Of the two refuge units,
birders most often visit the one surrounding **Lake Lowell,**
a popular recreational facility. Take Idaho 45 (12th Avenue
South) south from Nampa and turn west on Lake Lowell
Avenue. In 3.8 miles, after the road turns south, turn northeast on Upper Embankment Road toward the headquarters.

From the park at the east end of the dam and from the
headquarters you can scan Lake Lowell for a wide variety
of waterbirds. Geese and ducks can number in the tens of
thousands in spring and fall. The commonest species usually include Canada Geese (check the smaller numbers of
Snow Geese for rare Ross's), American Wigeon, Mallard,
Northern Pintail, and Green-winged Teal; Tundra Swan is

an uncommon migrant. Bald Eagles gather around the lake in winter; Golden is less common but is seen often. Late summer can bring postbreeding Great and Snowy Egrets and White-faced Ibis. Nesting birds here include Eared, Western, and Clark's Grebes; Black-crowned Night-Heron; Redhead; Virginia Rail; Sora; American Avocet; Ring-billed and California Gulls; and Caspian and Black Terns.

Pick up a refuge map at headquarters and use it to make your way around the lake, stopping at some of the many access points. Water level varies throughout the year, and when mudflats are exposed, migrant shorebirds can be abundant. Look through flocks of the commoner species such as Semipalmated Plover, Marbled Godwit, and Western Sandpiper for rare American Golden-Plover (fall), Snowy Plover (spring), and Stilt Sandpiper (late summer).

Though it's not a birding site, the **World Center for Birds of Prey,** south of Boise, repays a tour with close looks at some of the rarest and most beautiful raptors on earth. To reach it from I-84, take South Cole Road south 4.3 miles to Flying Hawk Lane, which leads to the center. The captive-breeding programs here aid the recovery of North American birds such as Aplomado and Peregrine Falcons, as well as more exotic species such as the Harpy Eagle of Central and South America and the African Taita Falcon. The center is operated by the Peregrine Fund.

31 Just south of Hagerman, **Hagerman Wildlife Management Area** is home to great concentrations of waterfowl in winter on its ponds and marshes, as well as to a good variety of other species in wetland vegetation and surrounding trees, shrubs, and grassland. Look for a highway rest area on the east side of US 30 about 2 miles south of Hagerman, from which you can scan for Tundra Swan (Trumpeter is found as a migrant), geese, and ducks attracted to spring-fed waters that remain largely open throughout winter. Canada Geese and Mallards are the primary species, present in thousands. Other common wintering ducks include Wood Duck, Gadwall, American Wigeon, Northern Shoveler, Northern Pintail, Redhead, Ring-necked Duck, Lesser Scaup (watch for occasional Greater), Bufflehead, and Common Goldeneye. Wintering

Bald and Golden Eagles and Red-tailed and Rough-legged Hawks are seen frequently. Continue south a short distance and turn east into the wildlife management area. Here you can walk along the levees between the ponds for more viewing opportunities. In nesting season, the area hosts Pied-billed Grebe, Black-crowned Night-Heron, Ruddy Duck, Gray Partridge, California Quail, Virginia Rail, Spotted Sandpiper, Plumbeous and Warbling Vireos, Horned Lark, Marsh Wren, Common Yellowthroat, Yellow-breasted Chat, Spotted Towhee, Yellow-headed Blackbird, and Bullock's Oriole, among many other species.

A staff member displaying a Peregrine Falcon at the World Center for Birds of Prey near Boise

32 Waterbirds, shorebirds, and Bald Eagles make a visit to **American Falls** a productive one. Several good viewing areas can be found near the town of American Falls, just off I-86. From the Idaho 39 bypass in the north part of town, take Fort Hall Avenue and Marina Road north to the marina, where you can scan the reservoir for loons, grebes, and waterfowl in spring and fall. From midsummer through fall, return to Fort Hall Avenue; don't turn south but proceed southwest on Pacific Road (*take care on old roads here*).

American Falls reservoir in south-eastern Idaho, one of the state's top spots for waterbirds

Mudflats along the reservoir attract large numbers of shore-birds and occasional herons, egrets, and White-faced Ibis.

Return to Fort Hall Avenue and drive south, continu-ing on Lincoln Street (Idaho 37) and turning west on Falls Avenue. Follow it to its end, where you can view the Snake River below the dam. You'll find additional river view-points by returning east on Falls Avenue a few blocks, turning south on McKinley Road, and in 0.4 mile turning west into a cemetery; 0.3 mile south of the cemetery, turn west off McKinley and drive past the landfill. The river attracts ducks and gulls from fall through spring, along with several Bald Eagles, which roost in riverside trees, and migrant Osprey. Look for Common and Barrow's Gold-eneyes; Hooded, Common, and Red-breasted Mergansers; and an occasional surprise such as scoters or Oldsquaw.

33 Areas in the **Caribou National Forest** south of Pocatello make for a productive birding trip in nesting season. From Pocatello, take South Main Street southeast, following it as it becomes Bannock Highway. About 3.4 miles from the crossing of the Portneuf River, turn south on Bannock Highway (Forest Road 231) and drive 3.2 miles to the national forest. Just past a cattle guard, park and walk the old road up **Kinney Creek** to the east. Look here for Common Poorwill; Calliope and Broad-tailed Hummingbirds; Gray and Dusky Flycatchers; Plumbeous Vireo; Western Scrub-Jay; Juniper Titmouse; Blue-gray Gnatcatcher; Orange-crowned, Virginia's, Yellow, Black-throated Gray, and MacGillivray's Warblers; Green-tailed and Spotted Towhees; and Lesser Goldfinch.

Calliope Hummingbird

The smallest North American bird is of course a member of the hummingbird clan: the Calliope, a summer resident of meadows and clearings in northwestern highlands, south to southern California. Both sexes have a very short bill and tail, and the male sports a distinctive gorget that often looks striped, iridescent purple over white. In his courtship display the male flies in a shallow U-pattern, showing off as well as he can with a body only a bit over 3 inches long.

Continue on Mink Creek Road about 0.5 mile to the **Cherry Springs Nature Area,** where trails are good for many of the same species, along with forest- and riparian-habitat birds such as Ruffed Grouse, Willow Flycatcher, Black-capped Chickadee, Gray Catbird, Cedar Waxwing, Yellow-breasted Chat, Fox Sparrow, and Black-headed Grosbeak. Less than a mile farther south on Mink Creek Road, turn east on Forest Road 001 and drive up to the **Scout Mountain Campground,** where higher-elevation breeding birds include Blue Grouse, Flammulated and Northern Saw-whet Owls, Northern Pygmy-Owl, Red-naped Sapsucker, Hairy Woodpecker, Hammond's and Cordilleran Flycatchers, Clark's Nutcracker, Mountain Chickadee, Red-breasted Nuthatch, Brown Creeper, Golden-crowned and Ruby-crowned Kinglets, Swainson's and Hermit Thrushes, Western Tanager, Lincoln's Sparrow, and Red Crossbill.

34 Leave I-15 at Hamer, drive north on the frontage road for 3 miles, then cross over the interstate to reach **Camas National Wildlife Refuge,** known for concentrations of migratory waterfowl, as well as for some notable breeding species. In addition, trees near the refuge headquarters serve as a "migrant trap" not only for western species but for strays from the East. Along with Canada Goose and many varieties of ducks nesting here, look also for Trumpeter Swan in the lakes and marshes south of the headquarters. Peregrine Falcon was reintroduced at Camas in 1983 and can be seen on the refuge throughout the year. Ferruginous Hawk, a declining species throughout the West, is an uncommon breeder, and both Bald and Golden Eagles are seen here regularly.

Long-billed Curlew, a shorebird that nests in grasslands

Nesting waders and waterbirds include Eared and Western Grebes; American White Pelican; Double-crested Cormorant; American Bittern; Great Blue Heron; Great, Snowy, and Cattle Egrets; Black-crowned Night-Heron; White-faced Ibis; Sandhill Crane; Black-necked Stilt; American Avocet; Willet; Long-billed Curlew; and Wilson's Phalarope. In the grasslands and scrub, look for Gray Partridge; Ring-necked Pheasant; Short-eared Owl (scarce); Common Nighthawk; Horned Lark; Sage Thrasher; and Vesper, Savannah, and Grasshopper Sparrows.

35 Only a short drive south, **Market Lake Wildlife Management Area** offers much the same sort of birding: lots of waterfowl in migration and nesting wetland species from grebes and waders to Marsh Wren and Yellow-headed Blackbird. To reach it from Roberts, drive north on County Road 2880 East, bearing right in 0.5 mile onto County Road 2850 East at a Y-intersection. In about a mile, turn east on County Road 800 North and follow signs to the area headquarters. Several large marshy impoundments to the north, accessible by road or by walking dikes, allow viewing of waterfowl, shorebirds, gulls, and terns. To reach the main part of the area, return to County Road 2850 East and drive north, passing along a dike between Triangle and Main Marshes.

MONTANA

36 **Glacier National Park**'s landscape of mountains and lakes makes it Montana's most popular natural area. Not surprisingly, you'll find excellent birding here. Simply driving the **Going-to-the-Sun Road** (*closed in winter*) up and over 6,646-foot Logan Pass and stopping at picnic areas and overlooks can bring sightings of Red-naped Sapsucker; Northern Flicker; Hammond's Flycatcher; Gray and Steller's Jays; Clark's Nutcracker; Winter Wren; Golden-crowned and Ruby-crowned Kinglets; Townsend's Solitaire; Hermit, Swainson's, and Varied Thrushes; Cedar Waxwing; Yellow-rumped, Townsend's, and MacGillivray's Warblers; Western Tanager; Black-headed Grosbeak; Red Crossbill; and Pine Siskin. Walking trails might turn up less common birds such as Blue Grouse, Three-toed Woodpecker, or Pine Grosbeak. Osprey and Bald Eagle nest in the park, so watch for them around any of the lakes.

Look for American Dipper at the road bridge that crosses McDonald Creek just north of **Lake McDonald.** Watch for Barrow's Goldeneye (uncommon) on the lake and for Harlequin Duck anywhere along the creek above this point. At the **Avalanche Creek** picnic area, look for the rare Black Swift, which nests on nearby cliffs. Vaux's Swift also nests in this area. At **Logan Pass,** walk the nature trail across the tundra for a chance to see White-tailed Ptarmigan, American Pipit, and Gray-crowned Rosy-Finch. This is a popular spot (with a small parking lot), so get here early.

The **Inside North Fork Road** (*closed in winter*) on the west side of the park leads to good birding areas. Wet meadows along the road may have nesting Le Conte's Sparrow; for one likely spot, hike up the **Camas Creek Trail** about a half mile. Continuing up toward **Rogers Lake** may bring a sighting of a Boreal Chickadee. Black-capped, Mountain,

- Rocky Mountain species at Glacier National Park
- Migrant waterfowl and shorebirds at Freezout Lake
- Prairie species at Bowdoin National Wildlife Refuge

Information section p. 59

White-tailed Ptarmigan showing the protective coloration of its winter plumage in Montana's Glacier National Park

and Chestnut-backed Chickadees also nest in the park. Check meadows all along this road for Great Gray Owl. Continue north beyond Polebridge to an area that burned in 1988, where you might find Black-backed Woodpecker. Clay-colored Sparrow has nested here, as has Northern Hawk Owl, a very rare breeding species in the lower 48 states.

The timberline race of Brewer's Sparrow, which may someday be designated a separate species, is another park specialty. Among other locations near timberline, look for this sparrow about a mile up the trail to **Iceberg Lake** in the Many Glacier area, on the park's east side, and about a mile up the trail to Scenic Point, at **Two Medicine Lake.**

37 A viewing area and a short nature trail off US 93, about 7 miles south of Ronan, make it easy to observe some of the nesting and migrant birds at **Ninepipe National Wildlife Refuge.** Breeders on and around the reservoir here include Red-necked, Eared, and Western Grebes; Double-crested Cormorant; American Bittern; Great Blue Heron;

Canada Goose; several species of ducks; Osprey (which often attempt nesting on platforms at the south end of the reservoir); Sora; American Avocet (uncommon); Marsh Wren; and Yellow-headed Blackbird. From US 93, drive about 1.6 miles west on Mont. 212, turn south to the dam; from here, follow a gravel road atop the dam and dike south and back east to US 93 for more views of waterbirds. (*Road closed seasonally, but you may use county roads along the edge of the refuge to return to US 93.*)

The glacially formed terrain of this intermountain valley encompasses extensive grassland and many small ponds. In fall and winter, raptor viewing can be excellent in this vicinity, though numbers fluctuate with populations of rodents and other prey. Look for Bald Eagle, Northern Harrier (nests), Red-tailed (nests) and Rough-legged Hawks, Golden Eagle, Peregrine and Prairie Falcons, and Short-eared Owl (nests)—and hope for a rarity such as Gyrfalcon or Snowy Owl. Swainson's Hawk, an uncommon breeder, is absent in winter.

Sunrise at Freezout Lake Wildlife Management Area, one of Montana's most popular birding sites

38 As you approach **Freezout Lake Wildlife Management Area** from Fairfield along US 89, a high point on the road offers a view of grassland, fields, and a broad expanse of water, bounded by low hills on the horizon. You're looking at one of Montana's finest birding sites, where spectacular numbers of waterfowl stop to rest in spring and fall migration, and many species of waterbirds breed. In early spring, Canada Geese and Tundra Swans arrive in the area by the thousands, along with 15 to 20 species of ducks. Look for Eurasian Wigeon, uncommon but regular here in spring. Tens of thousands of Snow Geese arrive in March, and their restless flocks will incorporate a high percentage of the slightly smaller Ross's Goose.

In April and May, Freezout hosts a good variety of migrant shorebirds. Remaining to nest will be Killdeer, Black-necked Stilt, American Avocet, Willet, Upland Sandpiper, Long-billed Curlew, Marbled Godwit, and Wilson's Phalarope. Other breeding waterbirds include all six Montana species of grebes (Horned is rare); American Bittern; Black-crowned Night-Heron; Green-winged Teal; Ring-necked Duck; Sora; Franklin's, Ring-billed, and California Gulls; and Common, Forster's, and Black Terns. American White Pelican summers, but doesn't breed. Look in grasslands for nesting Northern Harrier; Gray Partridge; Ring-necked Pheasant; Short-eared Owl; Clay-colored, Vesper, and Savannah Sparrows; Lark Bunting; and Chestnut-collared Longspur.

Stop at area headquarters just off US 89 to pick up the excellent birding guide to Freezout, and follow roads that wind around the wetlands. Though waterfowl are abundant here in fall, this is a popular hunting area, and birding activity is limited.

39 Just a short drive north of Great Falls, **Benton Lake National Wildlife Refuge** is known for most of the same waterfowl and marsh birds as Freezout. To reach it, take US 87 north about a mile past the Missouri River and turn north on **Bootlegger Trail.** The refuge auto tour route passes wetlands alive in breeding season with grebes, ducks, American Coot, gulls (including thousands of nesting Franklin's), and terns. Migrant shorebirds can be abundant with proper water levels in impoundments. Look too for Burrowing Owl on the prairie, along with Northern Harrier, Sharp-tailed Grouse (males "dance" on their leks, or courtship grounds, in spring), Upland Sandpiper, Short-eared Owl, Sprague's Pipit (occasional), Savannah and Grasshopper Sparrows (and rarely Baird's), as well as Chestnut-collared Longspur. Swainson's Hawk is common here except in winter, and Ferruginous Hawk and Gyrfalcon occasionally appear. Rough-legged Hawk is a frequent winter visitor.

American Avocet, a common breeder in Montana wetlands

40 Offering wetland habitat in an environment that receives only 12 inches of rain a year, **Bowdoin National Wildlife Refuge** near Malta attracts migrant and breeding waterfowl and shorebirds. Sought-after grassland species also reward a trip to this refuge way out in the flat Big Sky Country, just 40 miles or so from Canada. Where the fluting song of Western Meadowlark sounds over short-grass and mid-grass prairie, look for Sprague's Pipit and Baird's Sparrow, two birds that have suffered declines as this habitat has been plowed and overgrazed. McCown's and Chestnut-collared Longspur perform their song flights in spring and early summer. Sharp-tailed Grouse, Burrowing Owl, Horned Lark, and a variety of sparrows in addition to Baird's also nest on the prairie.

The refuge auto tour route circles Lake Bowdoin, allowing looks at breeding birds including Western and Clark's Grebes; American White Pelican (abundant here); Great Blue Heron; Black-crowned Night-Heron; White-faced Ibis; Franklin's, Ring-billed, and California Gulls; and Common and Black Terns. Close study of shallow-water areas or mudflats in summer can turn up an excellent variety of shore-birds; several rarities have been found here over the years.

Three-toed Woodpecker

As its name states, the Three-toed Woodpecker has only three toes; except for its close relative the Black-backed Wood-pecker, other U.S. woodpeckers have four. Both the Three-toed and Black-backed are found in coniferous forests in western mountains, and both prefer to feed on dead trees with bark still loosely attached. Recently burned areas are good sites to look for these species, which can be difficult to find. In this part of the country, the Three-toed is generally more common than the Black-backed, though only the latter is normally found in California.

41 In eastern Montana the Missouri River has been impounded as the huge **Fort Peck Lake,** sprawling through some of the state's most remote areas. The tailwaters of the **Fort Peck Dam,** at the town of Fort Peck, are known for attracting numbers of gulls in late fall and winter. November and December are the best months to check gatherings of Ring-billed, California, and Herring Gulls for Thayer's, Glaucous (both regular), and other uncommon to rare species. Fourteen species of gull have been found here, including Mew, Glaucous-winged, and Great Black-backed. Roads and recreation areas below the dam provide several good access points.

A few eastern birds can be found around Fort Peck at the edge of their normal nesting range. Check around the campground along the Missouri River downstream from the dam for Orchard and Baltimore Orioles (as well as the western Bullock's), and watch the skies overhead around town for Chimney Swift. From the dam, follow Mont. 24 east about 2 miles to a spillway; 0.2 mile east of that, take a gravel road *(can be impassable in wet weather)* north to the river and turn west through a gate into a wooded area. Red-headed Woodpecker, Blue Jay, Eastern Bluebird, and Field Sparrow nest here, and Black-and-white Warbler has been seen in summer and may nest here.

Piping Plover breeds around Fort Peck Lake, and can often be seen with a spotting scope from the west end of the dam in spring and summer. For a chance to find nesting Least Tern, drive to the **Bear Creek Recreation Area** on the lake, about 7 miles east of the spillway, south off Mont. 24.

42 In April, male Sharp-tailed Grouse perform their earnest courtship displays at **Medicine Lake National Wildlife Refuge,** in northeastern Montana. Call the refuge office a week or more in advance to reserve space in a blind, and you'll be able to watch from just a few feet away as male grouse strut in their tail-up, spread-wing posture and show off for watching females. The movements of mating Sharp-tailed and other species of grouse inspired some Native American ceremonial dances, and the ancient courtship ritual remains a thrilling thing to behold.

Here in the transition zone between tallgrass and short-grass prairies, nesting birds include grassland species such as Gray Partridge; Ring-necked Pheasant; Upland Sandpiper; Burrowing and Short-eared Owls; Sprague's Pipit; Clay-colored, Vesper, Lark, Savannah, Grasshopper, Baird's (a specialty of the refuge), Le Conte's (a rare breeder in Montana and not easy to find), and Song Sparrows; Lark Bunting; and Chestnut-collared Longspurs. Look for these as you drive the auto tour route *(open May–Sept.)*, and scan the coves and islands of Medicine Lake for breeding grebes, American White Pelican (the colony on Big Island is one of the most important in the United States), ducks, American Avocet, Wilson's Phalarope, gulls, and terns. The threatened Piping Plover nests at the water's edge, with up to 30 pairs present some years. In migration, flocks of Sandhill Cranes rest here, along with thousands of waterfowl.

43 Birders eager to add warblers and other songbirds to their Montana list visit the small town of **Westby** *(Chamber of Commerce 406-385-2445)*, on the North Dakota state line, where the very small **Onstad Memorial** municipal park *(off Mont. 5)* seems to act as a magnet for migrants in spring and fall. The trees here provide an island of green in an expanse of prairie, and eastern vagrants as well as western species home in on the park. Visit early in the morning, since many birds don't stay all day and concentrations may be gone by noon. Westby lies in the prairie pothole region, where it is surrounded by hundreds of glacier-formed ponds and marshes. Such rarities as Yellow Rail and Le Conte's and Nelson's Sharp-tailed Sparrows nest in these wetlands, and Piping Plovers breed on alkali ponds.

Bald Eagle, increasingly common at lakes and reservoirs throughout the Northwest

44 If you happen to be in **Billings** *(Visitor Center 406-252-4016)* during spring or fall migration, a visit to **Two Moon County Park** can be worthwhile. To reach it, take Main Street (US 87) north; just past Metra Park turn southeast on Bench Boulevard, and in 0.6 mile turn east to enter the park. This riparian area on the Yellowstone River is popular with local birders, who search its trees, shrubby vegetation, and wetlands for migrant flycatchers, vireos, wrens, thrushes, warblers, sparrows, and a variety of other species.

45 One of the best winter waterbird sites in south-central Montana is part of **Bighorn Canyon National Recreation Area,** 85 miles east and south of Billings. Check at the Yellowtail Dam Visitor Center just south of Fort Smith on Mont. 313 for maps and information, and scan the water of the Bighorn River below Yellowtail Dam for loons, waterfowl, gulls, and Bald Eagle. Observation areas provide viewpoints. As you approach the area from I-90, watch the roadside for Northern Shrike, and the sky for Rough-legged Hawk, Golden Eagle, and Prairie Falcon—and, with luck, a Peregrine Falcon as well.

Northwest
Information

? Visitor Center/Information   **⑤** Fee Charged   **♬** Food

♿ Rest Rooms   **🏃** Nature Trails   **🚗** Driving Tours   **♿** Wheelchair Accessible

Be advised that facilities may be seasonal and limited. We suggest calling or writing ahead for specific information. Note that addresses may be for administrative offices; see text or call for directions to sites.

Rare Bird Alerts

Washington:
Statewide *425-454-2662*
Southeast *208-882-6195*
Lower Columbia Basin
  509-943-6957

Oregon:
Statewide *503-292-0661*
Northeast *208-882-6195*

Idaho:
North *208-882-6195*
Southwest *208-368-6096*
Southeast *208-236-3337*

Montana:
Statewide *406-721-9799*
Big Fork *406-756-5595*

WASHINGTON

Bayview State Park
(Page 19)
10905 Bayview-Edison Rd.
Mount Vernon, WA 98273
360-757-0227

♿ **&**

Washington State Ferries *(Page 20)*
801 Alaskan Way
Seattle, WA 98104
206-464-6400

⑤ **♬** **♿** **&**

Olympic National Park
(Page 21)
600 East Park Avenue
Port Angeles, WA 98362
360-452-0330

? **⑤** **♬** **♿** **🏃** **🚗** **&**

Dungeness National Wildlife Refuge *(Page 21)*
33 South Barr Road
Port Angeles, WA 98362
360-457-8451

⑤ **♿** **🏃** **&**

Ocean Shores Environmental Interpretive Center
(Page 23)
336 Nimble Hill Road
Newington, NH 03801
603-431-7511

? **⑤** **♬** **♿** **🏃** **🚗** **&**

Grays Harbor National Wildlife Refuge *(Page 23)*
Nisqually NWR Complex
100 Brown Farm Road
Olympia, WA 98516
360-753-9467

♿ **🏃** **🚗** **&**

Shorebird festival with workshops, lectures, and guided field trips during peak migration

Willapa National Wildlife Refuge *(Page 24)*
3888 Wash. 101
Ilwaco, WA 98624
360-484-3482

♿ **🏃** **&**

Leadbetter Point State Park *(Page 25)*
P.O. Box 488
Ilwaco, WA 98624
360-757-0227

♿ **🏃** **&**

Ridgefield National Wildlife Refuge *(Page 25)*
301 North Third Avenue
Ridgefield, WA 98642
360-887-4106

♿ **🏃** **🚗** **&**

Portions of refuge closed seasonally Oct.-May

Mount Rainier National Park *(Page 25)*
Tahoma Woods, Star Route
Ashford, WA 98304
360-569-2211

? **⑤** **♬** **♿** **🏃** **🚗** **&**

Turnbull National Wildlife Refuge *(Page 28)*
26010 South Smith Road
Cheney, WA 99004
509-235-4723

⑤ **♿** **🏃** **🚗** **&**

Okanogan National Forest *(Page 29)*
P.O. Box 579
Winthrop, WA 98862
509-996-4000

⬡ 🚻 🚶 ⛵ ♿

Administers Hart's Pass area

OREGON

Sauvie Island Wildlife Area *(Page 30)*
18330 NW Sauvie Island
   Road
Portland, OR 97231
503-621-3488

⬡ 🛏 🚻 ♿

Closed Oct.–mid-April

Fort Stevens State Park
(Page 31)
Ridge Road
Hammond, OR 97121
503-861-1671

❓ ⬡ 🚻 🚶 ♿

Oregon Coastal Refuges
(Page 32)
2127 SE Osu Drive
Newport, OR 97365
541-867-4550

❓ 🚻 🚶 ♿

Administers Oregon Islands National Wildlife Refuge (rocks, reefs, and islands as well as Coquille Point); Cape Meares National Wildlife Refuge and State Park; Three Arch Rocks National Wildlife Refuge; and Bandon Marsh National Wildlife Refuge.

Boiler Bay State Scenic Viewpoint *(Page 33)*
Oregon Parks and
   Recreation Department
1115 Commercial Street NE
Salem, OR 97310
541-265-4560

🚻 ♿

Yaquina Head Outstanding Natural Area *(Page 34)*
750 Lighthouse Drive
Newport, OR 97365
541-574-3100

❓ ⬡ 🚻 🚶 ♿

Hatfield Marine Science Center *(Page 34)*
Oregon State University
2030 South Marine
   Science Drive
Newport, OR 97365
541-867-0226

❓ 🚻 🚶 ♿

William L. Finley National Wildlife Refuge *(Page 35)*
26208 Finley Refuge Road
Corvallis, OR 97333
541-757-7236

❓ 🚻 🚶 ♿

Fern Ridge Wildlife Area *(Page 36)*
26969 Cantrell Road
Eugene, OR 97402
541-935-2591

🚻 🚶 ⛵ ♿

Seasonal access restrictions to protect wintering waterfowl

Perkins Peninsula Park
(Page 37)
U.S. Army Corps of
   Engineers
26275 Clear Lake Road
Junction City, OR 97448
541-688-8147

❓ ⬡ 🚻 🚶 ⛵ ♿

Deschutes National Forest *(Page 37)*
P.O. Box 249
Sisters, OR 97759
541-549-2111

⬡ 🚻 🚶

Crater Lake National Park *(Page 37)*
P.O. Box 7
Crater Lake, OR 97604
541-594-2211

❓ ⬡ 🛏 🚻 🚶 ⛵ ♿

Lower and Upper Table Rocks *(Page 38)*
The Nature Conservancy
821 SE 14th Avenue
Portland, OR 97214
503-230-1221

🚻 🚶

Summer Lake Wildlife Area *(Page 38)*
36981 Highway 31
Summer Lake, OR 97640
541-943-3152

❓ 🚻 ⛵ ♿

Malheur National Wildlife Refuge *(Page 39)*
HC 72, Box 245
Princeton, OR 97721
541-493-2612

❓ 🚻 🚶 ⛵ ♿

IDAHO

Heyburn State Park
(Page 41)
Route 1, Box 139
Plummer, ID 83851
208-686-1308
🚹🚻🧑‍🦽♿

**Deer Flat National
Wildlife Refuge** *(Page 43)*
13751 Upper
  Embankment Road
Nampa, ID 83686
208-467-9278
❓🚻🧑‍🦽♿

**World Center for Birds
of Prey** *(Page 44)*
566 West Flying Hawk Lane
Boise, ID 83709
208-362-8687
❓🅿️🚻♿

**Hagerman Wildlife
Management Area**
(Page 44)
Idaho Fish and Game
868 East Main Street
Jerome, ID 83338
208-324-4350
🚻

Caribou National Forest
(Page 47)
Westside Ranger District
250 South 4th Avenue
Pocatello, ID 83201
208-236-7500
🚻🧑‍🦽♿

*Administers Kinney Creek and
Cherry Springs Nature Areas*

**Camas National Wildlife
Refuge** *(Page 47)*
2150 East 2350 North
Hamer, ID 83425
208-662-5423

**Market Lake Wildlife
Management Area**
(Page 48)
804 North 2900 East
Roberts, ID 83444
208-228-3131
🚻🧑‍🦽

MONTANA

Glacier National Park
(Page 49)
West Glacier, MT 59936
406-888-7800
❓🅿️🍴🚻🧑‍🦽♿

**Ninepipe National
Wildlife Refuge** *(Page 50)*
c/o National Bison Range
132 Bison Range Road
Moiese, MT 59824
406-644-2211
🚻🧑‍🦽♿

*Parts of refuge closed during
nesting season (mid-
March–mid-July) and hunting
season (Sept.-Jan.)*

**Freezout Lake Wildlife
Management Area**
(Page 52)
US 89
Fairfield, MT 59436
406-467-2646
🚻🧑‍🦽♿

**Benton Lake National
Wildlife Refuge** *(Page 53)*
922 Bootlegger Trail
Great Falls, MT 59404
406-727-7400
🚻🧑‍🦽♿

**Bowdoin National
Wildlife Refuge** *(Page 53)*
HC 65, Box 5700
Malta, MT 59538
406-654-2863
🚻♿

Fort Peck Dam and Lake
(Page 54)
East Kansas
Fort Peck, MT 59223
406-526-3411
🚻🧑‍🦽♿

**Medicine Lake National
Wildlife Refuge** *(Page 55)*
223 North Shore Road
Medicine Lake, MT 59247
406-789-2305
🚻♿

**Bighorn Canyon
National Recreation
Area** *(Page 56)*
5 Avenue B
Fort Smith, MT 59035
*406-666-3234 or
  406-666-2412*
❓🅿️🍴🚻🧑‍🦽♿

*Yellowtail Dam Visitor Center
open Mem. Day–Labor Day*

Central
Rockies

Some of the birding highlights of this expansive and diverse region are very high, indeed. In Colorado's Rocky Mountain National Park, to choose one of the most famous examples, Trail Ridge Road ascends past tree line to wander through alpine tundra at over 12,000 feet, an elevation that can leave you breathless in more ways than one. Lucky birders sometimes find White-tailed Ptarmigan or Brown-capped Rosy-Finch near the highway, and even the not-so-lucky will find some of the most spectacular scenery in the country as consolation. The view of Long's Peak and the Continental Divide from Trail Ridge rates with the best in a state filled with magnificent panoramas.

Colorado's Mount Evans Scenic Byway (the highest paved road in the United States), southern Wyoming's Snowy Range Scenic Byway, Utah's Mirror Lake Scenic Byway, and Nevada's Great Basin National Park are just a few of the other highland areas where Clark's Nutcrackers and Mountain Bluebirds brighten already beautiful landscapes. Birds of pine, spruce, and fir forests in these places range from the common Steller's Jay, always noisy and conspicuous, to the elusive Blue Grouse, usually found by accident when a birder is walking along a woodland trail, thinking of something else entirely.

Preceding pages: Trumpeter Swans (one with an identifying neckband) and grazing bison in Wyoming's Yellowstone National Park *Above:* Black-billed Magpie

CENTRAL ROCKIES

If the mountains are the postcard destinations of this chapter, they're by no means the only worthwhile ones. In northeastern Colorado, Pawnee National Grassland invites birders to drive for miles through prairie where McCown's Longspurs perform their song flights in spring and summer; Ferruginous Hawk and Mountain Plover, both declining species, find homes here in the rolling steppe country. On the other side of the Continental Divide, rugged terrain with juniper, pinyon pine, and sagebrush—such as at Dinosaur National Monument, on the Colorado-Utah line—hosts a different set of birds, including Gray Flycatcher, Pinyon Jay, and Juniper Titmouse. Farther west, the Corn Creek area of Desert National Wildlife Refuge near Las Vegas, Nevada, ranks with the best desert-oasis "migrant traps" in the country.

A number of fine wetlands can be found in each of the states of this chapter, the most renowned of which may be

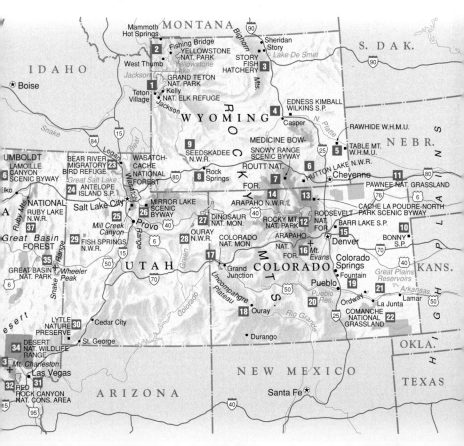

Bear River Migratory Bird Refuge, on the shore of Utah's Great Salt Lake west of Brigham City. Grebes, geese, swans, ducks, shorebirds, and other waterbirds rest at the refuge in migration, and many species remain to nest. Wyoming's Seedskadee National Wildlife Refuge and Nevada's Lahontan Valley, while not as well known as Bear River, offer their own very respectable lists of breeders and migrants. In the Arkansas River Valley of eastern Colorado, waders and

Sage Thrasher

Special Birds of the Central Rockies

	Lesser Prairie-Chicken	Three-toed Woodpecker	Cassin's Sparrow
Clark's Grebe	Snowy Plover	Gray Flycatcher	Black-chinned Sparrow
Trumpeter Swan	Mountain Plover	Gray Vireo	Sage Sparrow
Barrow's Goldeneye	Wilson's Phalarope	Pinyon Jay	McCown's Longspur
Ferruginous Hawk	Flammulated Owl	Chihuahuan Raven	Chestnut-collared Longspur
Chukar	Great Gray Owl	Juniper Titmouse	Gray-crowned Rosy-Finch
Himalayan Snowcock	Boreal Owl	Sage Thrasher	Black Rosy-Finch
Sage Grouse	Black Swift	Curve-billed Thrasher	Brown-capped Rosy-Finch
White-tailed Ptarmigan	Lewis's Woodpecker	Le Conte's Thrasher	Pine Grosbeak
Blue Grouse	Williamson's Sapsucker	Phainopepla	
		Virginia's Warbler	

shorebirds frequent a series of shallow lakes that dot the High Plains.

So as you drive or hike to some of the enticing mountain birding spots here, take time to look around when you reach the top. Arrayed around you down below (figuratively speaking, anyway) will be a splendid range of other destinations, from grassland to marsh to desert, all with great birding possibilities.

This chapter begins in Wyoming and moves south to visit Colorado and Utah before ending beside the blue water of Nevada's Lake Tahoe. ∎

WYOMING

1 The jagged peaks, glacier-carved valleys, and tree-lined lakes of Grand Teton National Park and the surrounding area make it a beautiful birding spot, and diverse habitats make it a rewarding one. From marshes and riparian vegetation along the Snake River to sagebrush flats, and from spruce-fir forest to alpine tundra, there's a lot to keep a birder busy here.

From Jackson, it's just a short drive north off Broadway to the **National Elk Refuge,** where wetlands are home to migrant and breeding waterfowl including Trumpeter Swans and Sandhill Cranes, which nest here and in other wet grassland throughout Jackson Hole. Keep watch for such open-country birds as Prairie Falcon, Long-billed Curlew, and Mountain Bluebird. On US 89/191 just north of town, the Jackson Hole and Greater Yellowstone Information Center sits alongside a marsh worth checking for various waterbirds. Farther north, pull-offs along the highway allow scanning of National Elk Refuge wetlands.

Continue northward into **Grand Teton National Park.** Just after crossing the Gros Ventre River, turn east on the Gros Ventre Road toward the community of Kelly. With luck, you might find Sage Grouse in the sagebrush flats here, along with Mountain Bluebird, Sage Thrasher, Green-tailed Towhee, and Brewer's and Savannah Sparrows. The national park campground 4 miles up the road can be productive for species such as Western Wood-Pewee, Cordilleran Flycatcher, Warbling Vireo, Tree and Violet-green Swallows, Black-capped Chickadee, Yellow Warbler, and Bullock's Oriole. Three miles north of the Gros Ventre Road, turn west off US 89/191 toward the Jackson Hole Airport. The sagebrush north of the entrance road is probably the best place in the area for Sage Grouse. In spring,

- **Mountain and wetland birds at Grand Teton National Park**
- **Waterbirds and grassland species in the Torrington area**
- **High-elevation species along the Snowy Range Scenic Byway**

Information section p. 105

Birding by canoe on the Snake River at Grand Teton National Park

male grouse gather to "dance" at courtship grounds here. Check with park personnel for viewing information.

In summer, you'll find Black Rosy-Finch, one of the park's special birds, by taking the aerial tramway from Teton Village to the top of **Rendezvous Mountain,** at an elevation of 10,446 feet. These little finches prefer rocky areas and cliff faces, especially those bordering snowbanks, and it may take some exploring to find them; walk up from the tram to check cirques and snowfields. You can return on the tram, but for a real adventure hike the **Granite Canyon Trail** back down to the village. It's a 12.4-mile walk with an elevation change of more than 4,000 feet—but it's all downhill, and you'll travel from tundra through coniferous forest to sage country along the way. In winter, rosy-finches gather at feeders in Jackson and elsewhere in the valley.

From the park's Moose Visitor Center, drive north on the main park road (*closed in winter*). On trails at popular **Jenny** and **String Lakes** and up to **Hidden Falls,** you'll have a chance at many of the regular nesting species of western montane forests, such as Northern Goshawk, Blue Grouse, Williamson's and Red-naped Sapsuckers, Dusky Flycatcher, Gray and Steller's Jays, Clark's Nutcracker, Mountain Chickadee, Red-breasted Nuthatch, American Dipper (along rocky streams), Ruby-crowned Kinglet, Townsend's Solitaire, Swainson's and Hermit Thrushes, Yellowrumped Warbler, Western Tanager, Pine Grosbeak, Cassin's Finch, and Pine Siskin. Farther north, the **Signal Mountain Road** can also be productive for the same species.

Just ahead lies some of the park's best birding. Stop at the **Jackson Lake Dam** to scan for loons, grebes, and waterfowl. Check the **Oxbox Bend Turnout, Willow Flats Overlook,** and **Christian Pond** for wetland and meadow species such as Western Grebe, American White Pelican, American Bittern, Trumpeter Swan, Barrow's Goldeneye, Common Merganser, Osprey, Bald Eagle, Northern Harrier, Sora, California Gull, Calliope Hummingbird, Willow Flycatcher, Marsh Wren, MacGillivray's and Wilson's Warblers, and Lincoln's Sparrow.

Black Rosy-Finch, a species that nests on high mountain peaks

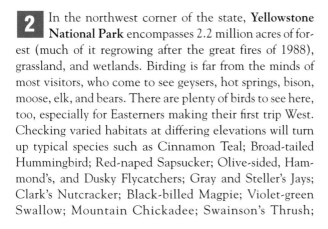

2 In the northwest corner of the state, **Yellowstone National Park** encompasses 2.2 million acres of forest (much of it regrowing after the great fires of 1988), grassland, and wetlands. Birding is far from the minds of most visitors, who come to see geysers, hot springs, bison, moose, elk, and bears. There are plenty of birds to see here, too, especially for Easterners making their first trip West. Checking varied habitats at differing elevations will turn up typical species such as Cinnamon Teal; Broad-tailed Hummingbird; Red-naped Sapsucker; Olive-sided, Hammond's, and Dusky Flycatchers; Gray and Steller's Jays; Clark's Nutcracker; Black-billed Magpie; Violet-green Swallow; Mountain Chickadee; Swainson's Thrush;

Yellowstone River flowing through Hayden Valley in Yellowstone National Park

MacGillivray's Warbler; and Western Tanager. As always, there are certain montane birds it takes a bit of luck to see, such as Northern Goshawk, Blue Grouse, Williamson's Sapsucker, Pine Grosbeak, and Red Crossbill. For these species, time spent walking trails may eventually pay off.

After you've seen Old Faithful, some of the park's best birding can be found by driving from West Thumb, on Yellowstone Lake, east and north to Tower and west to Mammoth Hot Springs. Depending on the size of your map, this may not seem like much distance, but note that it's actually 73 miles. As you skirt **Yellowstone Lake** to Fishing Bridge and a bit beyond, stop where you can to scan for Common Loon, American White Pelican, Double-crested Cormorant, Trumpeter Swan, Barrow's Goldeneye, California Gull, and other waterbirds, as well as Osprey and Bald Eagle.

Heading north along the **Yellowstone River,** you'll find White-throated Swift flying through canyons; American Dipper flits from rock to rock along rapids; and with luck you might see Harlequin Duck (ask park personnel about this scarce bird). Where roads cross meadows, stop to check surrounding trees—and hope to find a huge Great Gray Owl looking back at you. If you're not successful, you could spot a Sandhill Crane nesting or a beautiful sky blue Mountain

Bluebird. In sagebrush areas, look for Sage Thrasher and Brewer's Sparrow.

Three-toed and Black-backed Woodpeckers frequent burned woodland, and the Yellowstone fires of 1988 provided vast areas of such habitat. Ask park naturalists about any recent sightings and about the chances of seeing these often elusive species.

3 In north-central Wyoming, the small town of **Story** (*Chamber of Commerce 307-672-2485*) and nearby **Lake De Smet** constitute a popular birding destination. In Story, Wyo. 194 (Fish Hatchery Road) leads west to **Story Fish Hatchery,** set in a mature ponderosa pine forest where you can find nesting Broad-tailed Hummingbird; Dusky Flycatcher; Plumbeous Vireo; Mountain Chickadee; Red-breasted, White-breasted, and Pygmy Nuthatches; Ruby-crowned Kinglet (Golden-crowned appears in winter); and Yellow-rumped Warbler. Drive back east into town and turn south on County Road 145 (Wagon Box Monument Road). In spring and early summer, stop and check for Calliope Hummingbird along **South Piney Creek** behind the Catholic church on the west. As you continue south down the road alongside **Little Piney Creek,** nesting birds include

Veery, Yellow and MacGillivray's Warblers, American Redstart, Ovenbird, Common Yellowthroat, and Lazuli Bunting. In grassland farther south, you may find Sharp-tailed Grouse and Bobolink.

From I-90 south of Story, take the Shell Creek exit and cross to the east side of the interstate. Take Monument Road north a short distance and turn east to the southern part of Lake De Smet, a fine place for loons, grebes, waterfowl, and gulls in spring and fall. Many rarities have been seen here over the years, and Gray Partridge is sometimes found along the shore.

Cinnamon Teal, a familiar nesting duck of Wyoming wetlands

4 If you're visiting Casper in spring or fall, a walk along the **Platte River Parkway** on the north side of town may result in a nice list of migrants. A paved, 2.5-mile trail along the Platte River, it can be accessed from Crossroads Park, off Poplar Street, or from the Bryan Stock Trail Bridge over the Platte to the east. Just a few miles east of Casper, off US 20/26/87, **Edness Kimball Wilkins State Park** is also excellent in migration and hosts riparian breeding species such as Red-headed Woodpecker, Western and Eastern Kingbirds, Blue Jay, Yellow Warbler, Black-headed Grosbeak, Lazuli Bunting, and Bullock's Oriole.

5 The region around Torrington, near the Nebraska border in southeastern Wyoming, is noted for water-birds and grassland species. The ponds and marshes at **Table Mountain Wildlife Habitat Management Area** (*take Wyo. 92 S beyond Huntley, then drive 3.5 miles S on Wyo. 158*) host migrant shorebirds and waterfowl, with thousands of Snow Geese present at times. American Bittern and Snowy Egret are here in summer and have nested, and Great and Cattle Egrets are occasionally seen. Black-crowned Night-Heron, Virginia Rail, Sora, American Avocet, and Wilson's Phalarope breed, and Wyoming's first Great-tailed Grackle nest was found here in 1998. Cars aren't allowed into this area before Memorial Day, but you can walk in. Birding is not advisable during the fall waterfowl hunting season.

CENTRAL ROCKIES

The grasslands in this area comprise one of the best places in Wyoming to see McCown's and Chestnut-collared Longspurs, though the latter is much less common than the former. As you drive the back roads through the plains, look also for Swainson's and Ferruginous Hawks, Burrowing Owl (check around prairie-dog towns), Western and Eastern Kingbirds (most years Cassin's is present, as well), Horned Lark, and Lark Bunting.

From Torrington, drive northwest on US 26/85 and in 6 miles turn south to the **Rawhide Wildlife Habitat Management Area,** where the riparian habitat can be excellent for spring migrant songbirds. Nesting species here include Red-headed Woodpecker, Blue Jay, and Eastern Bluebird. The last two birds are among several species that have been steadily expanding their ranges westward along rivers. Dams have tamed the floods that once annually scoured riverbanks of vegetation, allowing cottonwoods and willows to grow up and create new habitat.

Burrowing Owl

With its fierce yellow eyes and long legs adapted to a terrestrial life, the Burrowing Owl is one of the most appealing birds of the plains. It often bobs up and down rather comically while standing on the ground. Though still widely distributed through much of the West, this species has suffered serious declines nearly everywhere it occurs and has been extirpated in some areas. The owl nests in holes dug by prairie dogs and other burrowing animals, and the destruction of prairie dog colonies is one factor in its dwindling population.

6 One of the best places for waterbirds in southern Wyoming is the **Hutton Lake National Wildlife Refuge,** southwest of Laramie. To reach it, take Wyo. 230 southwest from I-80 about 10 miles; turn east on County Road 37 and drive 7 miles to County Road 34. Turn northeast and drive 3.5 miles to the entrance. Hutton Lake has no staff or facilities, and roads are primitive. Don't try to visit in wet weather or winter. As you travel the grassland to the refuge, watch for Mountain Plover (scarce) and McCown's Longspur. Once you're inside, check the five small lakes for migrant grebes, American White Pelican, waterfowl, gulls, and terns. In April, as many as 20,000 ducks may throng the wetlands. Nesting species here include Pied-billed, Eared, and Western Grebes; Canvasback; Redhead; Ruddy Duck; Northern

The Snowy Range Scenic Byway, an excellent high-elevation birding route west of Laramie

Harrier; Virginia Rail; Sora; American Avocet; Forster's and Black Terns; Marsh Wren; possibly Sage Thrasher; Vesper, Lark, and Savannah Sparrows; and Yellow-headed Blackbird. Look for Snowy and occasional Cattle Egrets in summer. In summer and early fall, Hutton Lake can host good numbers of shorebirds.

7 West of Centennial, the **Snowy Range Scenic Byway** (Wyo. 130) through **Medicine Bow-Routt National Forest** ascends to 10,847-foot Snowy Range Pass before heading down the western side of the Medicine Bow Mountains. Open usually from late May into October, its upper sections provide an opportunity to see such nesting species as Northern Goshawk (rare); Blue Grouse; Olive-sided, Dusky, and Cordilleran Flycatchers; Gray and Steller's Jays; Clark's Nutcracker; Mountain Chickadee; Red-breasted Nuthatch; American Dipper; Townsend's Solitaire; Swainson's and Hermit Thrushes; Orange-crowned and Yellow-rumped Warblers; White-crowned Sparrow; and Pine Grosbeak. Rarities such as Boreal Owl and Three-toed Woodpecker are possible here, as well.

Stop at the visitor center a mile west of Centennial, then

CENTRAL ROCKIES

continue about 7 miles to the turn north to **Brooklyn Lake,** an excellent birding location. About 3.5 miles west on Wyo. 130, turn north to **Lewis Lake** for more birding. From here you can hike up 12,013-foot **Medicine Bow Peak** where you'll find nesting American Pipit and, with luck, Brown-capped Rosy-Finch on rocky slopes.

8 You'll find a far different landscape south of **Rock Springs** (*Chamber of Commerce 307-362-3771*), where birders go in late spring and early summer to find species of arid pinyon pine-juniper habitat. From the Flaming Gorge Road exit (exit 99) on I-80 just west of town, drive south on US 191 for 4.2 miles and turn west on gravel Little Firehole Road, which runs south for about 11 miles to meet Firehole Canyon Road, where you can turn east back to US 191. Stop often along this productive route to look for Gray and Ash-throated Flycatchers; Plumbeous Vireo; Western Scrub-Jay; Pinyon Jay; Juniper Titmouse; Bushtit (rare); Rock, Canyon (rare), and Bewick's Wrens; Blue-gray Gnatcatcher; Sage Thrasher; Virginia's and Black-throated Gray Warblers; Sage Sparrow; and Scott's Oriole (scarce).

9 From I-80, take Wyo. 372 north about 28 miles, a mile past Wyo. 28, to **Seedskadee National Wildlife Refuge.** This is a fine destination any time of year for both waterbirds, attracted to marshes along the Green River, and land birds of riparian and arid terrain. Some of the birds you'll see in summer include Western Grebe, American White Pelican, Great Blue Heron (a heronry is located on the refuge), White-faced Ibis, Canada Goose, several species of duck, Osprey, Bald Eagle (an uncommon breeder, but more common in winter), Northern Harrier, Swainson's and Ferruginous (uncommon, and seen more often off the refuge) Hawks, Golden Eagle, Prairie Falcon, Sora, Sandhill Crane, Short-eared Owl, Warbling Vireo, Mountain Bluebird, Sage Thrasher, Vesper and Sage Sparrows, and Yellow-headed Blackbird.

Ask refuge personnel about the chances of seeing Sage Grouse and Mountain Plover, two special birds not easy to find here. You might run across moose or pronghorn while visiting Seedskakee, as well.

COLORADO

Colorado means mountains to many people, and it's certainly true that the Rockies offer fabulous scenery, great recreational opportunities, and equally wonderful birding. You'll be making a mistake, though, to look on the eastern part of the state as simply blank space on the map. Several sites in the High Plains reward traveling birders with sought-after regional specialties, concentrations of migrants—and more wide-open sky than some people see in an average year.

10 Just 25 minutes or so north of I-70 via US 385, **Bonny Lake State Park,** on the shores of Bonny Reservoir, attracts waterbirds and some eastern species unusual in this area; it's also a fine spot to look for vagrant warblers and other songbirds in spring. Check cottonwoods and willows at the **Foster Grove Campground** on the north shore, and the **Wagon Wheel Campground** on the south shore, for Wild Turkey, Yellow-billed Cuckoo, Red-headed and Red-bellied Woodpeckers, Eastern Kingbird, Warbling Vireo, Blue Jay, Gray Catbird, Brown Thrasher, Lazuli and Indigo Buntings, Orchard and Bullock's Orioles, and, of course, for migrants. Scan the reservoir from the dam and other lookout points for grebes and waterfowl. When low water in late summer exposes mudflats, watch for migrant shorebirds. In open places around the lake, you may find Loggerhead Shrike, Eastern Bluebird, several species of sparrow, and Dickcissel. Bonny is a popular hunting, fishing, and recreation area, so plan your visit accordingly.

11 East of Fort Collins, the **Pawnee National Grassland** attracts birders who drive back roads through the rolling short-grass steppe country from late April through

early July looking for Swainson's and Ferruginous Hawks; Mountain Plover; Long-billed Curlew; Burrowing Owl; Lark Bunting; Cassin's, Brewer's, and other sparrows; and McCown's and Chestnut-collared Longspurs. The area northwest of Briggsdale is a productive one, and with a map of the Pawnee you can explore on your own for hours (noting that much private property is mixed with federal land). Your best bet, though, is to get a copy of the grassland's birding-route map, available at the office in Greeley or at **Crow Valley Recreation Area** just north of Briggsdale off County Road 77. While you're at the latter spot, check the

Pawnee Buttes on the Pawnee National Grassland, home of nesting Golden Eagles and Prairie Falcons riparian vegetation along Crow Creek for migrants and breeders such as Yellow-billed Cuckoo, Western and Eastern Kingbirds, Northern Mockingbird, Brown Thrasher, and Orchard and Bullock's Orioles.

Lark Bunting and McCown's Longspur are easy to find many places on the grassland, especially when males are performing their song flights (see sidebar this page), and seeing Ferruginous Hawk is a matter of keeping your eyes on the sky and having a bit of luck. Burrowing Owl is found in prairie-dog towns, and since these little rodents have suffered losses recently from plague and other problems, it might pay to ask Pawnee personnel about likely locations. Mountain Plover can be tricky to find—look in habitat where vegetation height is less than 4 inches, as well as in prairie-dog towns. Chestnut-collared Longspur likes grass a bit longer than McCown's, and is usually not as easy to see. For one likely spot, take US 85 north of Ault for 16 miles, turning east into the **Central Plains Experiment Range.** Stop along the entrance road and walk the field just to the south.

Northeast of Keota, Golden Eagle and Prairie Falcon nest on cliffs at the picturesque **Pawnee Buttes,** and close approach is prohibited from March through June. You can observe from a distance, and you might see either of these species anywhere in the area.

Singing in the Air

Male birds in forested areas often perch in high places when they sing, to help their song carry farther, or to make themselves more conspicuous. Prairie birds have no such perches available, so many have evolved song flights in which they sing while hovering or flying slowly well above the ground. Explore Colorado's **Pawnee National Grassland** (see p. 74) from late May through early July and you'll see and hear Horned Lark, Lark Bunting, and McCown's and Chestnut-collared Longspurs displaying characteristic song flights above the rolling grassland. At the same time, males often show prominent plumage markings, such as the white tail feathers of Horned Lark and the longspurs and the white wing patches of Lark Bunting.

12 There could hardly be a more beautiful spot to see high-country birds than **Rocky Mountain National Park,** encompassing more than 400 square miles of meadows, coniferous woodland, and tundra, all lying astraddle the Continental Divide. The park's famed **Trail Ridge Road** (*usually open Mem. Day–mid-Oct.*) climbs through spruce-fir forest to run for several miles above tree line, offering an alpine experience for those unable to climb, and other roads provide access to a varied habitats. For those who enjoy hiking, the potential for exploration is limitless.

Entering the park from Estes Park at the Beaver Meadows entrance, turn south toward Bear Lake. At Moraine Park, turn west to the **Cub Lake Trail** and walk through the marshy riparian area of the Big Thompson River and up the valley toward the lake. Look for Northern Pygmy-Owl (rarely seen, but listen for the "scolding" notes of songbirds mobbing an owl they've spotted in daylight), Broad-tailed Hummingbird, Williamson's and Red-naped Sapsuckers, Northern Flicker, Western Wood-Pewee, Plumbeous Vireo, Steller's Jay, Black-billed Magpie, Violet-green Swallow, Black-capped and Mountain Chickadees, Pygmy Nuthatch, Townsend's Solitaire, MacGillivray's and Wilson's Warblers, Western Tanager, Lincoln's Sparrow, and Black-headed Grosbeak, among others. (Farther north, the road to the **Endovalley Picnic Area** offers excellent spots for most of these species.)

Backtrack to Bear Lake Road, where, past Hollowell Park, you'll be driving along **Glacier Creek.** Stop anywhere here, sit on a streamside rock, and the odds are pretty good that an American Dipper will fly up before long. Farther on, the flat, easy loop around **Sprague Lake** is a good place to look for many of the same birds mentioned for the Cub Lake Trail. The road climbs to end at 9,475 feet at **Bear Lake,** where Hammond's Flycatcher, Gray Jay, Clark's Nutcracker, Yellow-rumped Warbler, and Cassin's Finch might be found. Looking south from the parking lot at dusk, some people have been lucky enough to see Black Swifts flying toward nesting sites behind nearby waterfalls.

From Bear Lake, and from **Glacier Gorge Junction** back down the road a short distance, some of the park's nicest trails head out through deep forests to such stunning destinations as **Mills Lake, The Loch,** and **Odessa Lake.** Many of the park's special birds, such as Northern Goshawk, Blue Grouse, Northern Pygmy-Owl, Williamson's Sapsucker, Three-toed Woodpecker, Pine Grosbeak, and Red Crossbill, are present but irregular in occurrence. To see them, you simply need to walk trails and stay alert—the more you walk, the better your chances.

The same can be said for White-tailed Ptarmigan, that elusive resident of the tundra. If you trudge along trails above tree line long enough, you'll eventually find this chickenlike bird in its brownish summer plumage. From Bear Lake, the trail up to **Flattop Mountain** and **Hallett Peak** is as good as any. If you're not ready for a strenuous hike, ptarmigan are regularly found along Trail Ridge Road.

Take this awesomely scenic route west from Deer Ridge

American Dipper, known for its characteristic bobbing movement on streamside rocks

Junction, stopping at **Rainbow Curve,** just past the "Two Miles Above Sea Level" sign, to enjoy the view and the Gray Jays and Clark's Nutcrackers that are always present. Soon you'll enter the tundra world; about 2 miles from Rainbow Curve, watch for a parking area for the **Old Ute Trail** on the south. You might find ptarmigan by hiking a bit of this trail, or farther on at the **Tundra Nature Trail** at the popular Rock Cut area. (Be aware that simply walking at this elevation requires great exertion and can be dangerous for those with health problems.) Brown-capped Rosy-Finch is also found along Trail Ridge Road at times, but can be quite elusive. Look in rocky areas and along the edges of snowbanks and ice fields. The Lava Cliffs area, a short distance west, is often productive. Continue to the Alpine Visitor Center for rest rooms and refreshment. Just beyond, at **Medicine Bow Curve,** a trail from the parking area leads northeast across the tundra. Ptarmigan are sometimes seen a quarter mile or so along this path, downhill near the wind-stunted shrubs.

13 Colo. 14 running from Fort Collins to Walden, the **Cache la Poudre-North Park Scenic Byway,** follows the Cache La Poudre River through the **Roosevelt National Forest,** where picnic areas and trails offer the chance to see montane species and watch American Dippers dip on river rocks. The road crests at 10,276-foot **Cameron Pass,** known as a spot where the very elusive Boreal Owl can sometimes be heard on quiet nights in spring and fall. Walk the dirt road leading south from the

pass (if snow levels make this possible), and also check the area around **Joe Wright Reservoir,** about 3 miles east, where the owl has been heard.

Long's Peak, the highest point in Rocky Mountain National Park, as seen from Trail Ridge Road

14 In the intermontane basin called North Park, just south of Walden, **Arapaho National Wildlife Refuge** is home to birds of dry sagebrush, ponds, and marsh, and in migration shorebirds can throng edges of shallow wetlands. Nesting ducks of many species are abundant, and when you drive the 6-mile tour route in summer, you'll also find Eared Grebe; Northern Harrier; American Avocet;

Willet; Wilson's Phalarope; Forster's and Black Terns; Sage Thrasher; Brewer's, Vesper, and Savannah Sparrows; and Yellow-headed and Brewer's Blackbirds. Drive the road from refuge headquarters north back to Colo. 14, along the Illinois River, and watch for Willow Flycatcher, Mountain Bluebird, Tree Swallow, and Yellow Warbler—and for moose, which you may find feeding in riparian areas. The sage flats along this road are particularly good for Sage

Eared Grebes nesting at Arapaho National Wildlife Refuge in north-central Colorado

Thrasher and sparrows. Walk around a little and you could find Sage Grouse, as well.

You might be lucky enough to see Sage Grouse in the refuge, but for the best chance, call the North Park Chamber of Commerce (970-723-4600) and ask about tours to leks (courtship grounds) in April and May. On the western edge of Walden, be sure to scan **Walden Reservoir** for water-birds and migrant shorebirds. California Gull nests here.

15 In the Denver area, **Barr Lake State Park** has recorded nearly 350 species over the years, testament to its habitat (attractive to waterbirds and migrants) and to intense coverage by local birders. Bald Eagles have begun nesting at the lake, and other breeders include Pied-billed and Western Grebes; Double-crested Cormorant; Great Blue Heron; Snowy and Cattle Egrets; Black-crowned Night-Heron; Blue-winged, Cinnamon, and Green-winged Teals; American Avocet; Say's Phoebe; Western and Eastern Kingbirds; Horned Lark; Common Yellowthroat; and American Goldfinch.

Barr is an irrigation lake where the shoreline advances and recedes with water use; in late summer and fall, shorebirding is excellent on mudflats. In both spring and fall you should check trees and shrubs along the lake's south and east sides for migrant songbirds. A 9-mile trail circles the lake, with several observation points for scanning the water.

16 Within **Arapaho National Forest,** the **Mount Evans Scenic Byway** (*fee*) south of Idaho Springs climbs nearly to the top of 14,264-foot Mount Evans, making it the highest paved road in the United States. Open from around Memorial Day to Labor Day, the drive usually offers a better chance than does Rocky Mountain National Park's Trail Ridge Road (see p. 76) to see Brown-capped Rosy-Finch. A few miles before the top, stop at **Summit Lake** (at 12,830 feet, it's the only handicapped-accessible alpine lake in Colorado) to look for the rosy-finches, which frequent rocky places, cliffs, and the edges of snowbanks. American Pipit nests on this alpine tundra, and if luck is truly with you, a White-tailed Ptarmigan might put in an appearance.

Fewer than 4 miles west as the Common Raven flies, **Guanella Pass** is known as an excellent (though not sure-fire) place to see White-tailed Ptarmigans in their pure white winter plumage (see sidebar p. 82). Tightly twisting, partly paved, partly gravel County Road 381 runs south from Georgetown on I-70 to Grant on US 285, topping out at 11,669 feet at the pass. Though the road is kept plowed to the pass, this is obviously not a trip to undertake when bad weather threatens. From the parking area at the pass, scan the hillside to the southeast. Sometimes birders see ptarmigans from their cars, but other times they may have to walk toward the hill and explore a bit to find them. Before or after this winter (*Nov.-March*) trip, drive around Georgetown and check feeders for Gray-crowned, Black (uncommon), and Brown-capped (also uncommon) Rosy-Finches, as well as Pine and Evening Grosbeaks and Cassin's Finch. Chances are best when there's lots of snow cover.

17 Westward nearly to Utah, just south of I-70 and west of Grand Junction, **Colorado National Monument** delights the eye with strikingly sculptured cliffs of red sandstone and deep canyons cutting into the Uncompahgre Plateau. Pinyon pine and juniper create habitat far different from the spruce, fir, and ponderosa pine forests of the Rockies. Here the list of nesting birds includes Gambel's Quail, Black-chinned Hummingbird, Gray and Ash-throated Flycatchers, Gray Vireo (uncommon), Western Scrub-Jay, Pinyon Jay, Juniper Titmouse, Bushtit, Blue-gray Gnatcatcher, Black-throated Gray Warbler (uncommon), Black-throated Sparrow, and Lazuli Bunting.

The **Devils Kitchen** picnic area and adjacent 0.75-mile trail, near the east entrance to the park, provide a good introduction to the area. Several other trails, ranging from 0.25 to 8.5 miles, offer additional possibilities. As you follow the scenic **Rim Rock Drive,** watch for Golden Eagles, Peregrine and Prairie Falcons, White-throated Swift, and Mountain Bluebird, and listen for the songs of Rock, Canyon, and Bewick's Wrens. The pinyon-juniper habitat around **Saddlehorn Campground** is another fine birding location.

White-tailed Ptarmigan

All birds molt at least once a year to replace worn feathers. The White-tailed Ptarmigan, a grouselike bird of high elevations, molts three times annually, changing its plumage to match its environment. In winter, pure white feathers blend with snow-covered terrain; in summer, mottled brown and white provides camouflage on tundra where patches of snow and ice may linger; more white appears in the plumage in fall. White-tailed Ptarmigans can be elusive, but are usually approachable once located.

18 The mountain town of **Ouray** (*Chamber of Commerce 970-325-4746*), which calls itself the Switzerland of America for its alpine surroundings, has a reputation among birders as one of the best places anywhere to see the scarce and elusive Black Swift. The species nests at **Box Canyon Falls Park,** located just a half mile south of town off US 550, and can be seen on the rock face at the base of the falls, which drop 285 feet through sheer cliffs. Be here in early morning or just before dusk, because the birds spend the day feeding away from nest sites.

By continuing on County Road 361, which follows Canyon Creek up toward Yankee Boy Basin, you may find

nesting birds such as Blue Grouse; Williamson's and Red-naped Sapsuckers; Hammond's, Dusky, and Cordilleran Flycatchers; Gray Jay; Clark's Nutcracker; Mountain Chickadee; Orange-crowned and MacGillivray's Warblers; and Pine and Evening Grosbeaks.

Mountain goat on the tundra of Mount Evans, west of Denver

19 In Fountain, just south of Colorado Springs, **Fountain Creek Regional Park and Nature Center** (*N of town, W of US 85*) rates highly with local birders for its spring and fall songbird migration. A 2.5-mile-long linear park stretching along the cottonwood-lined creek, it also hosts an excellent variety of breeding birds such as Great Blue and Green Herons, Wood Duck, Virginia Rail, Sora, Red-headed Woodpecker, Western and Eastern King-birds, Violet-green Swallow, Yellow Warbler, Common Yellowthroat, Lazuli Bunting, Bullock's Oriole, and Lesser and American Goldfinches.

Stop at the nature center for advice and to check the nearby marsh. Then drive to the north part of the park, where you can investigate the area's ponds, marshes, and riparian woods for more good birding.

Red sandstone cliffs at Colorado National Monument, near Grand Junction

20 The region around **Pueblo Reservoir** combines lake, shallow ponds, riparian areas, and pinyon-juniper habitat, a variety that makes it an excellent birding destination, productive for fall and winter waterbirds, migrants, and local breeders. From the intersection of Colo. 96 and Colo. 45 in Pueblo, take Colo. 96 west 2.5 miles and turn north to **Valco Ponds State Wildlife Area,** along the Arkansas River just below the reservoir's dam.

Explore the riverbank (a trail follows the river eastward) and wetlands for migrant songbirds (warblers sometimes linger here well into winter) and summering Green Heron (scarce), Wood Duck, Osprey, Mississippi Kite, Yellow-billed Cuckoo, Red-headed Woodpecker, Blue Jay, Bewick's and House Wrens, Blue-gray Gnatcatcher, Northern Mockingbird, Brown Thrasher, Blue Grosbeak, and Lazuli and Indigo Buntings. Don't be shocked if you see the gorgeous Mandarin Duck here: Introduced from Asia, this exotic species breeds along the river. In fall and winter, check the ponds for ducks and gulls.

Return to Colo. 96 and drive west 3 miles to **Lake Pueblo State Park,** on Pueblo Reservoir. From fall into spring, use lookout points at reservoir marinas and at the dam to scan for loons, grebes (six species have been present simultaneously), ducks, and gulls. Several Bald Eagles

CENTRAL ROCKIES

usually winter here. In breeding season, pinyon-juniper areas both south and north of the lake host Scaled Quail, Greater Roadrunner, Western Scrub-Jay, Pinyon Jay, Juniper Titmouse, and Bushtit.

21 Following US 50 and the Arkansas River eastward from Pueblo onto the plains leads to some fine birding sites. Check a map and you'll notice a number of lakes and reservoirs along the way, many of which are popular birding spots. From Ordway, drive east 1.9 miles on Colo. 96 and turn north to **Lake Henry,** where grebes, waders, and shorebirds are present from spring through fall, and waterfowl and gulls congregate in fall and winter. The woodland on the west side of the lake attracts migrant songbirds in spring and fall.

Not far southeast, **Lake Cheraw** (north of La Junta) is bisected by Colo. 109. A good birding site year-round, it can be excellent for migrant shorebirds. Northwest of Lamar, US 287 passes several shallow lakes, of which the most popular for birding may be **Nee Noshe Reservoir,** just east of the highway, and **Neeso Pah Reservoir,** to the west. At any or all of these lakes you may find nesting Western and Clark's Grebes, Snowy Plover, Black-necked Stilt, and American Avocet.

22 The **Comanche National Grassland** south of Springfield is best known for its Lesser Prairie-Chicken leks, where males gather in spring to "dance" for females at dawn. This scarce species is found in Colorado only in Baca and Prowers Counties, where its leks are usually located on high spots in sage-grassland. If you're going to explore this area, contact the Comanche office in advance to buy a map and get travel advice. To reach one traditional lek site, take County Road J east from Campo 8 miles to County Road 36. Go south 2 miles to County Road G and turn east for 4 miles. Just before a road culvert, turn south through a gate and drive 1.2 miles. The lek is on the west side of the road. The prairie-chickens perform from mid-March into May. You should arrive well before dawn and take care not to disturb them. This habitat is also home to Ferruginous Hawk, Scaled Quail, Northern Bobwhite, and Lark Bunting.

The spirited spring courtship antics of Lesser Prairie-Chickens at a lek, or display ground

To reach the national grassland's **Carrizo Canyon Picnic Area,** a popular birding site with several local specialties, drive west from Campo on County Road J for 15 miles to County Road 13. Go north 3 miles to County Road M and drive west about 8.5 miles to the turnoff south to the picnic area. As you drive these roads, look for Long-billed Curlew, Burrowing Owl (in prairie-dog towns), Cassin's Kingbird, Chihuahuan Raven, and Cassin's and Grasshopper Sparrows. In the canyon you may find Scaled Quail; Greater Roadrunner; Black-chinned Hummingbird; Ladder-backed Woodpecker; Ash-throated Flycatcher; Juniper Titmouse; Bushtit; Rock, Canyon, and Bewick's Wrens; Curve-billed Thrasher; Spotted and Canyon Towhees; and Rufous-crowned Sparrow.

Return to County Road M and follow it west about 4 miles to County Road J. Take it south through **Cottonwood Canyon,** an excellent place to find Lewis's Woodpecker. Continuing through the canyon about 7 miles, you'll reach County Road 5, which you can follow northeast back to County Road M.

UTAH

Utah's **Great Salt Lake** may not be quite as famous as Yellowstone or Yosemite, but in its own way it ranks with the West's outstanding wonders. The largest natural lake in the continental United States west of the Mississippi, it stretches northwest of Salt Lake City over some 2,000 square miles—though its flat basin means small changes in water level cause large variations in surface area. Broad expanses around the lake are covered in shallow marshland attractive to nesting and migratory waterbirds of all kinds. The Great Salt Lake has no outlet; losing water only through evaporation, it has accumulated such a high concentration of salts that no fish can survive there.

23 The most famous birding area on the lake—indeed, one of the most famous in the West—is **Bear River Migratory Bird Refuge,** west of Brigham City (*exit I-15 onto Forest St. and drive W 15 miles*). As you drive to the refuge, you'll cross marshes adjoining the Bear River where wading birds and waterfowl can be abundant, so don't rush to reach the entrance. Many of the species listed for the refuge below can be found here, and in fact the birding is sometimes better along the road than in the refuge itself. Snowy Plover can be found along the road when water levels aren't too high (look for whitish alkali flats), and Long-billed Curlew can be common.

Bear River refuge suffered great damage in the mid-1980s when the Great Salt Lake rose 7 to 11 feet above its normal level, washing out dikes, flooding buildings, and destroying habitat. After much work, which involved moving more than a million cubic yards of earth, the refuge reopened for visitation in the early 1990s, and it is again a regional birding hot spot. From the old headquarters site,

- **Waterfowl and shorebirds on the Great Salt Lake**
- **Highland sites along the Mirror Lake Scenic Byway**
- **Migrants and varied breeders at Ouray National Wildlife Refuge**

Information section p. 106

American White Pelicans at Bear River Migratory Bird Refuge, west of Brigham City

a 12-mile loop auto-tour route *(call for spring road conditions)* passes ponds and marshes diked to control water level and salinity.

In spring and summer, you can practice differentiating Western and Clark's Grebes (look for the yellow-orange bill and more extensively white "face" on the latter), watch nesting Black-necked Stilt, American Avocet, and Willet, and with luck glimpse a Virginia Rail or Sora walking through the marsh grass. Other breeding-season birds here include Eared Grebe, American White Pelican (nests on islands in the Great Salt Lake), Double-crested Cormorant, American Bittern (rarely seen), Great Blue Heron, Snowy and Cattle Egrets, Black-crowned Night-Heron, White-faced Ibis, several species of duck, Northern Harrier, Ring-necked Pheasant, California Gull, Forster's and Black Terns, Horned Lark, Marsh Wren, and Savannah and Song Sparrows.

Migration brings a wider variety of species to Bear River, with thousands of ducks stopping to feed, and as many as 50,000 Tundra Swans present in November. In summer and fall, common shorebirds include Greater and Lesser Yellowlegs, Marbled Godwit, Western and Least Sandpipers, Long-billed Dowitcher, and Wilson's and Red-necked

Phalaropes, though many other species are possible. Peak shorebird variety occurs the second week of August.

24 **Antelope Island State Park** occupies the largest island in the Great Salt Lake, reached by a 7.2-mile causeway (Utah 127/1700 Street South) from Syracuse. The causeway and island are known for migrant waterbirds and shorebirds, as well as some interesting land birds. In summer and fall, billions of brine flies swarm along the Great Salt Lake shoreline (don't worry; they don't bite). In addition, though the lake is too salty for fish, tiny brine shrimp provide another food source. The result is vast congregations of Eared Grebes, shorebirds (look for Snowy Plover, among many others, along the causeway, and for Wilson's and Red-necked Phalaropes in the lake), and gulls, among other species. From the causeway and island, birders scan the open lake for migrant and wintering waterfowl. The causeway is probably the best place on the entire lake to look for rarities such as scoters, Oldsquaw, and Barrow's Goldeneye in late fall.

At the state park, look for such grassland and aridcountry birds as Chukar (check near the visitor center), Burrowing Owl, Common Poorwill, Say's Phoebe, Rock and Canyon Wrens, Sage Thrasher, and Brewer's and Sage Sparrows. Bridger Bay Beach here is probably the best swimming area on the Great Salt Lake, and a good place to see how easy it is to float (in fact, how impossible it is to sink) in the buoyant salty water. A herd of bison thrives on Antelope Island, and both pronghorn and bighorn sheep have been introduced. Sixteen miles of backcountry trails allow hiking and wildlife viewing.

Black-necked Stilt nesting at Antelope Island State Park

Just to the south, **Farmington Bay Waterfowl Management Area** (*main entrance located S and W of Farmington on W. Glover Ln./Rte. 925 South*) offers a chance to see many of the same waders, waterfowl, and shorebirds listed for Bear River refuge. The shallow impoundments and marshes here have nesting Western and Clark's Grebes, Great Blue Heron, and Snowy Plover, and as many as 200,000 ducks may be present in fall. Driving and/or walking are allowed on some dikes at certain times of year, but parts of the area are closed seasonally to lessen disturbance of the birds.

25 Part of Utah's great diversity of habitats is, of course, the beautiful high country of the Rocky Mountains, a favorite destination for summer birders just as it is for winter skiers. The Wasatch Range provides easy access from Salt Lake City to many of the typical nesting birds of the mountains in the **Wasatch-Cache National Forest.** From Utah 190 (Wasatch Boulevard, closed in winter), which parallels I-215, take 3800 South Street eastward up into **Mill Creek Canyon.** Several picnic areas are located along the 9 miles of this road, offering the chance to look for White-throated Swift; Black-chinned and Broad-tailed Hummingbirds; Red-naped Sapsucker; Olive-sided, Dusky, and Cordilleran Flycatchers; Plumbeous and Warbling Vireos; Steller's Jay; Clark's Nutcracker; Mountain Chickadee; American Dipper (along the creek); Townsend's Solitaire; Swainson's and Hermit Thrushes; Orange-crowned, Virginia's, and MacGillivray's Warblers; Western Tanager; Green-tailed Towhee; Song and Lincoln's Sparrows; Black-headed Grosbeak; and Cassin's Finch. You'll have to be lucky to see a Northern Goshawk, Blue Grouse, or Northern Pygmy-Owl, but all are possible.

About 3 miles into the canyon, watch for signs designating the **Desolation Trail;** a climb of less than 2 miles, ascending 1,250 feet above the trailhead, will take you to a fine overlook of the Great Salt Lake, and you can continue on the trail as far as you have time and energy. At the end of the road, the **Upper Mill Creek Canyon Trail** climbs 9 miles to join with the **Wasatch Crest Trail,** for those ready for a serious hike. Checking varied habitats, including aspen groves, conifers, and meadows, will turn up the greatest diversity of species.

Most of these same birds can be found in **Big Cottonwood Canyon,** about 5 miles south. From Wasatch Boulevard, drive on Utah 190 east into the canyon. **Spruces Recreation Area,** at 7,400 feet, makes a good stop, but many other spots also offer birding opportunities. About 14 miles

up the canyon, bear right to Brighton. Go behind the general store here to reach a trail around pretty **Silver Lake.** You can continue 1.5 miles to **Lake Solitude,** or even farther if you like, for solitude and more birding.

Tracks on mudflats along the shore of the Great Salt Lake

26 East of Salt Lake City, Utah 150 is known as the **Mirror Lake Scenic Byway** from Kamas east and north toward Wyoming. Along the way it crosses the Uinta Mountains, the highest east-west range in the lower 48 states. About 26 miles from Kamas, stop at **Trial Lake,** at 9,500 feet, to look for mountain birds such as Blue Grouse, Williamson's Sapsucker, Three-toed Woodpecker, Olive-sided and Hammond's Flycatchers, Gray and Steller's Jays, Clark's Nutcracker, Mountain Chickadee, Brown Creeper, Townsend's Solitaire, Pine Grosbeak, Cassin's Finch, Red Crossbill, and Pine Siskin.

In 3 miles, at Bald Mountain Pass, turn toward the parking area for the **Bald Mountain Trail,** known as a good spot

Big Cottonwood Canyon, a fine location for highland birds in the Wasatch-Cache National Forest

to find Black Rosy-Finch. Check rocky slopes, especially around the edges of ice fields and snowbanks, for this little bird, which nests only above timberline. You'll also find American Pipit up here at around 10,700 feet. The 2-mile trail to the top of Bald Mountain, at 11,943 feet, offers fabulous views of Uinta peaks and lakes. It's normally walkable only from mid-July to October. In 3 more miles, the **Mirror Lake** campground and picnic area is another popular birding spot. It is also just plain popular: The parking area here is full nearly every day in summer. After you've birded around the lake and picnic grounds, you can walk a short spur trail that leads to the **Highline Trail,** passing through meadows where you may find Calliope Hummingbird and Mountain Bluebird, as well as forests of Engelmann spruce and subalpine fir where there's a chance you'll see Blue Grouse, Three-toed Woodpecker, and other woodland birds. Keep an eye out for Northern Goshawk and Golden Eagle soaring overhead.

27 Over on the Colorado state line east of Vernal, **Dinosaur National Monument** is a fine place to see birds, as well as the bones of the creatures that may have been their ancestors. In the Dinosaur Quarry building, the fossil bones of *Stegosaurus, Apatosaurus,* and other dinosaurs are displayed in the rock where they were found. Outside is an arid, rocky landscape of sagebrush, greasewood, pinyon pine, and juniper, where breeding birds include White-throated Swift; Black-chinned and Broad-tailed Hummingbirds; Gray Flycatcher (rare); Say's Phoebe; Plumbeous Vireo (occasional); Western Scrub-Jay; Pinyon Jay; Juniper Titmouse; Rock, Canyon, and House Wrens; Mountain Bluebird; Virginia's (occasional) and Black-throated Gray Warblers; Spotted Towhee; Chipping, Lark, and Sage Sparrows; Lazuli Bunting; and Bullock's Oriole.

Steller's Jay, common and conspicuous in western mountains

The area around the **Josie Morris Cabin,** 10 miles past Dinosaur Quarry, is a spectacularly beautiful place of rugged box canyons, productive for several riparian and pinyon-juniper birds. Also check the nature trail at Split Mountain Campground, and riparian areas along the Green River. You might see a Golden Eagle or a Prairie Falcon anywhere around the park. Recently, thanks to restoration efforts, there probably have been more Peregrine Falcons in the park than Prairies, as this magnificent predator continues its comeback from endangered status. By taking the **Harpers Corner Scenic Drive** (partly in Utah and partly in Colorado), you have a chance of seeing Sage Grouse, fairly common many places in the park. In spring, ask naturalists about viewing Sage

Grouse leks (traditional courtship "dancing" sites), most of which are located outside the park.

28 Downstream on the Green River, **Ouray National Wildlife Refuge** ranks with Utah's best birding sites. The marshes and impoundments of this 11,987-acre refuge, stretching along 12 miles of the river, serve as an oasis in a desert region where rainfall averages only about 7 inches a year. Drier habitat around the wetlands adds to the diversity of possible species. As you drive south from US 40 toward the refuge on Utah 88, stop in about 2 miles and check the sage flats to the east for Brewer's and Sage Sparrows. At **Pelican Lake** (*about 7 miles S of US 40*), check for waders and other waterbirds, and for shorebirds feeding around the lake edge in migration. Then continue south another 6 miles to the Ouray refuge entrance on the east.

Driving the 9-mile auto tour route, look for nesting waterbirds including Pied-billed, Eared, Western, and Clark's Grebes; Double-crested Cormorant; Great Blue Heron; Snowy Egret; Black-crowned Night-Heron; White-faced Ibis; Canada Goose; several ducks including all three teals, Redhead, Common Merganser, and Ruddy Duck; Virginia Rail; Sora; Black-necked Stilt; American Avocet; Wilson's Phalarope; and Forster's and Black Terns. In migration, many other species of shorebirds visit the refuge, along with occasional flocks of Sandhill Cranes. An observation tower at Sheppard Bottom provides an overview of the area, and it is a good place to look for American Bittern.

Burrowing Owl is sometimes seen at the prairie dog town on the tour route, and other species of the brushlands and grasslands include Northern Harrier; Ring-necked Pheasant; Say's Phoebe; Western and Eastern Kingbirds; Horned Lark; Loggerhead Shrike; Sage Thrasher (uncommon); Vesper, Lark, and Sage (scarce) Sparrows; and Lazuli Bunting. Marsh Wren, Yellow Warbler, and Yellow-headed Blackbird breed in and around wetlands, and a few Lewis's Woodpeckers nest in riverside cottonwoods. From spring through fall, Lewis's Woodpecker is more likely to be found by driving a few miles south on Utah 88 to the town of **Ouray** and crossing the bridge over the Green River, where these birds frequent the cottonwoods.

29 Out—far out—in west-central Utah, **Fish Springs National Wildlife Refuge** is another desert oasis, where springs and seeps provide water for a 10,000-acre marsh complex, attracting nesting grebes; waders, including American Bittern, Great Blue Heron, and Snowy Egret (Great and Cattle Egrets are sometimes present); ducks; Snowy Plover (uncommon); Willet; and Long-billed Curlew. Sage Thrasher is a possibility in desert scrub, as is Black-throated Sparrow. In fall and winter, Tundra Swan is common, and some Trumpeter Swans winter here. And, of course, any wetland area this isolated in the desert will attract more than its share of rarities.

The Josie Morris Cabin, one of the best birding sites in Dinosaur National Monument, east of Vernal

The birds of Fish Springs are tempting, but be advised that when planning a visit, travelers should realize that reaching it requires a long drive on gravel roads through uninhabited desert—a journey not to be undertaken without preparation. From Salt Lake City take I-80 west to Utah 36 (Tooele exit). Travel south about 27 miles until you reach the old Pony Express route and follow this approximately 63 miles to the refuge.

30 The most famous birding spot in southwestern Utah is not one of the well-known national parks or monuments, but the small **Lytle Nature Preserve,** off the beaten track just a few miles from both Nevada and Arizona. Here several birds of the Mojave Desert extend their ranges into Utah, and a small creek creates a riparian oasis in an arid landscape of shrub-dotted cliffs. From St. George, drive west on US 91 through Santa Clara; at Shivwits, continue on US 91 southwestward toward Arizona. About 7 miles from Shivwits, you'll reach Utah Hill, the crest of the Beaver Dam Mountains. Gray Vireo and Black-chinned Sparrow have been found here in spring and early summer. Also watch for Western Scrub-Jay and Scott's Oriole. In about 4 more miles, at Cattle Cliff, turn west onto a dirt road, following signs 11 miles to the preserve. Reservations aren't necessary for day visits, but if you'd like to camp here, call in advance for information and fees. Drinking water and rest rooms are available.

Gambel's Quail perched atop a Joshua tree at Lytle Nature Preserve

Some of the birds you might find include Common Black-Hawk (very rare); Gambel's Quail; White-winged Dove; Greater Roadrunner; Costa's Hummingbird; Ladder-backed Woodpecker; Vermilion, Ash-throated, and Brown-crested Flycatchers; Black Phoebe; Loggerhead Shrike; Bell's Vireo; Verdin; Cactus and Bewick's Wrens; Black-tailed Gnatcatcher; Crissal Thrasher; Lucy's Warbler; Summer Tanager; Abert's Towhee; Black-chinned Sparrow; Hooded and Scott's Orioles; and Lesser Goldfinch. Several trails lead up the wash and into the low hills, passing through cottonwoods, desert scrub, and old fields and an orchard from the days when this was a working ranch. Look down occasionally, instead of always up for birds, and you might be lucky enough to spot a Gila monster, that beautiful, orange-and-black poisonous lizard of the southwestern desert.

NEVADA

31 If you're visiting Las Vegas and you happen to be more interested in birding than betting, be of good cheer: Several spots in and near the city let you escape ersatz Egyptian monuments and neon nightlife. To see a good selection of typical desert birds, visit **Sunset Regional Park,** just 3 miles or so east of the southern end of The Strip, at the corner of Sunset Road and Eastern Avenue. This is a popular spot, so get here early for the least disturbance and best birding. Much of the park is developed for recreation, but check the remaining areas of natural scrub toward the south. You'll find Gambel's Quail scooting through the underbrush, and possibly a Greater Roadrunner as well. Look for Ladder-backed Woodpecker, Verdin, Cactus (uncommon) and Bewick's Wrens, Black-tailed Gnatcatcher, Crissal Thrasher (uncommon), Phainopepla, and Abert's Towhee here all year, joined in nesting season by Ash-throated Flycatcher, Bell's Vireo (scarce), Lucy's Warbler, and Hooded and Bullock's Orioles. Check the park pond for migrant waterfowl and swallows.

Drive east on Sunset Road for 6 miles, and a half mile after crossing Boulder Boulevard (Nev. 582), turn north on Moser Drive to the **Henderson Bird Viewing Preserve,** known to birders for years as the Henderson sewage ponds (*open daily 6 a.m.-3 p.m.*). An excellent example of cooperation between public officials and local birders, the more than 90 acres of ponds and adjacent land here are managed to benefit migrant and nesting waterbirds, and the result is one of Nevada's birding hot spots. The highlights are migrant waterfowl, shorebirds, gulls, and terns, but any time of year you'll find something to see.

Resident wetland species include Great and Snowy Egrets, Cinnamon Teal, Ruddy Duck, Virginia Rail, Ring-billed

- **High-elevation birds on Mount Charleston**
- **Famed desert oasis at the Corn Creek Field Station**
- **Wetland species in the Lahontan Valley**

Information section p. 107

and California Gulls, and Belted Kingfisher. Look, too, for such residents as Black and Say's Phoebes, Horned Lark, Verdin, Bushtit, and Rock Wren. Present in nesting season are Black-chinned Hummingbird, Common Yellowthroat, Blue Grosbeak, and Yellow-headed Blackbird.

32 Less than a half hour west of Las Vegas, **Red Rock Canyon National Conservation Area** (*take Charleston Blvd. W and continue on Nev. 159*) offers marvelous scenery as well as good birding for Mojave Desert species. Stop at the visitor center operated by the Bureau of Land Management, and then take the 13-mile drive through the rocky hills. **Willow Spring Picnic Area** and **Pine Creek Canyon** can be good for Chukar; Gambel's Quail; Black- chinned, Anna's, and Costa's Hummingbirds; Ladder-backed Woodpecker; Ash-throated Flycatcher; Gray Vireo; Western Scrub-Jay; Juniper Titmouse; Bushtit; Cactus and Canyon Wrens; Blue-gray and Black-tailed Gnatcatchers; Spotted Towhee; and Black-chinned and Black-throated Sparrows. Check the sky occasionally and you might spot a Golden Eagle, Prairie Falcon, or White-throated Swift.

Farther south on Nev. 159, riparian areas at **Spring Mountain Ranch State Park** and **Wheeler Camp Spring** (for the latter, look for the inconspicuous sign between Bonnie Springs and Blue Diamond) might add Crissal Thrasher, Summer Tanager, and Hooded Oriole to your list. At Nev. 160, drive west about 12 miles to Mount Potosi Road; turn south and check the pinyon-pine-juniper habitat along the road from early May through June for Gray Vireo, Black-chinned Sparrow, and Scott's Oriole.

33 Take US 95 northwest from Las Vegas and in just a few miles turn west on Nev. 157, which ascends Kyle Canyon toward 11,918-foot **Mount Charleston** in the **Humboldt-Toiyabe National Forest.** Near the top you can drive north on Nev. 158 to Nev. 156, and then descend Lee Canyon back to US 95. One of the region's favorite birding routes, this 41-mile drive takes you from desert through pinyon-pine-juniper woods up through ponderosa pine forest and higher to spruce-fir habitat. In one morning you can

find the desert's Cactus Wren and the highlands' Mountain Chickadee, and a fine selection of in-between species as well.

You can see Pinyon Jay on the middle levels of the drive, though this species is irregular in its movements: You often find either ten or none. Explore picnic areas, campgrounds, and trails for such montane species as Band-tailed Pigeon (rare), Calliope (scarce) and Broad-tailed Hummingbirds, Red-naped Sapsucker, Olive-sided Flycatcher, Plumbeous Vireo, Steller's Jay, Clark's Nutcracker, Pygmy Nuthatch, Brown Creeper, Townsend's Solitaire, Hermit Thrush, Virginia's and Grace's Warblers, Western Tanager, Dark-eyed Junco, Cassin's Finch, and Red Crossbill. In spring and early summer, Flammulated Owl hoots at the end of the road up Kyle Canyon, Whip-poor-will calls in ponderosa pine below, as does Common Poorwill in the desert scrub.

34 East off US 95 between Nev. 156 and Nev. 157 you will find the entrance to **Desert National Wildlife Range;** covering 1.6 million acres, it's the largest refuge in the lower 48 states. The vast spaces of desert, shrubby slopes, and mountains are dedicated to preserving bighorn

The picturesque landscape of Red Rock Canyon National Conservation Area, near Las Vegas sheep, but birders are most interested in a small area called the **Corn Creek Field Station,** 4 miles from US 95. Here, spring-fed ponds create an oasis in a land where rain averages only about 4 inches a year. On the way into the refuge, check the desert scrub for Le Conte's Thrasher and Brewer's and Sage Sparrows. Early morning in spring is when you're most likely to hear the thrasher singing.

At Corn Creek, vegetation around the ponds and plant-

ings left from an old orchard are at their best in migration for species both expected and vagrant. Corn Creek ranks with America's best desert oases. In spring and fall you'll nearly always find a great variety of flycatchers, vireos, thrushes, warblers, sparrows, and other birds here.

Mojave Desert species such as Ash-throated Flycatcher and Phainopepla can be found in the environs. The refuge's Mormon Wells Road leads up into coniferous habitat with good birding, but it's a long, lonely drive over fairly primitive roads—check with refuge staff before setting out.

35 **Great Basin National Park** is one of America's newest parks, established in 1986 to protect part of the southern Snake Mountain Range and the desert around it. A drive up to its highest point at 13,063-foot Wheeler Peak lets visitors experience the range of life zones within Great Basin and the surrounding public lands, from sagebrush through pinyon-juniper

An ancient bristle-cone pine at Great Basin National Park

woods into forests of Engelmann spruce, Douglas-fir, and aspen, and upward to terrain where gnarled limber and bristlecone pine give way to rocky peaks above timberline. No matter how bird-oriented a traveler might be, a bit of tree-watching is in order here: Some of these bristlecone pines have been growing for more than 3,000 years, and one was discovered to be almost 5,000 years old—one of the oldest known living things on the planet.

Take **Wheeler Peak Scenic Drive** from near the park visitor center to the Wheeler Peak Campground, gaining 3,400 feet in elevation to finish at 10,000 feet. The drive is usually open from late May through September, depending on weather. After seeing Western Scrub-Jay, Pinyon Jay, Mountain Chickadee, Juniper Titmouse, Bushtit, Sage Thrasher, and Green-tailed Towhee at the bottom, you'll soon be hearing the *kra-a-a* call of Clark's Nutcracker, and spotting Steller's Jay, Red-breasted Nuthatch, Brown Creeper, American Dipper (along streams), Golden-crowned and Ruby-crowned Kinglets, Mountain Bluebird, Townsend's Solitaire, Yellow-rumped and MacGillivray's Warblers, and Dark-eyed Junco. Other species of the highland forests include Northern Goshawk, Blue Grouse, Flammulated Owl (rare), Northern Pygmy-Owl, Calliope Hummingbird, Williamson's and Red-naped Sapsuckers, Hammond's and Dusky Flycatchers, Cassin's Finch, and Pine Siskin. A look at a soaring Golden Eagle is possible nearly anywhere in the park, and Canyon Wren is sometimes seen along cliffs. Hike up from the trailhead near the Wheeler Peak Campground and you might find Black Rosy-Finches flitting around cliffs above tree line. Try the 2.7-mile **Alpine Lakes Loop,** or, if you're fit and willing, the 4.3-mile climb to the top of Wheeler Peak.

36 Mountain birds—including one unique species—are the attraction of the **Lamoille Canyon Scenic Byway** in Humboldt-Toiyabe National Forest. The drive begins near the small town of Lamoille, 20 miles southeast of Elko, and winds 13.5 miles up the picturesque glacially carved canyon into the Ruby Mountains to end at an elevation of 8,800 feet. Stop as you ascend to look for Blue Grouse, Clark's Nutcracker, Mountain Bluebird, Townsend's Solitaire, Virginia's Warbler, Western Tanager, White-crowned Sparrow, and many other highland birds. At the end of the road, trails head up above timberline where American Pipit and Black Rosy-Finch nest.

But the bird for which the Ruby Mountains are known is the exotic Himalayan Snowcock, an Asian species introduced as a game bird in the 1960s and surviving here above tree line in what must be a reasonable facsimile of its native Himalayan heights. It takes some effort to find the snowcock. At the least you must hike 2 miles, gaining about 800 feet in elevation, to the area around **Island Lake.** The **Liberty Pass** and **Wines Peak** areas also are home to the birds. The best time to visit is mid-July through August, when snow has left the trails, but even then there's no guarantee you'll find this scarce species.

37 Set in a high valley on the east side of the Ruby Mountains, **Ruby Lake National Wildlife Refuge** might be off the beaten path, but nesting and migrant waterbirds make the effort to reach it worthwhile. From Elko, take Nev. 227 to Nev. 228. Drive south 28 miles, and turn west to cross the mountains on the Harrison Pass Road (Forest Road 113), then drive south to the refuge headquarters. Look for Lewis's Woodpecker along Harrison Pass Road.

More than 160 springs flow into the area from the Ruby Mountains (Nevada's wettest mountain range), creating a marsh where many species of waterfowl breed—including Trumpeter Swan, introduced from Montana. Sandhill Crane also nests, and other breeding species of wetlands and riparian areas include Pied-billed and Eared Grebes, American Bittern, Great and Snowy Egrets, Black-crowned Night-Heron, White-faced Ibis, Northern Harrier, Virginia Rail, Sora, Black-necked Stilt, American Avocet, Long-billed Curlew, Forster's and Black Terns, Short-eared Owl, Tree and Violet-green Swallows, Marsh Wren, and Orange-crowned and MacGillivray's Warblers. In sagebrush and shrubby areas, look for Gray Flycatcher, Western Scrub-Jay, Juniper Titmouse, and Brewer's and Vesper Sparrows.

38 Wetlands near **Fallon,** in western Nevada, are home to sometimes spectacular numbers of nesting and migrant waders, waterfowl, and shorebirds. Located in the **Lahontan Valley,** a basin that was filled by a glacial lake at the end of the last ice age, these lakes and marshes can vary greatly in size and somewhat in depth from year to year, but collectively the Lahontan Valley wetlands compose one of the most important waterbirds habitats in the west.

To reach **Stillwater National Wildlife Refuge,** take US 50 east from Fallon 5 miles and continue east on Nev. 116 another 11 miles. In spring and fall migration, tens of thousands of shorebirds may feed along lake edges here, with the most common species Western and Least Sandpipers, Long-billed Dowitcher, and Red-necked Phalarope. Also common, and remaining to nest on the refuge, are Black-necked Stilt, American Avocet, and Wilson's Phalarope. Snowy Plover and Long-billed Curlew are uncommon breeders, and more than a dozen other species are seen regularly in migration. Other nesting birds on the refuge include Eared, Western, and Clark's Grebes; Great, Snowy, and Cattle Egrets; Black-crowned Night-Heron; White-faced Ibis; ducks including Gadwall, Cinnamon Teal, and Redhead; and Forster's Tern. American White Pelicans are common from spring through fall. Migration can bring vast numbers of geese and ducks (sometimes in the hundreds of thousands), including perhaps half the Pacific flyway's

A marsh at Stillwater National Wildlife Refuge, part of the wetlands complex of the Lahontan Valley

Canvasbacks in fall, and up to 6,000 Tundra Swans in late fall. Many Tundras remain through the winter, as do good numbers of Bald Eagles; look also for wintering Rough-legged Hawk, Golden Eagle, Prairie Falcon, and Northern Shrike. From Fallon, drive south on US 95 for 8.8 miles, turn east on Pasture Road, and drive 2 miles to **Carson Lake,** another part of the region's wetland complex that can offer terrific birding for much of the year. This is a managed hunting area, so you must check in at the entrance before birding. Access is restricted during the fall waterfowl season. Migrant waterfowl and shorebirds highlight Carson Lake, but breeding species of waders and waterfowl include those listed above for Stillwater. Three viewing towers allow easy scanning of the area.

Wilson's Phalarope

Wilson's Phalarope is one of many shorebirds that nest far from ocean shores. In breeding season it can be found on shallow lakes throughout much of the Great Plains and Great Basin. In fall migration huge flocks gather at spots such as Utah's Great Salt Lake and Mono Lake in California. As is true for all phalaropes, in Wilson's the sex roles are reversed: The female is more colorful than the male, and it's the latter that incubates the eggs and raises the young.

39 The coniferous forests around lovely Lake Tahoe, southwest of Reno, host montane species from the raucous and conspicuous Steller's Jay to the unassuming little Dark-eyed Junco. **Lake Tahoe Nevada State Park,** situated on the lake between Incline Village and Carson City, is a good place to begin your exploration. At **Spooner Lake,** trails lead up into the mountains; the **Tahoe Rim Trail** follows the crest of the Carson Range, but there are less strenuous trails, too. White-headed Woodpecker is possible in these forests, as are Williamson's, Red-naped, and Red-breasted Sapsuckers. Watch also for Blue Grouse; Band-tailed Pigeon; Calliope and Broad-tailed Hummingbirds; Hammond's, Dusky, and Cordilleran Flycatchers; Mountain Chickadee; Pygmy Nuthatch; Yellow-rumped and Hermit Warblers; Western Tanager; Cassin's Finch; and Red Crossbill. For more mountain birding, take Nev. 431 north from Incline Village, stopping at picnic and recreation areas in the Humboldt-Toiyabe National Forest along the way. Trails lead westward into the **Mount Rose Wilderness** area, for those seeking a solitary backcountry experience.

Central Rockies
Information

? Visitor Center/Information   **$** Fee Charged   **¶** Food

Rest Rooms   **Nature Trails**   **Driving Tours**   **Wheelchair Accessible**

Be advised that facilities may be seasonal and limited. We suggest calling or writing ahead for specific information. Note that addresses may be for administrative offices; see text or call for directions to sites.

Rare Bird Alerts

Wyoming:
Statewide *307-265-2473*

Colorado:
Statewide *303-424-2144*

Utah:
Statewide *801-538-4730*

Nevada:
Northwest *702-324-2473*
South *702-390-8463*

WYOMING

National Elk Refuge
(Page 65)
P.O. Box 510
Jackson, WY 83001
307-739-9322

? ¶ &

Grand Teton National Park *(Page 65)*
P.O. Drawer 170
Moose, WY 83012
307-739-3300

? $ ¶ ¶ ⚡ ～ &

Yellowstone National Park *(Page 67)*
P.O. Box 168
Yellowstone NP, WY 82190
307-344-7381

? $ ¶ ¶ ⚡ ～ &

Interior of park closed to vehicles early Nov.–late April

Story Fish Hatchery
(Page 69)
311 Fish Hatchery Road
Story, WY 82842
307-683-2234

? ¶ &

Edness Kimball Wilkins State Park
(Page 70)
P.O. Box 1596
Evansville, WY 82636
307-577-5150

$ ¶ ⚡ &

Table Mountain and Rawhide Wildlife Habitat Management Areas
(Pages 70, 71)
Wyoming Fish and Game
5400 Bishop Boulevard
Cheyenne, WY 82006
307-777-4600

Hutton Lake National Wildlife Refuge *(Page 71)*
c/o Arapaho NWR
P.O. Box 457
Walden, CO 80480
970-723-8202

Medicine Bow-Routt National Forest *(Page 72)*
2468 Jackson Street
Laramie, WY 82070
307-745-2300

? ¶ ⚡

Seedskadee National Wildlife Refuge *(Page 73)*
P.O. Box 700
Green River, WY 82935
307-875-2187

? ¶ ～ &

Open June-Oct.

COLORADO

Bonny Lake State Park
(Page 74)
30010 County Road 3
Idalia, CO 80735
970-354-7306

$ ¶ ⚡ &

Pawnee National Grassland *(Page 74)*
660 O Street
Greeley, CO 80631
970-353-5004
❓👫🚶🏊♿

Central Plains Experiment Range
(Page 76)
58009 Wells County
Road 37
Nunn, CO 80648
970-897-2226

Rocky Mountain National Park *(Page 76)*
Estes Park, CO 80517
970-586-1206
❓🅿️🍴👫🚶🏊♿

*Toll road open Mem. Day–
Columbus Day. Trails closed
mid-April–late May*

Roosevelt National Forest *(Page 78)*
240 Prospect Road
Ft. Collins, CO 80526
970-498-1100
❓👫🚶🏊♿

Arapaho National Wildlife Refuge *(Page 79)*
P.O. Box 457
Walden, CO 80480
970-723-8202
👫🚶🏊♿

*Auto tour route and most other
roads closed in winter*

Barr Lake State Park
(Page 80)
13401 Picadilly Road
Brighton, CO 80601
303-659-6005
❓🅿️👫🚶♿

Arapaho National Forest
(Page 81)
Clear Creek Ranger District
P.O. Box 3307
Idaho Springs, CO 80452
303-567-2901
❓🅿️👫🚶🏊♿

*Administers Mount Evans
and Guanella Pass areas*

Colorado National Monument *(Page 82)*
Fruita, CO 81521
970-858-3617
❓🅿️👫🚶🏊♿

Box Canyon Falls Park
(Page 82)
P.O. Box 468
Ouray, CO 81427
970-325-4464
❓🅿️👫🚶

Fountain Creek Regional Park and Nature Center *(Page 83)*
320 Pepper Grass Lane
Fountain, CO 80817
719-520-6745
❓👫🚶♿

Valco Ponds State Wildlife Area *(Page 84)*
Pueblo Service Center
600 Reservoir Road
Pueblo, CO 81005
719-561-4909
🚶

Lake Pueblo State Park *(Page 84)*
640 Reservoir Road
Pueblo, CO 81005
719-561-9320
❓🅿️👫🚶🏊♿

Comanche National Grassland *(Page 86)*
P.O. Box 127
Springfield, CO 81073
719-523-6591

UTAH

Bear River Migratory Bird Refuge *(Page 87)*
58 South 950 West
Brigham City, UT 84302
435-723-5887
👫🚶🏊♿

Antelope Island State Park *(Page 89)*
4528 West 1700 South
Syracuse, UT 84075
801-773-2941
❓🅿️🍴👫🚶🏊♿

Farmington Bay Waterfowl Management Area *(Page 89)*
515 East 5300 South
Ogden, UT 84405
801-451-7386
👫🚶🏊♿

Wasatch-Cache National Forest *(Page 90)*
8236 Federal Building
125 South State Street
Salt Lake City, UT 84138
801-524-3900
❓🅿️🍴👫🚶♿

*Administers Mill Creek
Canyon, Big Cottonwood
Canyon, and Mirror
Lake Scenic Byway areas*

Dinosaur National Monument *(Page 93)*
4545 East US 40
Dinosaur, CO 81610
970-374-3000
⬛⬛⬛⬛⬛

Ouray National Wildlife Refuge *(Page 94)*
266 West 100 North,
Suite 2
Vernal, UT 84078
435-789-0351
⬛⬛⬛

Fish Springs National Wildlife Refuge *(Page 95)*
P.O. Box 568
Dugway, UT 84022
435-831-5353
⬛⬛⬛⬛

Lytle Nature Preserve
(Page 96)
290 MLBM, Brigham
Young University
Provo, UT 84602
801-378-5052
⬛⬛⬛⬛

NEVADA

Sunset Regional Park
(Page 97)
Clark County Parks and
Recreation Department
2601 East Sunset Road
Las Vegas, NV 89120
702-455-8293
⬛⬛⬛

Henderson Bird Viewing Preserve *(Page 97)*
Henderson Parks and
Recreation Department
240 Water Street
Henderson, NV 89015
702-565-4264
⬛⬛

Also known as the Henderson sewage ponds

Red Rock Canyon National Conservation Area *(Page 98)*
HCR 33, Box 5500
Las Vegas, NV 89124
702-363-1921
⬛⬛⬛⬛⬛⬛

Spring Mountain Ranch State Park *(Page 98)*
Box 124
Blue Diamond, NV 89004
702-875-4141
⬛⬛⬛⬛

Humboldt-Toiyabe National Forest *(Page 98)*
2881 South Valley View,
Suite 16
Las Vegas, NV 89102
702-873-8800
⬛⬛⬛⬛⬛⬛

Desert National Wildlife Range *(Page 99)*
1500 North Decatur
Boulevard
Las Vegas, NV 89108
702-646-3401
⬛⬛⬛⬛⬛

Great Basin National Park *(Page 100)*
Baker, NV 89311
775-234-7331
⬛⬛⬛⬛⬛⬛

Ruby Lake National Wildlife Refuge
(Page 102)
HC 60 Box 860
Ruby Valley, NV 89833
775-779-2237
⬛⬛⬛⬛⬛

Stillwater National Wildlife Refuge
(Page 103)
P.O. Box 1236
1000 Auction Road
Fallon, NV 89406
775-423-5128
⬛⬛

Carson Lake *(Page 104)*
Nevada Division of Wildlife
380 West B Street
Fallon, NV 89406
775-423-3171
⬛⬛

Lake Tahoe Nevada State Park *(Page 104)*
P.O. Box 8867
Incline Village, NV 89452
702-831-0494
⬛⬛⬛⬛

California

Without question, California has within its borders a greater variety of terrain than any other state. Stretching more than 800 miles corner to corner, it encompasses Mojave Desert scrub and redwood forests, Pacific Ocean cliffs and Sierra Nevada peaks, salt marshes and Great Basin sagebrush, to list only a few of its many habitats. This sort of diversity, of course, means a correspondingly long list of birds. In fact, more than 600 species have been found in California—about 70 percent of the total seen in the lower 48 states.

Some of the state's specialties are obvious from a quick scan of a checklist. You probably won't have much trouble adding California Quail, California Thrasher, or California Towhee to your life list, since all are common and easily seen. You'll have to work a little harder to see the threatened California Gnatcatcher (once considered a race of Black-tailed Gnatcatcher), found in the southern part of the state in coastal sage scrub, a habitat nearly obliterated by development. The endangered California Condor (see sidebar p. 131), once teetering on the verge of extinction, has been reintroduced into southern California, years after all the remaining wild birds were rounded up for a captive-breeding program. Though they don't have "California" in their names, the Island Scrub-Jay of Santa Cruz Island and the Yellow-billed Magpie of the Central Valley are among the most special of the specialties, since neither has ever been found in any other state or country.

Highlights of California birding include the Salton Sea, that strangely

Preceding pages: Double-crested Cormorants, Sonny Bono Salton Sea National Wildlife Refuge *Above:* California Gnatcatcher *Below:* Observation platform, Tijuana Slough National Wildlife Refuge

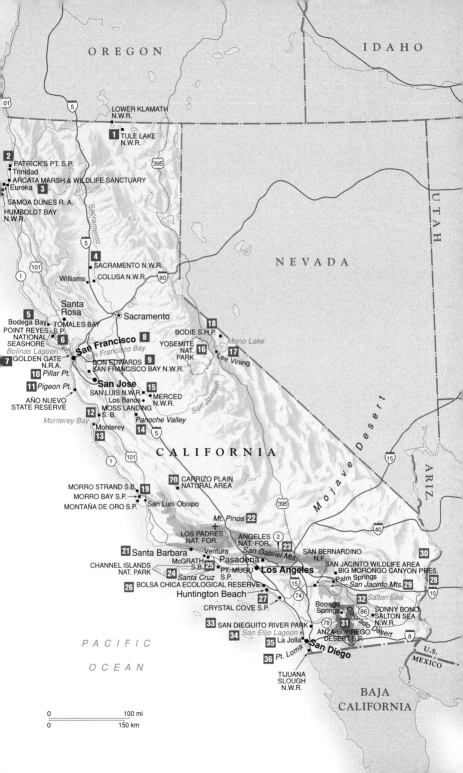

accidental lake in the southern desert where odd waterbirds appear regularly, and pelagic trips out into the Pacific from Monterey Bay, where keen observers search for wandering seabirds from around the globe. Great flocks of waterfowl winter in the Klamath Basin in the north and in Central Valley refuges. Yosemite National Park, famed for its scenery, is home to a tempting array of high-country nesting birds; Point Reyes National Seashore is one of the

Yellow-billed
Magpie

Special Birds of California

Pacific Loon	Pacific Golden-	Anna's Hummingbird	Oak Titmouse
Black-footed	Plover	Costa's	Verdin
Albatross	Mountain Plover	Hummingbird	California
Buller's Shearwater	Wandering Tattler	Allen's	Gnatcatcher
Black-vented	Black Turnstone	Hummingbird	Varied Thrush
Shearwater	Surfbird	Red-breasted	Wrentit
Ashy Storm-Petrel	Rock Sandpiper	Sapsucker	California Thrasher
Black Storm-Petrel	Heermann's Gull	Nuttall's	Le Conte's Thrasher
Brandt's Cormorant	Mew Gull	Woodpecker	Phainopepla
Pelagic Cormorant	Thayer's Gull	White-headed	Hermit Warbler
California Condor	Yellow-footed Gull	Woodpecker	California Towhee
Ross's Goose	Elegant Tern	Black-backed	Black-chinned
Eurasian Wigeon	Common Murre	Woodpecker	Sparrow
Barrow's Goldeneye	Pigeon Guillemot	Pacific-slope	Sage Sparrow
White-tailed Kite	Marbled Murrelet	Flycatcher	Golden-crowned
Chukar	Xantus's Murrelet	Cassin's Vireo	Sparrow
Sage Grouse	Cassin's Auklet	Hutton's Vireo	Tricolored Blackbird
Blue Grouse	Rhinoceros Auklet	Island Scrub-Jay	Hooded Oriole
Mountain Quail	Tufted Puffin	Yellow-billed	Scott's Oriole
California Quail	Spotted Owl	Magpie	Gray-crowned
Black Rail	Great Gray Owl	Chestnut-backed	Rosy-Finch
Clapper Rail	Black Swift	Chickadee	Lawrence's
			Goldfinch

state's finest sites for both land birds and waterbirds; excellent coastal reserves from San Diego northward are home to waders, waterfowl, shorebirds, gulls, and terns. No single trip can take in all of California's diversity, so avid birders return time after time to sample more of its destinations.

This chapter begins in the Klamath Basin, on the Oregon state line, and ends in San Diego, just a short distance from the Mexican border. ■

NORTHERN CALIFORNIA

1 Wildlife refuges with lots of wintering waterfowl are certainly not rare in the United States; neither is it unusual to find numbers of Bald Eagles and other raptors congregating in such places to feed on sick and injured ducks and geese. Even so, the **Klamath Basin National Wildlife Refuges Complex** stands out for the spectacle it offers, with more than a million waterfowl present at times in fall migration. Common species include Tundra Swan; Greater White-fronted, Snow, Ross's, and Canada Geese; and a host of dabbling and diving ducks. In addition, the Klamath Basin is home to the greatest concentration of wintering Bald Eagles in the lower 48 states, with most years seeing peak populations ranging from 500 to 1,000.

The six refuges in this complex straddle the California-Oregon border north and south of Klamath Falls, Oregon. Two refuges in California, **Lower Klamath National Wildlife Refuge** and **Tule Lake National Wildlife Refuge,** make the best destinations, since most others are either closed to the public or difficult to access. To reach Lower Klamath from the town of Tulelake, drive northwest on Calif. 139 for 4 miles, turn west on Calif. 161, and drive 10 miles. For the latter, turn south off Calif. 161 onto Hill Road 2 miles west of the Calif. 139/161 junction. Auto tour routes at both refuges lead through wetlands where you'll enjoy looking over masses of birds from fall through spring (though midwinter freeze-up pushes many birds farther south). With luck you might find a rarity such as Emperor Goose (best chance in fall at Tule Lake), Trumpeter Swan, Oldsquaw, or Barrow's Goldeneye. Eurasian Wigeon is uncommon but regular in flocks of American Wigeon. In addition to Bald Eagle, look for other winter raptors including Red-tailed (nests) and Rough-legged Hawks, Golden

- **Excellent diversity at Point Reyes National Seashore**
- **Seabirds at Año Nuevo State Reserve and other coastal sites**
- **Pelagic trips from Monterey Bay**
- **Mountain species at Yosemite National Park**

Information section p. 145

Eagle (nests), Merlin, and Peregrine Falcon, and for that diminutive predator, the Northern Shrike.

By no means are Lower Klamath and Tule Lake refuges only winter birding sites. Great numbers of waders, waterfowl, and other waterbirds breed here, including Pied-billed, Red-necked (uncommon), Eared, Western, and Clark's Grebes; American White Pelican; Great and Snowy Egrets; White-faced Ibis; many ducks; Virginia Rail; Sora; Snowy Plover (nesting areas are closed, but ask refuge personnel about viewing this shorebird at White Lake); Black-necked Stilt; American Avocet; Long-billed Curlew; Wilson's Phalarope; and Caspian, Forster's, and Black Terns. Other nesters include California Quail, Sandhill Crane, Short-eared Owl, Ash-throated Flycatcher, Western Scrub-Jay, and Tricolored and Yellow-headed Blackbirds—though this is only a sampling of what you might find.

2 There's excellent seabird-watching, and good land birding, too, at **Patrick's Point State Park,** just west of US 101, 5 miles north of Trinidad. Follow the 2-mile **Rim Trail,** and from the cliffs of this rocky headland (especially near Wedding Rock) look for Common Murre, Pigeon Guillemot, Cassin's and Rhinoceros Auklets, and with luck Tufted Puffin (April through July is best), plus occasional Marbled Murrelet; and for Red-throated, Pacific, and Common Loons; Brandt's, Double-crested, and Pelagic Cormorants; Brown Pelican; and wintering sea ducks including rare Harlequin and all three scoters (Black is uncommon). Black Oystercatcher nests here, and three other "rocky shorebirds"—Wandering Tattler (mostly in migration), Black Turnstone, and Surfbird—are present except in early summer. In woodland of spruce, fir, pine, and hemlock, you'll find resident California Quail, Band-tailed Pigeon, Anna's Hummingbird, Pileated Woodpecker, Black Phoebe, Hutton's Vireo, Gray and Steller's Jays, Chestnut-backed Chickadee, Bushtit, Varied Thrush, and Wrentit. Nesting-season birds include Allen's Hummingbird, Olive-sided and Pacific-slope Flycatchers, Orange-crowned and Wilson's Warblers, Western Tanager, and Black-headed Grosbeak. As is true of many places along the coast, this is a good site for viewing migrating gray whales in spring and fall.

3 Not far to the south, in the town of Arcata, you can turn west on Calif. 255, drive less than a half mile, and turn south on either G or I Streets to enter the **Arcata Marsh and Wildlife Sanctuary.** Here, extensive trails border wetlands where you'll find waders, ducks, and other marsh birds, as well as migrant shorebirds. The sanctuary sits alongside **Humboldt Bay,** one of California's most productive birding areas. From fall through spring, loons, grebes, and waterfowl can be present in great numbers. The eelgrass beds here attract migrant Brant, with the greatest concentration in March and April, and mudflats along the shoreline draw migrant shorebirds.

From Eureka, take Calif. 255 west from US 101 and in 1.7 miles go south on New Navy Base Road for 4 miles to the **Samoa Dunes Recreation Area,** where a viewing platform overlooks the bay and Pacific coast. For more birding, return to US 101, drive south, and in about 3 miles take Hilfiker Lane west for additional bay access. About 6.5 miles south on US 101, take Hookton Road west to a section of **Humboldt Bay National Wildlife Refuge,** or keep west to **Table Bluff County Park,** both of which provide more bay views.

The rocky coast at Patrick's Point State Park, home to several species of nesting seabirds

4 Moving inland from the coast temporarily, you'll find tremendous flocks of wintering waterfowl at the **Sacramento National Wildlife Refuge Complex,** six associated refuges about 100 miles north of Sacramento. Ross's Goose is abundant here in winter with its larger relative, the Snow Goose. Greater White-fronted Goose is common, and the total numbers of waterfowl reach into the hundreds of thousands from October through February. **Sacramento National Wildlife Refuge** (*take Norman Rd. exit from I-5, drive E and immediately N on the frontage road*) and **Colusa National Wildlife Refuge** (*from Williams, E on Calif. 20*) both have auto tour routes from which you can view geese, ducks, and other marsh and waterbirds. These wetlands also attract migrant shorebirds and nesting waders, ducks, and rails. Look in spring and summer for breeding American Bittern; Great, Snowy, and Cattle (rare) Egrets; Black-crowned Night-Heron; White-faced Ibis; Common Moorhen; Black-necked Stilt; and American Avocet. Yellow-billed Magpie, a central California specialty, is found here year-round.

Wetlands along Humboldt Bay, near Eureka

5 Back on the coast, the area around **Bodega Bay,** about 20 miles southwest of Santa Rosa, ranks with the region's best seabirding sites. Just north of the community of Bodega Bay, turn west off Calif. 1 on Eastshore Road and then west again onto Westside Road, which dead-ends at Bodega Head. Scan the bay along the way for loons, grebes, and ducks from fall through spring, and for Brant in spring. Black-crowned Night-Heron nests at the **Hole-in-the-Head Picnic Area,** and **Westside County Park** offers good bay views. At **Bodega Head,** check the rocks for resident Black Oystercatcher and migrant Wandering Tattler, Ruddy and Black Turnstones, and Surfbird, among other shorebirds. You might spot a wintering Rock Sandpiper, too. Migrant and wintering ducks may include Harlequin Duck, scoters, or Oldsquaw. Pelagic Cormorant, Western Gull, and Pigeon Guillemot nest on rocky cliffs. Return to Calif. 1, drive south, and in about a mile veer west onto Smith Brothers Road to check the bay for ducks, migrant shorebirds, and gulls. Just to the south, turn west off Calif. 1 onto Doran Beach Road to reach **Doran County Park,** another fine shorebirding site.

6 **Point Reyes National Seashore** earns its superb birding reputation on several levels. Beginners or visitors from outside the region will find many characteristic land birds of this area in forests (walk the **Bear Valley Trail**), scrub, and fields, including California Quail, Anna's and Allen's (absent fall through early winter) Hummingbirds, Nuttall's Woodpecker, Pacific-slope Flycatcher (spring and summer), Hutton's Vireo, Chestnut-backed Chickadee, Oak Titmouse, Pygmy Nuthatch, Wrentit, and California Towhee. Spots such as Limantour Beach can have concentrations of migrant shorebirds; walk along the Spit, and take the **Estero** and **Muddy Hollow Trails** north past ponds good for waterbirds. Walk to **Abbott's Lagoon,** on Pierce Point Road, to look for winter and migrant waterfowl, and visit **Drake's Estero** for waders and shorebirds.

The lighthouse area makes a great lookout for seabirds, including Red-throated and Pacific Loons, Sooty Shearwater (summer and early fall), Brown Pelican (summer and fall), Brandt's and Pelagic Cormorants, scoters (fall through spring), Black Oystercatcher and other rocky shorebirds, Common Murre, Pigeon Guillemot, Rhinoceros Auklet, and other alcids. Where Sir Francis Drake Boulevard turns west to the lighthouse, drive east toward Chimney Rock and check **Drake's Bay** for loons, grebes, and sea ducks.

Point Reyes offers some special birding challenges, too. The rare Spotted Owl is a possibility at adjacent **Tomales Bay State Park,** where trails provide good land birding, and the bay hosts Osprey and migrant and winter waterfowl. Pacific Golden-Plover is often found in pastures from fall through spring. Check along Sir Francis Drake Boulevard near the side road to Drake's Beach, or continue south 0.8 mile past Spaletta Ranch and pass through a gate on the east to check the field. Look also for wintering raptors and longspurs in these areas. Isolated patches of trees in this part of the park, including those around dairy farms, are famed migrant and vagrant traps in fall and late spring, when all sorts of eastern migrants may show up. Conditions are best for migrants when the sky is overcast or fog is present. (Dairy ranches are private, so use discretion when birding around them, and leave gates as you find them.) Point Reyes is a large and heavily birded area, so ask park naturalists about recent sightings and best locations for the time of your visit.

Just to the south, **Bolinas Lagoon** is also excellent for waders, waterfowl including migrant Brant, and resident Osprey. From Olema, drive south on Calif. 1 about 9 miles and turn south on Olema-Bolinas Road, scanning the water where you can. Also check the lagoon from pull-offs along Calif. 1 south of this road. Just north of Calif. 1 here, **Audubon Canyon Ranch** *(open mid-March–mid-July)* is home to a colony of Great Blue Herons and Great and Snowy Egrets nesting in redwood trees. An observation platform provides a great view of the lively, noisy business of raising a new generation of these waders.

7 In fall, visit the Marin Headlands area of the **Golden Gate National Recreation Area** *(take the Alexander Ave. exit from US 101 N of Golden Gate Bridge and drive W)*, where Battery 129 on Conzelman Road is known to birders as "Hawk Hill." Peak months are September and October, when thousands of raptors, including Osprey; Northern Harrier; accipiters; Red-shouldered, Broad-winged (rare), and Red-tailed Hawks; Golden Eagle; Merlin; and Peregrine Falcon pass over the region's most famous hawk-watching site. Visitors to San Francisco without time to travel far from the city will also find **Marin Headlands** a pleasant place to see typical area birds such as California Quail, Chestnut-backed Chickadee, and Wrentit, and exploring its coastline and **Rodeo Lagoon** will always turn up waterbirds.

8 Many an out-of-state visitor has seen his or her first Glaucous-winged Gull, Anna's Hummingbird, Western Scrub-Jay, Chestnut-backed Chickadee, Bushtit, Pygmy

Nuthatch, Wrentit, or California Towhee right in the heart of San Francisco at **Golden Gate Park.** To this list can be added nesting Allen's Hummingbird and wintering Mew Gull, Red-breasted Sapsucker, Varied Thrush, and Golden-crowned Sparrow. Wooded areas and plantings in the western part of this expansive park offer the best land birding, but local bird-watchers keep an eye on all the park lakes for waterfowl and gulls. Eurasian Wigeon appears here regularly in winter, and the very rare Tufted Duck has been found a number of times.

Next drive just to the northeast, at the western end of Point Lobos Avenue, where the **Cliff House** area of the Golden Gate National Recreation Area provides visitors with an excellent viewpoint for finding seabirds and shorebirds year-round. Black Oystercatcher is a nesting resident on the rocks below, and other "rocky shorebirds" are present except in midsummer. Look also for Brandt's and Pelagic Cormorants, Brown Pelican, gulls (Western nests here, and Heermann's is present much of the year), Elegant Tern (in summer), Common Murre, Pigeon Guillemot (absent in winter), and any number of other waterbirds, including possible wintering Harlequin Duck, scoters, and Oldsquaw. Walking down to the old Sutro Baths (where waterfowl rest on ponds) and the Point Lobos area offers additional birding opportunities.

Tomales Bay at Point Reyes National Seashore, one of California's most popular birding sites

San Francisco and the Golden Gate Bridge, as seen from the Marin Headlands, Golden Gate National Recreation Area

9 Waders, waterfowl, shorebirds, and other wetlands species can be found at several accessible sites on the southern end of San Francisco Bay. To reach the **Don Edwards San Francisco Bay National Wildlife Refuge,** take the Paseo Padre Parkway/Thornton Avenue exit from Calif. 84, just east of the Dumbarton Bridge at Newark, and drive south 0.8 mile to the entrance. The **Tidelands Trail,** a 1-mile loop, traverses marshland where Pied-billed and Eared Grebes, American Bittern, Great and Snowy Egrets, dabbling ducks, Common Moorhen, Black-necked Stilt, and American Avocet are present all year, and an array of shorebirds, gulls, and terns changes with the seasons. Follow Marshlands Road (*closed April–Aug. to protect nesting Snowy Plover*) to its end to walk the **Shoreline Trail** along the edge of the bay, where with luck (and high tide, which pushes birds up to drier ground) you might see a Clapper Rail—or with lots of luck, a Black Rail in winter. The trail leads north about 4 miles to **Coyote Hills Regional Park,** where more trails provide access to freshwater marsh. You can also reach the park by taking the Paseo Padre Parkway/Thornton Avenue exit off Calif. 84 and driving 1.5 miles north to Patterson Ranch Road, which leads to the entrance. White-tailed Kite might be seen here or at the refuge.

To reach another unit of the national wildlife refuge, at Milpitas take Calif. 237 west from I-880 for 1.2 miles, turn north on Zanker Road, and continue 2.1 miles to the refuge Environmental Education Center. The **Mallard Slough** and **Alviso Slough Trails** are excellent birding walks for wetland species. For more similar marsh habitat, take Embarcadero Road east from US 101 in Palo Alto, on the west side of the bay, to **Palo Alto Baylands Preserve,** where birders also look for Clapper Rail and, at high tide in winter, for the elusive Black Rail and Nelson's Sharp-tailed Sparrow.

10 Following Calif. 1 south from the Bay Area along the Pacific coast will take you past a number of excellent sites for observing seabirds and shorebirds. Just north of Half Moon Bay, drive west through the community of Princeton toward **Pillar Point,** a fine spot from which to scan the sea for loons, grebes, sea ducks, and alcids, and the rocky coast for shorebirds. The harbor here should be checked for waterfowl as well as seabirds; Brant can be common in spring. Check gull flocks for Thayer's, occurring regularly but in small numbers.

11 About 20 miles south, turn west off US 1 toward the lighthouse at **Pigeon Point,** one of the coast's very best seabird lookouts. Stop along the road north of the lighthouse for the best viewing, and keep in mind that this sort of birding can be exciting or dull, depending on circumstances of weather and luck. On good days, the sea and sky can be alive with loons, cormorants, ducks, gulls, and alcids from the common Common Murre to something as unusual as an Ancient Murrelet (winter) or Tufted Puffin (summer). In migration, a west wind pushes birds closer to shore. Pigeon Point is an excellent spot for Marbled Murrelet and for pelagics such as Sooty Shearwater (summer and fall); each spring a few Black-footed Albatrosses are seen from shore here.

The next stop, 6 miles south, is **Año Nuevo State Reserve,** famed for its colony of elephant seals (females give

Japanese Tea Garden in Golden Gate Park, San Francisco

birth from late December to early February), and for good birding. Brandt's and Pelagic Cormorants, Black Oystercatcher, Pigeon Guillemot, and Cassin's and Rhinoceros Auklets all nest on cliffs and/or offshore islands here, and the bluffs offer yet another good viewpoint for seabird-watching. Marbled Murrelet might be found year-round out beyond the surf line. Land birding at Año Nuevo can be interesting as well. Nesting birds include White-tailed Kite, California Quail, Band-tailed Pigeon, Acorn Woodpecker, Black Phoebe, Hutton's Vireo, Steller's Jay, Swainson's Thrush, California Thrasher, Wrentit, Wilson's Warbler, Spotted and California Towhees, White-crowned Sparrow, and Lesser Goldfinch. Keep a sharp eye out anywhere along this stretch of coast in fields and marshes for Tricolored Blackbird. In addition, the rare Black Swift breeds in sea caves at Año Nuevo, though you need to be present at dawn or dusk to see them leaving or returning to their nests; during the day they travel long distances to feed on insects high in the sky.

Acorn Woodpecker

The strikingly attractive Acorn Woodpecker is notorious for its habit of storing acorns in small holes it drills in the bark of trees, or in nearly any other sort of wood from utility poles to buildings. A single tree, which may be used year after year, can have thousands of acorn holes. Woodpeckers wedge the nuts in tightly to protect them from other birds and squirrels. Common throughout much of western and central California, the "clown-faced" Acorn Woodpecker also feeds on insects, tree sap, and fruit.

12 As you skirt Monterey Bay and approach the town of Moss Landing from the north along Calif. 1, turn west on Jetty Road toward **Moss Landing State Beach,** where migrant shorebirds can be abundant in marshes and on mudflats. Set up your spotting scope here and scan the bay for loons, grebes, cormorants, sea ducks, and whatever other waterbirds might be present from fall through spring. Because the seafloor drops off quickly to deep water in Monterey Bay, pelagic species such as shearwaters, storm-petrels, and jaegers sometimes approach fairly close to land. To reach **Elkhorn Slough National Estuarine Research Reserve,** which can have an excellent diversity of waterfowl and shorebirds, continue south on Calif. 1 toward Moss Landing. Drive east on Dolan Road 3.5 miles, turning north on

Elkhorn Road—the entrance is 2 miles ahead. In addition to waterbirds, land birding can be rewarding along the reserve trails.

13 Some of America's most famous pelagic trips leave from **Fisherman's Wharf** in Monterey, heading out to deep water for looks at oceanic species seldom or never seen from shore. Trips are offered by several tour companies, the most active of which is **Shearwater Journeys** *(831-637-8527)*. The list of possible species depends on the destination and time of year, ranging from year-round near certainties such as Black-Footed Albatross, Sooty Shearwater, Common Murre, and Rhinoceros Auklet to rarities such as Laysan Albatross and Streaked, Wedge-tailed, and Manx Shearwaters. In general, fall is best for diversity of species including Buller's and Black-vented Shearwaters and four species of storm-petrels. The January issue of the American Birding Association's newsletter, *Winging It*, includes a listing of nationwide pelagic trips with target species. Consult it for trip sponsors' expected sightings, or check with the trip organizers as far in advance as possible.

Elephant seals at Año Nuevo State Reserve, north of Santa Cruz

In Monterey, the city's municipal wharf *(N off Del Monte Ave.)* provides a view of the harbor and bay. As you continue southwest toward Point Pinos along Ocean View Boulevard, stop where you can to look for Black Oystercatcher and other rocky shorebirds, and to scan the bay. From **Point Pinos** you can often see a good number of seabirds such as shearwaters and alcids.

14 Moving inland, a driving tour through the **Panoche Valley** can bring good birding from late fall through early spring (summers are very hot and dry, and bird activity is low). To reach it, take the Little Panoche Road/Shields Avenue exit from I-5 about 20 miles south of Los Banos and drive west. Little Panoche Road curves to the south to join Panoche Road in about 20 miles; from here (when the road is dry) you can drive east back to I-5. While this isn't exactly the middle of nowhere, it is an isolated drive through an area with no services, so make sure you're prepared and your car is in good condition. Four miles from I-5, stop at **Little Panoche Reservoir** to see what might be around (Tricolored Blackbird is possible), and then continue west, looking for White-tailed Kite; Ferruginous and Rough-legged Hawks; Prairie Falcon; Chukar (rare); California Quail; Greater Roadrunner; Burrowing Owl; Lewis's and Nuttall's Woodpeckers; Loggerhead Shrike; Yellow-billed Magpie; Horned Lark (check flocks for rare winter longspurs); Bushtit; Mountain Bluebird; California Thrasher; Phainopepla, Rufous-crowned, Vesper, and Lark Sparrows; and Lesser and Lawrence's Goldfinches. Mountain Plover, one of the special birds of the area, is getting harder to find, but diligent searching in short-grass areas might turn up a small wintering flock between early November and early March.

15 Not far north, in the San Joaquin Valley, several wildlife areas attract masses of wintering waterfowl and host nesting waterbirds in the warmer months. To reach **Merced National Wildlife Refuge** from Los Banos, take Calif. 152 east 18 miles, turn north on Calif. 59, drive 6.5 miles, and turn west on Sandy Mush Road. For **Los Banos Wildlife Area,** take Calif. 165 north from Los Banos and in 3 miles turn east on Henry Miller Avenue. For **San Luis National Wildlife Refuge** get back on Calif. 165 north, then drive northeast 2 miles on Wolfsen Road.

Yellow-billed Magpie, an endemic species of central and northern California

At these sites and in the surrounding agricultural fields you'll find wintering Tundra Swan; Greater White-fronted, Snow, Ross's, and Canada Geese; ducks; and Sandhill Crane (mostly at Merced). Look also for Bald Eagle and Ferruginous and Rough-legged Hawks, among other raptors. Migrant shorebirds make a spring, late summer, or fall visit to these areas worthwhile. Long-billed Curlew is present year-round. A small sampling of nesting species includes Western and Clark's Grebes, American Bittern, Great and Snowy Egrets, White-faced Ibis, Wood Duck (at San Luis), White-tailed Kite, Northern Harrier, Swainson's Hawk, Burrowing Owl, Yellow-billed Magpie, and Tricolored and Yellow-headed (uncommon) Blackbirds.

16 One of America's most beautiful natural areas, **Yosemite National Park** is also one of California's most popular destinations—a fact that causes personnel some concern as they try to maintain the park's wild character in the face of throngs of visitors. Birders who go to Yosemite (the best time is between early June and August— earlier in lower-elevation areas) tend to get up early, and those who do will have an advantage here not only in bird-finding but in crowd-avoiding. The effort will be worthwhile, because Yosemite offers a fine list of montane species. Some, such as Vaux's and White-throated Swifts, Hammond's and Dusky Flycatchers, Clark's Nutcracker, Mountain Chickadee, Brown Creeper, Western Tanager, and Fox and Lincoln's Sparrows, are easy to find in proper habitat. But it takes a bit of luck to walk up on a Blue Grouse along a forest trail, or to spot a Black-backed Woodpecker chipping away at the bark of a lodgepole pine, or to look up just in time to see Northern Goshawk soaring overhead.

Drive **Glacier Point Road,** south of Yosemite Valley, to look for forest birds such as Band-tailed Pigeon; Williamson's Sapsucker; White-headed and Pileated Woodpeckers; Olive-sided Flycatcher; Cassin's Vireo; Golden-crowned Kinglet; Townsend's Solitaire; Hermit Thrush; Nashville,

Yosemite National Park's Bridalveil Falls, where the elusive Black Swift nests

Tufa formations at Mono Lake, near Lee Vining

Black-throated Gray, and Hermit Warblers; Pine Grosbeak; and Red Crossbill. A morning walk along the entrance road to Bridalveil Campground will bring looks at a good number of these species. Yosemite has many expansive meadows, in or around which you may find Mountain Quail, Calliope Hummingbird (Rufous doesn't nest but is common as a summer migrant), Red-breasted Sapsucker (look in aspens and willows around meadow edges), Mountain Bluebird, and MacGillivray's and Wilson's Warblers.

Great Gray Owl is one of the park's special species, and fortunate birders sometimes spot one perched in a tree at the edge of a meadow such as McGurk or Peregoy on Glacier Point Road or Crane Flat in the western part of the park. (If you're lucky enough to see this impressive bird, enjoy it from a distance—don't approach for "a better look.") Flammulated Owl can be heard giving its hollow hoots in late May and June, but it's rarely seen. The threatened Spotted Owl calls earlier in the year in old-growth forest, and is even less frequently seen.

Another much sought-after bird, the scarce Black Swift, nests near waterfalls. **Bridalveil Falls** is a favorite spot to look for this large swift, but be there at dawn or just before dusk to see the birds leaving or returning to their nests. Sometimes Black Swifts are seen from Glacier Point, flying with the much more common White-throated. Hiking

into the tundra around **Tioga Pass,** or behind the dam at Ellery Lake just east of there, may bring a sighting of Gray-crowned Rosy-Finch; early summer offers the best chance.

17 Eastward near the Nevada border, **Mono Lake** is famed not only for the number of migrants that appear here in summer and fall, but for the spectacular landscape of weirdly shaped towers of calcium-carbonate deposits called tufa, formed when the water level of this highly salty and alkaline lake was higher. Your first stop should be at the **Mono Basin National Forest Scenic Area Visitor Center** on US 395 just north of Lee Vining, where you can get maps and information. Four miles north of Lee Vining, turn east on Cemetery Road to reach **Mono Lake County Park,** the best spot on the lake for a variety of birds. Here you can check the cottonwoods and willows along DeChambeau Creek for nesting American Kestrel, Great Horned Owl, Northern Flicker, Western Wood-Pewee, Warbling Vireo, Yellow Warbler, Black-headed Grosbeak, and Bullock's Oriole, and for migrants in spring and fall. Then take the boardwalk to the lake, passing through a wetland where Green Heron, Virginia Rail, Sora, and Common Snipe nest.

California Gulls nest at Mono Lake in a colony of around 50,000 birds, making this species easy to find from spring through fall. The lake also sees enormous concentrations of migrant phalaropes. In summer, Wilson's Phalaropes arrive by the tens of thousands, joined in late July by Red-necked Phalaropes. As these shorebirds feed on flies and their larvae, building up fat reserves before continuing their southward migration, their numbers can reach 150,000. As the phalaropes depart, Eared Grebes arrive in the hundreds of thousands, at times covering the water in immense flocks totaling more than a million birds. Shorebirding can be excellent at Mono, as well, though rising water levels are changing the lake's configuration and inundating areas that once were mudflats.

Returning to Lee Vining, drive south on US 395 about 5 miles, then east on Calif. 120; in 4 miles turn north toward the **South Tufa** area. In the sagebrush scrub, look for Common Nighthawk, Say's Phoebe, Loggerhead Shrike, Western Scrub-Jay, Bushtit, Mountain Bluebird, Sage Thrasher, Green-tailed Towhee, and Brewer's and Sage Sparrows. Viewpoints here, as anywhere around the lake, can provide looks at a range of migrant and wintering waterfowl.

Two areas near Mono Lake offer the chance to see Sage Grouse. To visit a lek, where males "dance" to court females in spring, drive south on US 395; 5 miles past Calif. 203, turn northeast on Benton Crossing Road. Drive 1.1 miles, veer east, and in 0.7 mile east again. In a mile you'll come to a road leading south 0.3 mile to the lek. You need to be here before dawn from late March to early May to see the courtship display.

18 Sage Grouse are also seen in summer at **Bodie State Historic Park,** 20 miles northeast of Lee Vining. Six miles north of town, turn east on Calif. 167. As you travel this road, watch for Pinyon Jay. In 6.5 miles, turn north on Cottonwood Canyon Road, which leads to the park in about 10 winding miles. Grouse are commonly seen walking among the buildings of this ghost town in spring and summer. Other times you might, with luck, run across one by walking through the sagebrush in the area (which is also good for Common Nighthawk, Mountain Bluebird, Sage Thrasher, and Brewer's Sparrow), but call ahead for road conditions in bad weather. You can also reach Bodie via US 395 north from Lee Vining 17 miles, turning east on Calif. 270.

SOUTHERN CALIFORNIA

19 One of the landmarks of the central California coast, **Morro Rock** lifts its rugged cliff face 578 feet above the surf of Morro Bay. To reach it, drive north on Embarcadero, which runs beside the water in the town of Morro Bay, and turn west on Coleman Drive. Park in the south lot, from which you can scan the rock in spring and summer for Peregrine Falcon nesting on the cliffs. Brandt's and Pelagic Cormorants, Pigeon Guillemot, White-throated Swift, Violet-green Swallow, and Canyon Wren also breed here. Watch the water for sea otters, which can often be seen near shore.

In Morro Bay, take Main Street south and continue skirting the bay southward to **Morro Bay State Park.** Great Blue Heron, Snowy Egret, and Black-crowned Night-Heron nest in a heronry west of the road, north of the Morro Bay Natural History Museum. Past the museum, turn south to a marina from which you can scan the bay for waterbirds. Look for American White Pelican and Brant (the latter is attracted to eelgrass beds) in winter, Brown Pelican year-

- **Winter birds on the Carrizo Plain**
- **Highland species at Mount Pinos and the San Gabriel Mountains**
- **Migrants and desert birds at Anza-Borrego Desert State Park**
- **Waterbirds and rarities at the Salton Sea**

Information section p. 146

Fishing boats in Morro Bay, with Morro Rock in the background

round, and at any time of year for loons, grebes, sea ducks, gulls, and terns. Elegant Tern, a visitor from breeding grounds farther south, can be seen in late summer and fall.

Continuing through the park, you'll reach South Bay Boulevard. To look for Snowy Plover, turn north to US 1, drive 2.3 miles, and go west on Atascadero Road to its end. Walk the sandy beach of **Morro Strand State Beach** northward to find this little shorebird. Otherwise, turn south, drive 1.6 miles, and turn west on Santa Ysabel Avenue; drive 0.9 mile, turn north on Third Street, and then go a block to the bay. Here you can visit the **Morro Coast Audubon Overlook** and have another chance to check the bay for Willet, Whimbrel, Long-billed Curlew, Marbled Godwit, and other shorebirds, as well as the waterbirds mentioned above.

Return to South Bay Boulevard, drive south 1.3 miles to Los Osos Valley Road, turn west, and follow signs (the road changes to Pecho Valley Road) to **Montaña de Oro State Park,** an excellent year-round birding spot. Walk the **West Hazard Canyon Trail** or the **Campground Loop,** checking the pines and streamside vegetation for resident Anna's Hummingbird, Nuttall's Woodpecker, Hutton's Vireo, Chestnut-backed Chickadee, Bewick's Wren, Wrentit (more often heard than seen), California Thrasher, and Spotted and California Towhees. In nesting season look for Allen's Hummingbird and Pacific-slope Flycatcher, and in winter for Ruby-crowned Kinglet, Blue-gray Gnatcatcher, and Golden-crowned Sparrow. On the **Bluff Trail,** a 3-mile walk along the coast, scan the Pacific for loons, grebes, and sea ducks. Check the rocks for cormorants and "rocky shorebirds" such as Black Oystercatcher, Wandering Tattler, Black Turnstone, and Surfbird; the first is present all year, while the last three are fall-through-spring visitors.

20 **Carrizo Plain Natural Area** attracts birders with its notable wintering species. Some interesting birds nest here, but are best looked for in spring. Few people travel to this hot and remote semidesert area in summer. From US 101 9 miles north of San Luis Obispo, drive east on Calif. 58 about 45 miles (you'll see Yellow-billed Magpie along the way, and there's a chance in winter for Lewis's

Woodpecker) and turn south on Soda Lake Road toward California Valley. First paved, then dirt, Soda Lake Road enters the natural area 8 miles from Calif. 58. By driving southeast about 33 miles and turning north on Elkhorn Plain Road, which swings back west, you can make a circuit of around 70 miles, though you of course don't have to travel that far. (Be aware that dirt roads can be impassable in and immediately after wet weather.) Keep an eye out for wintering Ferruginous and Rough-legged Hawks, Sandhill Crane (watch for them coming to roost at Soda Lake in late afternoon), Mountain Plover (in bare and short-grass fields), Long-billed Curlew, Mountain Bluebird, Sage Thrasher, and Vesper Sparrow. Any time of year you might find White-tailed Kite, Northern Harrier, Golden Eagle, Prairie Falcon, Burrowing Owl, Horned Lark, and Common Raven. Le Conte's Thrasher and Sage Sparrow nest here, though the thrasher is rare and irregular in occurrence; try areas with scattered saltbrush/sagebrush for both species.

21 In Santa Barbara, take Mission Canyon Road north to reach the **Santa Barbara Museum of Natural History, Rocky Nook County Park,** and the **Santa Barbara Botanic Garden.** Oak woods at these sites host typical birds of the region, from California Quail to California Thrasher to California Towhee. Residents include Anna's Hummingbird, Nuttall's Woodpecker, Black Phoebe, Hutton's Vireo, Western Scrub-Jay, Oak Titmouse, Wrentit, Orange-crowned Warbler, Spotted Towhee, and Lesser Goldfinch. Among the nesting season species are Black-chinned and Allen's Hummingbirds, Pacific-slope and Ash-throated Flycatchers, Black-headed Grosbeak, and Hooded Oriole. The 5.5 miles of trails at the botanic garden also provide an excellent lesson in California native plants.

California Condor

One of the most famous endangered birds in the U.S., the California Condor was in such critically low numbers in the mid-1980s that all the remaining wild individuals (fewer than ten) were taken from their southern California range and added to a long-standing captive-breeding program. Since then, condors have been reintroduced into southern California in San Luis Obispo and Santa Barbara Counties and into northern Arizona, where they had not occurred since the 19th century. Controversy has followed many aspects of the condor recovery program, and it's too early to tell whether this fabulous bird will ever again find a place in a world so greatly changed from wilderness conditions.

The view from Mount Pinos, in Los Padres National Forest west of Gorman

Drive west on Foothill Road (Calif. 192) to Calif. 154; then head north 7 miles to the crest of San Marcos Pass, turning east on **East Camino Cielo Road,** which winds into **Los Padres National Forest.** A local birders' favorite, this picturesque route can produce Mountain Quail, Band-tailed Pigeon, Greater Roadrunner, California Thrasher, Wrentit, and Rufous-crowned Sparrow year-round; in spring and summer look for Costa's Hummingbird, Common Poorwill (predawn and dusk), Black-chinned Sparrow, and Lazuli Bunting. Drive east at least 7 miles to La Cumbre Peak, where you also might find Townsend's Solitaire in winter.

22 Higher-elevation species are the reward for a spring or summer visit to **Mount Pinos** in Los Padres National Forest. Leave I-5 at the Frazier Park exit just north of Gorman, and drive west; in 6.5 miles bear right on Cuddy Valley Road, and in about 5 miles turn south on Mount Pinos Road. Explore side roads as you drive up the mountain. Two favorite birding stops are **McGill Campground,** about 5 miles up, and **Iris Meadow,** near the Chula Vista Campground at the end of the paved road. You should walk the old road 1.5 miles to the 8,831-foot summit as well. Among the many birds nesting in the area are Mountain

Quail, Band-tailed Pigeon, Flammulated Owl (scarce), Northern Pygmy-Owl, Northern Saw-whet Owl (scarce), White-throated Swift, Calliope Hummingbird (check Iris Meadow), Williamson's (rare) and Red-breasted Sapsuckers, White-headed Woodpecker, Olive-sided and Dusky Fly-catchers, Steller's Jay, Clark's Nutcracker, Mountain Chick-adee, Oak Titmouse, Pygmy Nuthatch, Western Bluebird, Yellow-rumped Warbler, Western Tanager, Green-tailed Towhee, the large-billed subspecies of Fox Sparrow, Purple and Cassin's Finches, and Lawrence's Goldfinch.

23 A detour eastward: Most of these same highland birds can be found on a trip into the **San Gabriel Mountains** north of Los Angeles in the **Angeles National Forest.** From I-210 northwest of Pasadena, take Calif. 2 (Angeles Crest Highway) north. Explore some of the picnic areas and campgrounds as you ascend along 34 miles of winding road to **Buckhorn Campground** at 6,500 feet. Look for Nuttall's Woodpecker, Oak Titmouse, Wrentit, and California Thrasher at mid-elevations. As you climb, check spots such as **Charlton Flat** and the **Chilao Visitor Center** for Mountain Quail, White-headed Woodpecker, Dusky Flycatcher, Cassin's and Hutton's Vireos, Steller's Jay, Western Tanager, and Lawrence's Goldfinch. Even higher,

Santa Cruz Island, part of Channel Islands National Park

you might find Clark's Nutcracker, Townsend's Solitaire, Hermit Warbler, or Red Crossbill.

24 The oceanside town of Ventura is the embarkation site for boat trips to **Santa Cruz Island** in **Channel Islands National Park,** known to birders as the only place in the world where the Island Scrub-Jay can be found. Once a race of the Scrub Jay shown in most field guides, this species can sometimes be found in a grove of eucalyptus trees and other exotic plantings near the landing site at Scorpion Anchorage. If the jays aren't there, you can try finding them by walking about a mile up the seasonal stream to the west to stands of oaks and ironwood trees in the narrowing canyon above, or ask for directions to **Prisoners Harbor,** about 6 miles over water.

Cruises to Santa Cruz aren't just for the jay. Among the pelagic species you might see are Sooty Shearwater from spring through fall, Black-vented Shearwater between early fall and early spring, Ashy and Black Storm-Petrels from May to October, Least Storm-Petrel in late summer, Xantus's Murrelet in spring, and Common Murre and Cassin's and Rhinoceros Auklets from late fall to early spring. Other migrant seabirds include Red-necked and Red

Phalaropes and Pomarine and Parasitic Jaegers. Black Oystercatcher, Pigeon Guillemot, and Xantus's Murrelet nest on Santa Cruz; the oystercatcher is a permanent resident. Santa Cruz and other Channel Islands are also home to the nonmigratory race of Allen's Hummingbird. For information, contact the Channel Islands National Park or the boat concessioner, **Island Packers** *(805-642-1393; take Spinnaker Dr. W from Harbor Blvd. in Ventura)*, at Ventura Harbor.

25 Just a short distance south on Harbor Boulevard, **McGrath State Beach** can have excellent shorebirding. Take the nature trail to the estuary at the mouth of the Santa Clara River and look over mudflats for Black-necked Stilt, American Avocet, Willet, Marbled Godwit, Sanderling, Western Gull, and Forster's Tern, to list only a few of the most common species. Snowy Plover nests in the sand dunes here, and many rarities such as Sharp-tailed Sandpiper have appeared.

Island Scrub-Jay, found only on Santa Cruz Island

Drive south on the Pacific Coast Highway (a segment of Calif. 1, also known as the PCH) past the Point Mugu Naval Air Station and watch for parking at Point Mugu, within **Point Mugu State Park.** Mugu Rock is a favorite lookout from fall through spring for seabirds. The salt marsh and tidal flats bordering the PCH just north of the rock are often teeming with waders, waterfowl, and shorebirds.

26 On the other side of Los Angeles, in Orange County, **Bolsa Chica Ecological Reserve** rates with the area's top wetland birding sites. Located on the east side of the PCH about 4 miles south of Seal Beach (note that you must enter from the northbound lanes; look for a parking lot with a boardwalk), the reserve hosts nesting Snowy Plover; Black-necked Stilt; American Avocet; and Caspian, Royal, Elegant, Forster's, and Least Terns. The dark Belding's subspecies of Savannah Sparrow lives in cordgrass and pickleweed areas. You'll find lots of waders here, and shorebirds including Black-bellied and Semipalmated Plovers, Willet, Long-billed Curlew, Marbled Godwit, Red Knot, and Western and Least Sandpipers, are common from midsummer through spring. Waterfowl throng the reserve in winter, and from fall through spring you might find Pied-billed, Horned, Eared, Western, and Clark's Grebes.

27 A few miles farther south on the PCH, **Huntington Beach Pier** is a good lookout for scanning the Pacific for seabirds in early morning. Snowy Plover and Least Tern nest at nearby **Huntington State Beach.** Less than a mile south of Newport Bay, turn left (north) on Jamboree Road and, in 0.2 mile, west on Back Bay Drive. This road passes alongside **Upper Newport Bay Ecological Reserve,** where mudflats, marsh, and open water attract waders, waterfowl, shorebirds, gulls, and terns. Clapper Rail is found here, along with Virginia Rail and Sora. In about a mile, stop at a paved parking lot at the Big Canyon area; the endangered California Gnatcatcher is found in the coastal sage scrub near the pond across the road (listen for a rising and falling kittenlike mew). The endangered coastal race of Cactus Wren sings its chugging song on the bluffs. (At this writing an interpretive center for Upper Newport Bay, where visitors will be able to obtain birding advice, is planned to open in 2000.)

Return to the PCH and continue south. Three miles from Jamboree Road, turn west into the Pelican Point area of **Crystal Cove State Park.** Trails run through coastal sage scrub where you'll have another good chance to find California Gnatcatcher. South along the east side of the PCH, the back-country section of the park offers miles of hiking trails through coastal sage scrub, grassland, and oak-sycamore woods, where resident birds include White-tailed Kite (irregular), California Quail, Greater Roadrunner, Anna's Hummingbird, Black Phoebe, Western Scrub-Jay, Bushtit, Wrentit, and Spotted and California Towhees.

Birds, Plants, and Fire

The California coastal habitat called chaparral has dense shrubby vegetation well adapted to regular fires. Unfortunately, many people who build houses in chaparral discover nature's regimen for this environment too late, when blazes roar through the scrub with terrifying speed in the dry season. Several of the state's special birds make this habitat their home, including California Quail, Wrentit, California Thrasher, and California Towhee. The demand for coastal real estate has led to the destruction of a great percentage of the related southern California habitat called coastal sage scrub, found at lower elevation than the chaparral. The most famous bird of this environment is the seriously threatened California Gnatcatcher. Look for this long-tailed little bird at coastal southern California sites including **Crystal Cove State Park** (see p. 136), **San Elijo Lagoon** (see p. 143), and **Lake Hodges** (see p. 143).

28 Moving from the coast to the desert: The lush oasis of **Big Morongo Canyon Preserve** north of Palm Springs attracts a noteworthy array of breeding species. To reach it, drive north from I-10 on Calif. 62 for 10.5 miles to Morongo Valley; turn southeast on East Drive and watch for the preserve entrance on the east. As you walk through arid areas of yucca and juniper, riparian cottonwood-willow woodland, and marsh in spring and summer, you can

find a variety of species, including Virginia Rail; Black-chinned and Costa's Hummingbirds; Ladder-backed and Nuttall's Woodpeckers; Black and Say's Phoebes; Vermilion and Brown-crested (scarce) Flycatchers; Cassin's and Western Kingbirds; Bell's Vireo (rare); Verdin; Cactus and Marsh Wrens; Blue-gray and Black-tailed Gnatcatchers; Phainopepla; Lucy's Warbler (rare); Common Yellowthroat; Yellow-breasted Chat; Summer Tanager; Black-chinned, Lark, and Black-throated Sparrows; Blue Grosbeak; Lazuli Bunting; Hooded and Scott's Orioles; and Lesser and Lawrence's (irregular) Goldfinches.

Wetlands at Bolsa Chica Ecological Reserve, south of Seal Beach, one of California's best coastal wetland birding areas

29 Though the area around Palm Springs marks the transition zone between the Mojave and Colorado Deserts, it's not far to coniferous forest on the peaks of the **San Jacinto Mountains.** One picturesque nearby route has been designated the **Palms to Pines Scenic Byway** for its linkage of desert and highland habitats. Of course, traveling between two such differing environments will bring a correspondingly wide range of birds. From Palm Springs, take Calif. 111 to Palm Desert and turn south on Calif. 74. Stop at the Bureau of Land Management's visitor center just outside town for information.

From the desert, where Costa's Hummingbird, Ladder-backed Woodpecker, Verdin, Cactus Wren, Phainopepla, and Black-throated Sparrow reside, you'll ascend into pinyon-juniper scrub; within **San Bernardino National**

Joshua trees in the Morongo Valley, north of Palm Springs

Forest stop at the **Pinyon Flats Campground** for a chance at Pinyon Jay. Continue up into the pine forest; check the **Hurkey Creek Campground** (good for White-headed Woodpecker) 21 miles farther, and **Lake Hemet** across the highway. At Mountain Center turn north on Calif. 243, and at Idyllwild investigate national forest campgrounds, or hike part of the trail up Mount San Jacinto at **Mount San Jacinto State Park.** At these higher elevations, look for resident Mountain Quail, Band-tailed Pigeon, Steller's and Pinyon Jays, Mountain Chickadee, Pygmy Nuthatch, Townsend's Solitaire, Purple and Cassin's Finches, and Pine Siskin. Summer visitors include Olive-sided and Dusky Flycatchers, Western Tanager, and Black-headed Grosbeak. Calif. 243 then winds down back to the desert to meet I-10 at Banning.

30 Drive 6 miles west on I-10, take Calif. 60 west, and in 8 miles turn south on Theodore Street, continuing south on Davis Road (this dirt road can be difficult or impassable in wet weather). In 4.6 miles, turn east to **San Jacinto Wildlife Area,** a restored remnant of the once much larger wetlands of the San Jacinto Valley. Breeders in the area comprise a mix of marsh and scrub birds, including Pied-billed Grebe, several species of ducks, White-tailed Kite (irregular in occurrence), California Quail, Virginia Rail, Common Moorhen, Black-necked Stilt, American Avocet, Greater Roadrunner, Burrowing Owl, Bushtit, Rufous-crowned and Sage Sparrows, Blue Grosbeak, and Tricolored and Yellow-headed Blackbirds. Fall and winter bring flocks of waterfowl; raptors such as Ferruginous Hawk, Golden Eagle, and Prairie Falcon; and Mountain Bluebird. In winter you'll also have a chance to find Mountain Plover and longspurs in surrounding agricultural fields.

31 The vast, rugged expanse of **Anza-Borrego Desert State Park,** California's largest state park at more than 600,000 acres, provides good birding for desert species and migrants. Make your first stop at the visitor center on the west side of the town of Borrego Springs (Costa's Hummingbird sometimes nests around the partly underground structure), and then drive a short distance north to the **Borrego Palm Canyon Campground.** Here a walk on the 3-mile round-trip nature trail could turn up Gambel's Quail, Greater Roadrunner, Ladder-backed Woodpecker, Verdin, Cactus and Canyon Wrens, Black-throated Sparrow, and Hooded and Scott's Orioles, among other birds. This is a very popular trail, so arrive early. To look for Crissal Thrasher (rare) and Lucy's Warbler (spring and early summer), drive east on Palm Canyon Drive and turn south on Borrego Springs Road (Calif. S3); about 2 miles after this road turns east, go north on Yaqui Pass Road to its end and search the desert scrub. You'll also find Black-tailed Gnatcatcher and Phainopepla here, and in winter Brewer's Sparrow.

Return to Borrego Springs Road and drive south to **Tamarisk Grove Campground,** where Long-eared Owls are sometimes in residence (ask the park ranger for likely sites). Check this area and then take the road west across

Borrego Springs Road to the **Yaqui Well Nature Trail** for spring and fall migrants, and for California Quail, White-winged Dove, Anna's and Costa's Hummingbirds, Ladder-backed Woodpecker, Black-tailed Gnatcatcher, California Thrasher, and Phainopepla. To look for the scarce and elusive Le Conte's Thrasher, take Calif. 78 east about 7 miles from Tamarisk Grove and turn northwest on Borrego Springs Road. In less than a mile you'll cross the wash along **San Felipe Creek,** a good place to search.

For another Le Conte's Thrasher site, take the dirt road north off Calif. S22, just east of the intersection of Henderson Canyon Road and Calif. S22 in northeastern Borrego Springs. Drive about 3 miles and investigate the sparse scrub on the southwest side of **Clark Dry Lake.** The thrasher is most likely to be singing, and thus easier to find, in early morning in late winter and early spring.

32 The **Salton Sea** has a history as unusual as its reputation among birders is high. Formed in 1905 when an accidental break in a canal diverted water into the dry alkaline basin of the Imperial Valley, this saline lake (saltier than the Pacific Ocean) covers more than 380 square miles. At more than 200 feet below sea level, the Salton Sea area can be one of the hottest places in the United States in summer. Such a huge body of water in the desert attracts great numbers of waterbirds of all sorts, as well as regular coverage by birders hoping to find rare species.

If you're approaching the Salton Sea from the west on Calif. 78, turn north on Calif. 86 to the towns of Salton City, Salton Sea Beach, and Desert Shores, where you can make your way to the west shore of the sea to check for waterbirds including Yellow-footed Gull, a specialty here. This species, which might be found anywhere along the lakeshore, is present all year but is easiest to see from late June to October; only small numbers winter, and it's tough to find in that season.

Return south on Calif. 86. About 12 miles south of the intersection with Calif. 78, exit east on Bannister Road, then turn north on Vendel Road to reach **Unit 1** of the **Sonny Bono Salton Sea National Wildlife Refuge.** This area is excellent in winter for large numbers of Snow and Ross's

Geese and flocks of Long-billed Curlew. Herons, egrets, and White-faced Ibis are present year-round. Check along the roadside for Burrowing Owl as well. Return to Calif. 86, turn east, drive 5 miles to Westmoreland, and turn north on Forrester Road (Calif. S30). This turns into Gentry Road, which leads to the refuge headquarters.

Take the **Rock Hill Nature Trail** here to check freshwater marshes and the sea itself for grebes (Western and Clark's both nest), American White and Brown Pelicans, Wood Stork (summer), waterfowl from fall through spring, rails (Clapper nests; Virginia and Sora are found from fall through spring), shorebirds, gulls, and terns. Gull-billed Tern and Black Skimmer are uncommon breeders in the area. The Salton Sea area is home to more than just waterbirds, of course. Around refuge headquarters and elsewhere in the vicinity, look for land birds such as Gambel's Quail, Common Ground-Dove, Lesser Nighthawk (at dusk), Verdin, Cactus Wren, Phainopepla, and Abert's Towhee.

To reach another good spot for waterbirds, take Gentry Road just south of refuge headquarters to McKendry Road

Cholla and other desert vegetation in Anza-Borrego Desert State Park, home of Verdin and Black-tailed Gnatcatcher and go west to **Obsidian Butte.** This spot is also good in winter for Savannah Sparrow of the large-billed subspecies; many birders search out this sparrow in the hope that it could be reclassified as a separate species someday.

Next, take Sinclair Road a mile east from the refuge headquarters and turn north on Garst Road to the **Red Hill** area at the mouth of the Alamo River, another excellent place from which to scan for waterbirds. (The road west to the marina offers a good viewpoint.) This is one of the best areas around the sea for Yellow-footed Gull.

Brown Pelican on the Pacific coast near La Jolla

Drive east on Sinclair Road to Calif. 111 and turn south to the town of Calipatria. Drive 2.7 miles past the intersection with Calif. 115, then turn east to **Ramer Lake,** part of **Imperial Wildlife Area** (you'll want to avoid this spot in fall hunting season). After driving around the lake, go east on Quay Road, south on Kershaw Road, east on Titsworth Road, and south on Smith Road to **Finney Lake,** another unit of the wildlife area. At both lakes you'll find a good assortment of waterbirds, possibly including Fulvous Whistling-Duck in spring and summer. Finney Lake also has some of the region's best desert scrub, good for Lesser Nighthawk, Verdin, Cactus Wren, Black-tailed Gnatcatcher, Crissal Thrasher (rare), and Abert's Towhee.

Drive north on Calif. 111 through Calipatria about 8 miles to Niland. Turn west here on Noffsinger Road and drive 3.3 miles to Davis Road. By driving both south and north on Davis you can explore wetlands and roads running west to the Salton Sea in this unit of Imperial Wildlife Area. This is also a popular hunting spot in the fall season. Be very careful driving any of these dirt roads, and avoid them in wet weather. To reach another good viewpoint, go north on Davis Road to meet Calif. 111; drive north on Calif. 111 for 6.5 miles and turn south to Niland Marina.

The shoreline vegetation here may have wintering large-billed subspecies of the Savannah Sparrow.

33 Moving back toward the coast, drive 7 miles south of Escondido, leave I-15 on West Bernardo Drive, and go west following the road, which then turns south for 0.3 mile. Park in the dirt lot to the west of the road and walk the **Piedras Pintadas Interpretive Trail** across from the Casa de las Campanas retirement center into the **San Dieguito River Park's Bernardo Bay Natural Area at Lake Hodges.** The lake will have waterbirds (including Western and Clark's Grebes) from fall through spring, but specialties here are the threatened California Gnatcatcher and Sage Sparrow, both found in the coastal sage scrub along the trail. Look also for White-tailed Kite, Golden Eagle (irregular), California Quail, White-throated Swift, Anna's Hummingbird, Cassin's Kingbird, Cactus Wren, Wrentit, California Thrasher, and California Towhee.

34 Back on the shores of the Pacific, north of San Diego, exit I-5 on Lomas Santa Fe Drive toward Solana Beach, and in 0.7 mile turn north on North Rios Avenue to its end at **San Elijo Lagoon.** The coastal sage scrub fringing the lagoon along the path to the east is home to California Gnatcatcher, as well as Cassin's Kingbird, Wrentit, California Towhee, and Lesser Goldfinch. Large numbers of waders, waterfowl, shorebirds, and terns frequent the lagoon, as well.

35 To the south, the rugged coastline at **La Jolla** attracts the "rocky shorebird" group—Wandering Tattler, Black Turnstone, and Surfbird—from fall through spring. Black Oystercatcher is getting scarce this far south, but might also be found. Take Ardath Road west from I-5 and continue west where it merges with Torrey Pines Road. In a little less than a mile, turn right onto Prospect Place and then right onto Coast Boulevard toward Scripps Park and the lifeguard station, favorite lookouts for seabird-watching. Red-throated and Common Loons, Northern Fulmar (irregular), Black-vented Shearwater, Brandt's and Pelagic Cormorants, and of course a variety of gulls and terns might be seen in winter, and Sooty Shearwater is often spotted offshore from spring through fall.

36 In San Diego, take Calif. 209 southwest from I-5 toward **Cabrillo National Monument** and **Point Loma.** Birders visit this peninsula to look for migrants and vagrants in spring and fall. Check trees and shrubs in **Fort Rosecrans National Cemetery,** about a mile north of the national monument, and around the monument's visitor center and along its 2-mile **Bayside Trail.** The trail passes through sage scrub where you'll find California Quail, Anna's Hummingbird, Ash-throated Flycatcher, Bushtit, California Thrasher, Wrentit, and Rufous-crowned Sparrow. Continue south toward the Point Loma Light Station and follow the road west and back north to parking lots along the cliffs, good lookouts for seabirds and rocky shorebirds.

Back on I-5, drive south and take Calif. 75 (Palm Avenue) west toward Imperial Beach. In 1.3 miles turn north on Tenth Street, or continue west and take Seventh Street north, to reach spots from which you can see the south end of **San Diego Bay.** Gull-billed, Caspian, Elegant, and Least Terns and Black Skimmer nest here, and waders, shorebirds, and gulls are present year-round. Continue west and north on Calif. 75 (Silver Strand Boulevard) and look for a parking spot on the east from which you can scan the bay.

Turn around and return south on I-5 to the Coronado Avenue exit. Go west on Coronado (which turns into Imperial Beach Boulevard) to Third Street, which leads to the marsh and the visitor center for **Tijuana Slough National Wildlife Refuge.** After obtaining maps and information here, drive west to Seacoast Drive and go south to its end. Check the marsh and tidal channels here, and walk along the beach south to more marshes and mudflats at the mouth of the Tijuana River, just a couple of miles from the Mexican border. Waders, winter waterfowl, shorebirds, gulls, and terns can be found here in large numbers, and the endangered local race of Clapper Rail lives in the marsh. The beach at the mouth of the river is good for Snowy Plover and Least Tern. You can access another part of the area by driving south on Fifth Street from Imperial Beach Boulevard and following a trail southward toward the river.

California
Information

? Visitor Center/Information   **⑤** Fee Charged   **❚❚** Food

❖❖❖ Rest Rooms   **🏃** Nature Trails   **∾∾** Driving Tours   **♿** Wheelchair Accessible

Be advised that facilities may be seasonal and limited. We suggest calling or writing ahead for specific information. Note that addresses may be for administrative offices; see text or call for directions to sites.

Rare Bird Alerts

California:
Northern *415-681-7422*
Southeast *909-793-5599*
Southern *818-952-5502*
Sacramento *916-481-0118*
Santa Barbara
805-964-8240
Los Angeles *323-874-1318*
Orange County
949-487-6869
San Diego *619-479-3400*

NORTHERN CALIFORNIA

Klamath Basin National Wildlife Refuges Complex *(Page 113)*
Route 1, Box 74
Tulelake, CA 96134
530-667-2231

? ⑤ ❖❖❖ 🏃 ∾∾ ♿

Patrick's Point State Park *(Page 114)*
4150 Patrick's Point Drive
Trinidad, CA 95570
707-677-3570

? ⑤ ❖❖❖ 🏃 ♿

Arcata Marsh and Wildlife Sanctuary
(Page 115)
736 F Street
Arcata, CA 95521
707-826-2359

? ❖❖❖ 🏃 ∾∾ ♿

Samoa Dunes Recreation Area
(Page 115)
1695 Heindon Road
Arcata, CA 95521
707-825-2300

❖❖❖ 🏃 ♿

Humboldt Bay National Wildlife Refuge *(Page 115)*
1020 Ranch Road
Loleta, CA 95551
707-733-5406

? ⑤ ❚❚ ❖❖❖ 🏃 ∾∾ ♿

Sacramento National Wildlife Refuge Complex
(Page 115)
752 County Road 99W
Willows, CA 95988
530-934-2801

? ⑤ ❖❖❖ 🏃 ∾∾ ♿

Point Reyes National Seashore *(Page 117)*
Point Reyes Station,
   CA 94956
415-663-1092

? ❚❚ ❖❖❖ 🏃 ∾∾ ♿

Tomales Bay State Park *(Page 117)*
HCR-62
Inverness, CA 94937
415-669-1140

⑤ ❖❖❖ 🏃 ♿

Audubon Canyon Ranch
(Page 118)
4900 Highway One
Stinson Beach, CA 94970
415-868-9244

? ❖❖❖ 🏃 ♿

Open mid-March–mid-July

Golden Gate National Recreation Area
(Page 118)
Building 201, Fort Mason
San Francisco, CA 94123
415-556-0560

? ❚❚ ❖❖❖ 🏃 ♿

Golden Gate Park
(Page 119)
Recreation and Park
   Department
501 Stanyan Street
San Francisco, CA 94117
415-831-2745

? ⑤ ❚❚ ❖❖❖ 🏃 ♿

Don Edwards San Francisco Bay National Wildlife Refuge
(Page 120)
P.O. Box 524
Newark, CA 94560
510-792-0222

▨ ⊕ ♔ ﹠ ♿

Marshlands Rd. closed April-Aug. for nesting Snowy Plover

Coyote Hills Regional Park *(Page 120)*
8000 Patterson
  Ranch Road
Fremont, CA 94555
510-795-9385

▨ ⊕ ♔ ﹠ ♿

Palo Alto Baylands Preserve *(Page 121)*
2775 Embarcadero Road
Palo Alto, CA 94303
650-329-2506

▨ ♔ ﹠ ♿

Exhibit center open Mem. Day–mid-Oct.

Año Nuevo State Reserve *(Page 121)*
Highway 1
Pescadero, CA 94060
650-879-0227

▨ ⊕ ♔ ﹠ ♿

Moss Landing State Beach *(Page 37)*
c/o Marina State Beach
61 Reservation Road
Marina, CA 93933
831-384-7695

⊕ ♔ ﹠

Some areas periodically closed for nesting Snowy Plover

Elkhorn Slough National Estuarine Research Reserve *(Page 122)*
1700 Elkhorn Road
Watsonville, CA 95076
831-728-2822

▨ ⊕ ♔ ﹠ ♿

Shearwater Journeys *(Page 123)*
P.O. Box 190
Hollister, CA 95024
831-637-8527

⊕ ♔ ﹏

Merced and **San Luis National Wildlife Refuges** *(Page 124)*
P.O. Box 2176
Los Banos, CA 93635
209-826-3508

▨ ♔ ﹠ ﹏ ♿

Yosemite National Park *(Page 125)*
P.O. Box 577
Yosemite, CA 95389
209-372-0200

▨ ⊕ ♔ ﹠ ﹏ ♿

Mono Basin National Forest Scenic Area Visitor Center *(Page 127)*
Inyo National Forest
P.O. Box 429
Lee Vining, CA 93541
760-647-3044

▨ ⊕ ♔ ﹠ ﹏ ♿

Call for winter hours

Bodie State Historic Park *(Page 128)*
P.O. Box 515
Bridgeport, CA 93517
760-647-6445

▨ ⊕ ♔ ♿

Morro Bay State Park
(Page 129)
1 State Park Road
Morro Bay, CA 93442
805-772-2694

▨ ⊕ ♔ ﹠ ﹏ ♿

Montaña de Oro State Park *(Page 130)*
3550 Pecho Valley Road
Los Osos, CA 93402
805-528-0513

▨ ♔ ﹠

Carrizo Plain Natural Area *(Page 130)*
P.O. Box 3087
California Valley, CA 93454
805-475-2131

▨ ♔ ﹠ ﹏ ♿

Santa Barbara Museum of Natural History
(Page 131)
2559 Puesta del Sol Road
Santa Barbara, CA 93105
805-682-4711

▨ ⊕ ♔ ﹠ ♿

Santa Barbara Botanic Garden *(Page 131)*
1212 Mission Canyon Road
Santa Barbara, CA 93105
805-682-4726

▨ ⊕ ♔ ﹠

Los Padres National Forest *(Page 132)*
Mt. Pinos Ranger District
34580 Lockwood Valley Rd.
Frazier Park, CA 93225
805-245-3731

⊕ ﹠ ♿

Angeles National Forest
(Page 133)
701 N. Santa Anita Avenue
Arcadia, CA 91006
626-574-5200
🚻🛉🍴🚻🏃🏊👤♿

**Channel Islands
National Park** *(Page 134)*
1901 Spinnaker Drive
Ventura, CA 93001
805-658-5730
🚻🚻🏃♿

Island Packers *(Page 135)*
1867 Spinnaker Drive
Ventura, CA 93001
805-642-1393
🚻🛉🍴🚻🏃🏊

McGrath State Beach
(Page 135)
221 Harbor Boulevard
Oxnard, CA 93035
850-899-1400
🚻🛉🚻🏃♿

Point Mugu State Park
(Page 135)
1925 Las Virgines Road
Calabasas, CA 91302
818-880-0350
🛉🚻♿

**Bolsa Chica Ecological
Reserve** *(Page 135)*
3842 Warner Avenue
Huntington Beach,
    CA 92649
714-846-1114
🚻🚻🏃♿

Huntington State Beach
(Page 136)
18331 Enterprise Lane
Huntington Beach,
    CA 92648
714-536-1454
🚻🛉🍴🚻♿

**Upper Newport Bay
Ecological Reserve**
(Page 136)
600 Shellmaker Road
Newport Beach, CA 92660
949-640-6746
🚻🏃🏊👤

*Interpretive center scheduled to
open in 2000*

Crystal Cove State Park
(Page 136)
8471 Pacific Coast Highway
Laguna Beach, CA 92651
949-494-3539
🚻🛉🍴🚻🏃♿

**Big Morongo Canyon
Preserve** *(Page 137)*
P.O. Box 780
Morongo Valley, CA 92256
760-363-7190
🚻🏃♿

**San Bernardino National
Forest** *(Page 138)*
1824 South Commerce
    Center Circle
San Bernardino, CA 92408
909-383-5588
🚻🍴🚻🏃👤♿

**Mount San Jacinto State
Park** *(Page 138)*
P.O. Box 308
Idyllwild, CA 92549
909-659-2607
🚻🚻🏃♿

**San Jacinto Wildlife
Area** *(Page 139)*
P.O. Box 1254
Lakeview, CA 92567
909-654-0580
🛉🚻🏃👤♿

**Anza-Borrego Desert
State Park** *(Page 139)*
200 Palm Canyon Drive
Borrego Springs, CA 92004
760-767-5311
🚻🛉🚻🏃♿

**Sonny Bono Salton Sea
National Wildlife Refuge**
(Page 140)
906 West Sinclair Road
Calipatria, CA 92233
760-348-5278
🚻🚻🏃♿

**Bernardo Bay Natural
Area at Lake Hodges**
(Page 143)
San Dieguito River Park
1500 State Street
San Diego, CA 92101
619-235-5445
🏃♿

**Cabrillo National
Monument** *(Page 144)*
1800 Cabrillo
    Memorial Drive
San Diego, CA 92106
619-557-5450
🚻🛉🍴🚻🏃♿

**Tijuana Slough National
Wildlife Refuge**
(Page 144)
301 Caspian Way
Imperial Beach, CA 91932
619-575-3613
🚻🚻🏃♿

Southwest

The typical traveler is likely to visualize the southwestern deserts through a wide-angle lens: broad panoramas of arid terrain covered in forbiddingly spined cactus, ocotillo, and mesquite, with rocky, rugged hills on the horizon, all seen in the harsh light of midday.

A birder has a different, more tightly cropped image: a dry wash in the soft light of a cool spring morning, with the calls of wrens, thrashers, and sparrows accompanying the crunch of sand underfoot. The desert is a different world at dawn, when most folks are still abed and the birds who make this beautiful world their home are already active and going about their business.

Birders know, too, that there's much more to the Southwest than deserts. Cottonwood-lined streams create linear oases where Gray Hawks and Green Kingfishers nest. Mountains near the Mexican border host sought-after regional specialties such as Elegant Trogon and Red-faced Warbler, in lush canyons shaded by oaks, maples, and junipers. High country farther north is home to Blue Grouse and Three-toed Woodpecker, Clark's Nutcracker and Pine Siskin, resident in forests of Douglas-fir, spruce, and aspen. Reservoirs and wildlife refuges offer the opportunity to see waders, waterfowl, and shorebirds.

Preceding pages: Birders at Bosque del Apache National Wildlife Refuge, near Socorro, New Mexico
Above: Lucifer Hummingbird

150   SOUTHWEST

The Southwest encompasses two of America's finest birding locales. The first, southeastern Arizona, is considered by many to be their favorite overall location; certainly it ranks with southern Florida, the Texas Gulf Coast and lower Rio Grande Valley, and southern California as our best birding destinations. The "sky islands" here—mountain ranges surrounded by a sea of desert—along with riparian areas such as the San Pedro River make great diversity accessible in a relatively small area.

More than one traveling birder has fallen in love with the other of the Southwest's famed birding destinations: Texas' Big Bend National Park, a land that combines stark desert with green riparian areas and the strikingly picturesque Chisos Mountains. The tiny Colima Warbler lives

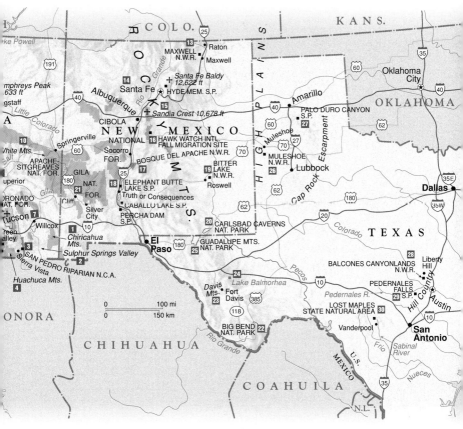

here and only here in the United States, rewarding hikers who make the climb up to the oak woods where it sings its trilling song in spring and early summer.

Many other excellent birding areas dot the southwestern map. Visit New Mexico's southwestern corner for many of the same specialties found in adjacent Arizona, and travel to Bosque del Apache National Wildlife Refuge for remarkable concentrations of geese and Sandhill Cranes.

Rose-throated Becard

Special Birds of the Southwest

Neotropic Cormorant	Violet-crowned Hummingbird	Vermilion Flycatcher	Bendire's Thrasher
Black-bellied Whistling-Duck	Blue-throated Hummingbird	Dusky-capped Flycatcher	Crissal Thrasher
Gray Hawk	Magnificent Hummingbird	Brown-crested Flycatcher	Phainopepla
Common Black-Hawk	Lucifer Hummingbird	Sulphur-bellied Flycatcher	Olive Warbler
Harris's Hawk	Elegant Trogon	Tropical Kingbird	Lucy's Warbler
Zone-tailed Hawk	Green Kingfisher	Thick-billed Kingbird	Grace's Warbler
Scaled Quail	Gila Woodpecker	Rose-throated Becard	Red-faced Warbler
Montezuma Quail	Strickland's Woodpecker	Black-capped Vireo	Painted Redstart
Mountain Plover	Northern Beardless-Tyrannulet	Gray Vireo	Hepatic Tanager
Whiskered Screech-Owl	Greater Pewee	Mexican Jay	Abert's Towhee
Elf Owl	Buff-breasted Flycatcher	Cave Swallow	Rufous-winged Sparrow
Spotted Owl		Bridled Titmouse	Cassin's Sparrow
Broad-billed Hummingbird		Verdin	Botteri's Sparrow
		Black-tailed Gnatcatcher	Yellow-eyed Junco
			McCown's Longspur
			Pyrrhuloxia
			Varied Bunting
			Bronzed Cowbird

The lovely Texas Hill Country offers a good selection of western birds for Easterners visiting Austin or San Antonio, as well as the endangered Golden-cheeked Warbler, which nests only in the oak-juniper woods here.

This chapter begins in southeastern Arizona, moving eastward to the Hill Country of central Texas. ■

ARIZONA

A glance at a map shows part of the reason southeastern Arizona ranks with the top American birding destinations: A certain number of notable birds, both regular breeders and strays, can be expected this close to the Mexican frontier. But you need a three-dimensional view truly to understand the region's allure. Then you see how mountains rise abruptly from the desert, creating a wide range of habitats in a relatively small area, home to equally diverse birdlife.

1 The **Chiricahua Mountains** have a place on every list of the country's best birding sites. From US 80 just north of Rodeo, New Mexico, drive west on Portal Road to the hamlet of **Portal,** stopping at the little store to check feeders for an array of hummingbirds that changes with the seasons but can include Broad-billed, Blue-throated, Magnificent, Black-chinned, Anna's, Costa's, Calliope, and Rufous, along with rarer species.

Just west of Portal, bear southwest toward **Cave Creek Canyon** on Forest Road 42. Stop at the **Coronado National Forest** station (*open spring–late summer*) for information and to check more hummingbird feeders. Along the road and in the campgrounds ahead, look for breeding birds including Montezuma Quail (usually very elusive); Acorn, Ladder-backed, and Strickland's Woodpeckers; Dusky-capped and Brown-crested Flycatchers; Plumbeous Vireo; Mexican Jay; Virginia's Warbler; Black-headed and Blue Grosbeaks; and Bullock's and Scott's Orioles.

Take the left turn to the **South Fork Picnic Area,** a legendary birding locale. Check along the entrance road and around the picnic grounds, and follow the trail up the South Fork of Cave Creek a mile or so, if you have time. In late spring and summer, your chances are excellent for finding

- Highland birds in the Chiricahua and Santa Rita Mountains
- Riparian species along the San Pedro River and Sonoita Creek
- Waterbirds in the Lake Havasu area

Information section p. 183

the beautiful Elegant Trogon, a top regional specialty. Look also for Peregrine Falcon; Band-tailed Pigeon; Cordilleran and Sulphur-bellied Flycatchers; Hutton's Vireo; Bridled Titmouse; Black-throated Gray, Grace's, and Red-faced Warblers; Painted Redstart; and Hepatic Tanager, among other nesting birds.

Return to the main road and ascend the Chiricahuas along a twisting road (first paved, then dirt; closed in winter) about 8 miles to Onion Saddle; keep left (south) here and continue to **Rustler Park.** At these heights, nesting birds include Northern Goshawk (rare), Northern Pygmy-Owl, Greater Pewee, Steller's Jay, Violet-green Swallow, Mexican Chickadee (this is the best spot in the United States for this species), Pygmy Nuthatch, Olive and Grace's Warblers, Western Tanager, and Yellow-eyed Junco.

2 To the west of the Chiricahuas, the **Sulphur Springs Valley** between Willcox and Douglas is known as an excellent winter birding destination. The main attractions here are great numbers of wintering Sandhill Cranes—often more than 10,000, and some years twice that— and raptors. Waterfowl and shorebirds are also seen seasonally on the shallow lakes that form in this flat basin, and in winter you'll find large mixed flocks of sparrows (Brewer's, Vesper, and White-crowned are the dominant species) and Lark Buntings. The uncommon Bendire's Thrasher is also a possibility here.

To reach one crane-viewing site, drive east from Willcox on Ariz. 186 for about 6 miles. Turn south on Kansas Settlement Road and drive 4 miles to **Willcox Playa.** To reach another, begin in Elfrida, about 25 miles north of Douglas. Take Central Highway 6 miles south to Davis Road, drive

Hummingbird Haven

True hummingbird aficionados travel south of the border, where countries such as Colombia and Venezuela are home to scores of species of these feathered jewels. In the United States, southeastern Arizona is the number one hummingbird hot spot. A dozen or more species can be found here at times. The best places to look are feeders in such famous hummer hangouts as **Cave Creek** (see p. 153), **Ramsey** (see p. 156), and **Madera** (see p. 158) **Canyons** and in **Patagonia** (see p. 158). While brilliantly colored males are usually readily identifiable, many females can be a challenge. Fortunately, birds at feeders often return regularly, allowing close observation of characteristics such as bill length and shape and tail color; call notes can also be important for identification. The greatest variety of species is present in late summer.

west a mile, then go south on Coffman Road to **Whitewater Draw Wildlife Area.** At either site, cranes gather each night and leave in the morning to feed in surrounding fields, so you may see (and hear) them anywhere in the area. Watch, too, for Northern Harrier; Bald and Golden Eagles; and Harris's, Red-tailed, Ferruginous, and Rough-legged (rare) Hawks, among other wintering birds of prey. Check the short-grass center-pivot irrigation fields about 5 miles north of Elfrida, near the intersection of US 191 and Rucker Canyon Road, for wintering Mountain Plover and possibly McCown's and Chestnut-collared Longspurs.

Cave Creek Canyon in the Chiricahua Mountains of southeastern Arizona, home of Elegant Trogon and Painted Redstart

3 The **San Pedro Riparian National Conservation Area** stretches 40 miles along the San Pedro River, running north from the Mexican border, east of Sierra Vista. **San Pedro House,** 7 miles east of Sierra Vista on US 90, is the area's visitor center, and the site of a hummingbird-banding station in spring and fall (*call 520-432-1388 for times*). Several trails radiating from San Pedro House provide excellent birding in spring and summer for species including Gray Hawk, Gambel's Quail, Yellow-billed Cuckoo, Gila Woodpecker, Gilded Flicker, Say's Phoebe, Vermilion Flycatcher, Verdin, Cactus Wren, Crissal Thrasher, Lucy's and Yellow Warblers, Yellow-breasted

Century plants in the Huachuca Mountains near Sierra Vista

Chat, Summer Tanager, Abert's Towhee, and Pyrrhuloxia. The tiny Green Kingfisher is a specialty of the river area. Look for this bird at **Kingfisher Pond,** south of San Pedro House. You might also find Tropical Kingbird, a bird of localized distribution in Arizona.

4 Just west of Sierra Vista, the **Huachuca Mountains** compose yet another of the Southwest's most celebrated birding haunts. Put the Nature Conservancy's beautiful **Ramsey Canyon Preserve** high on your visitation list, but be sure to call for reservations first (*520-378-2785*), as parking is strictly limited. The hummingbird feeders are always busy here, and a trail up the canyon through maples, oaks, junipers, and sycamores offers a chance to see many of the birds listed for the Chiricahuas, including Elegant Trogon, Acorn and Strickland's Woodpeckers, Sulphur-bellied Flycatcher, Mexican Jay, and Painted Redstart. Eared Trogon, a larger relative of the Elegant Trogon that is rarely seen north of Mexico, has taken up residence above Ramsey Canyon on occasion, attracting birders from far and wide.

Nearby **Fort Huachuca** is an active military base that allows birders to explore its birdy highlands. After entering the fort's main gate, at the western end of Fry Boulevard in Sierra Vista, take the road leading to Garden

Canyon. Picnic areas along the road make good stops (check for Montezuma Quail), but the best known birding areas lie beyond. **Scheelite Canyon,** less than a mile past the upper picnic area, has long been home to a pair of Spotted Owls, regularly seen along the rather steep trail leading up from the road. If you should be lucky enough to find them, enjoy the view briefly and leave the birds in peace, taking special care not to disturb them in any way. Continue up the road 2 miles to **Sawmill Canyon.** Exploring the trails here, you may find Elegant Trogon; Greater Pewee; Buff-breasted Flycatcher (a specialty of this site); Olive, Grace's, and Red-faced Warblers; Painted Redstart; and Yellow-eyed Junco. In late summer, check for flocks of migrant warblers that might include Hermit.

5 Part of pretty Sonoita Creek, which flows past the town of Patagonia, is protected in the Nature Conservancy's **Patagonia-Sonoita Creek Preserve,** reached by driving north from Ariz. 82 on Fourth Avenue and turning southwest at Pennsylvania Avenue. After crossing the creek, look for a private residence on the south side of the road where birders may observe hummingbird feeders. Many spring-through-fall visitors have seen their first Violet-crowned Hummingbird here, among the more common Broad-billed, Black-chinned, Anna's (fall through spring), and Rufous (late summer). In winter, seed feeders may attract Lazuli Bunting. Continue a short distance to the preserve entrance (*closed Mon.-Tues.*). Along the trails here in spring and summer you may find nesting birds including Gray Hawk (listen for its call, a series of high whistles), Yellow-billed Cuckoo, Northern Beardless-Tyrannulet (a very small, plain flycatcher), Vermilion and Brown-crested Flycatchers, Black Phoebe, Thick-billed Kingbird, Bell's Vireo, Bridled Titmouse, Curve-billed Thrasher, Lucy's Warbler, and Summer Tanager, to name only a few of the highlights. In winter, the sanctuary may be quiet at times, but hosts Hammond's and

Pyrrhuloxia, a cardinal-like species of the arid Southwest

Dusky Flycatchers, Green-tailed Towhee, and possibly a Green Kingfisher as well.

About 4 miles southwest of Patagonia on Ariz. 82 lies a picnic area birders call the **Patagonia roadside rest area.** In spring and summer, this is usually the best spot in the United States to find Rose-throated Becard, a flycatcher relative that is very rare and local north of Mexico. The birds build large hanging nests along Sonoita Creek, across the highway. (Be sure to obey the "No Trespassing" signs here, and do not cross fences.) Other birds found in the general area include Gray Hawk, Thick-billed Kingbird, and Rufous-crowned Sparrow.

A few miles farther southwest on Ariz. 82, turn north at the well-marked entrance to **Patagonia Lake State Park.** Past the ranger station, turn east and drive through the campground to the upper end of the lake and the start of the **Sonoita Creek Trail.** The park is best known as a good spot to see both Neotropic and Double-crested Cormorants year-round. In winter, several species of grebes and a variety of ducks including Common Merganser may be present. The trail leads through mesquite scrub and riparian areas good in winter for Hammond's and Dusky (riparian), Gray (mesquite), and Ash-throated (mesquite) Flycatchers, and for typical lowland birds throughout the year. Nutting's Flycatcher, a very rare visitor from south of the border, drew hundreds of birders to the park when it appeared in the winter of 1997–98.

Elegant Trogon

Trogons compose a colorful family of mostly tropical species, including in their number the Resplendent Quetzal of Central America, one of the world's most spectacularly beautiful birds. The Elegant Trogon ranks with the most sought-after specialties of southeastern Arizona. Its hoarse *co-ah* call is heard in spring and early summer in **Cave Creek** (see p. 153) and **Madera** (see p. 158) **Canyons** among other wooded riparian sites. The species is much less common in southwestern New Mexico. Its larger relative the Eared Trogon is found only rarely in southeastern Arizona mountains.

6 Located southeast of Green Valley (*Continental Road exit off I-19, then E through the town of Continental*), **Madera Canyon Recreation Area** in the Santa Rita Mountains offers the chance to see many regional specialties. Madera Canyon Road bends south from White House Canyon Road about 6.5 miles east of the railroad tracks.

Ocotillo growing in grassland near Madera Canyon, at the base of the Santa Rita Mountains

Within the first mile you'll cross two bridges over usually dry creek beds, or washes. Walking the second of these, Florida Wash, you can find typical desert breeding species including Gambel's Quail, Greater Roadrunner, Black-chinned and Costa's Hummingbirds (the latter performing its display flight in March), Verdin, Cactus Wren, Black-tailed Gnatcatcher, Curve-billed and Crissal Thrashers, Phainopepla, Rufous-winged (scarce) and Black-throated Sparrows, Pyrrhuloxia, and Varied Bunting. In grassland farther along the road, the look-alike Cassin's and Botteri's Sparrows sing after midsummer rains renew the vegetation.

Once you arrive in the oak woods of the lower canyon, check picnic areas and trails for Acorn and Strickland's Woodpeckers, Sulphur-bellied Flycatcher, Plumbeous and Hutton's Vireos, Mexican Jay, Bushtit, Hepatic Tanager, Black-headed Grosbeak, and Bronzed Cowbird. Feeders at the lodge offer fabulous hummingbird-watching. Madera Canyon is also known for its owls: Western Screech-Owl is found in the lower canyon, Whiskered Screech-Owl in the oaks of the middle canyon, and Flammulated Owl along trails higher up, past the end of the road. Tiny Elf Owls nest in telephone poles near the old lodge site. From trailheads at the end of Madera Canyon Road, trails lead up toward 7,600-foot Josephine Saddle and 9,453-foot Mount Wrightson. As you ascend, bird life includes Elegant Trogon;

Greater Pewee; Cordilleran Flycatcher; Steller's Jay; Pygmy Nuthatch; Black-throated Gray, Grace's, and Red-faced Warblers; Western Tanager; and Yellow-eyed Junco.

7 Visitors to Tucson can find good desert and mountain birding within a few miles of the city center. West of Tucson, the **Arizona-Sonora Desert Museum** provides an excellent introduction not just to the bird life but to the

overall environment of this ecological region. (There's plenty here to keep a nonbirding companion happy for a few hours, too.) Part zoo and part botanic garden, the museum hosts many wild birds on its extensive grounds, from Gambel's Quail scuttling through the scrub to Cactus Wrens singing their chugging song to Gila Woodpeckers on the feeders. Aviaries display many desert species, and the hummingbird exhibit is worth a visit in itself. To reach the museum, take Speedway Boulevard west from I-19 to Gates Pass Road and Kinney Road (the route is well marked). After visiting here, continue northwest on Kinney Road to the **Tucson Mountain District** of **Saguaro National Park** for more desert

Giant saguaro cactus in Saguaro National Park, near Tucson

birding opportunities. Birding in the desert is best early in the morning or late in the evening. At midday, you'll be better off admiring the impressive saguaro cactuses from your air-conditioned car. Gila Woodpeckers and Gilded Flickers excavate holes in the giant saguaros, and Elf Owls roost in old cavities.

8 In northeastern Tucson, following Tanque Verde Road east from Kolb Road brings you to the Catalina Highway, which leads uphill 30 miles to the top of 9,157-foot **Mount Lemmon,** part of **Coronado National Forest.** Driving this road takes you from desert, with Gila Woodpecker and Phainopepla, through middle elevations, with Acorn Woodpecker and Black-throated Gray Warbler, to pine and Douglas-fir highlands, with Hairy Woodpecker and Mountain Chickadee. You won't find Elegant Trogon in these Santa Catalina Mountains, but looking in the proper habitat will turn up many other regional specialties, including Zone-tailed Hawk; Magnificent Hummingbird; Strickland's Woodpecker; Greater Pewee; Dusky-capped and Sulphur-bellied Flycatchers; Mexican Jay; Bridled Titmouse; Olive, Grace's, and Red-faced Warblers; Painted Redstart; and Yellow-eyed Junco. Check campgrounds and recreation areas as you drive up Mount Lemmon to see the widest range of species. At overlooks, you may see White-throated Swifts or Common Ravens sailing along the rock faces, or, if you're lucky, a Peregrine Falcon.

9 On US 60 near Superior, about 50 miles east of Phoenix, the **Boyce Thompson Southwestern Arboretum** displays plants from deserts and arid areas around the world. It's a great place to get excellent looks at typical desert species, and the varied plantings attract interesting migrants (often including eastern vagrants) and winter residents. Look here for White-winged and Inca Doves, Gila and Ladder-backed Woodpeckers, Hutton's Vireo, Rock and Canyon Wrens, Curve-billed Thrasher, Canyon and Abert's Towhees, Northern Cardinal, and Pyrrhuloxia. Check **Ayer Lake** for an occasional waterbird such as Sora or Common Moorhen. Hummingbirds are attracted to all sorts of blooms; look for the beautiful little Costa's in spring and summer.

10 The **White Mountains** of east-central Arizona offer a chance to see montane species (some of which usually have the adjective "elusive" before their names) as well as lower elevation birds. From Eagar, just south of Springerville, drive 5 miles west on Ariz. 260, then south toward the South Fork Campground in the **Apache-Sitgreaves National Forest** (*closed Dec.-April*). Look for Western Scrub-Jay, Pinyon Jay, and Mountain Bluebird along the road, and for Gray Catbird and American Redstart (scarce) in riparian areas along the Little Colorado River, which the road crosses in less than 2 miles. American Dipper nests by the river. Continue to the campground for more birding.

Riparian vegetation in the White Mountains, near Eagar in the Apache-Sitgreaves National Forest

Return to Ariz. 260 and drive west about 12 miles to Ariz. 273; turn south and go 4 miles to the turn to Sunrise Peak ski area and campground. The forest here, on the **White Mountain Apache Reservation,** is home to Blue Grouse, Williamson's and Red-naped Sapsuckers, Three-toed Woodpecker, Cordilleran Flycatcher, Gray Jay, Clark's Nutcracker, Mountain Chickadee, Red-breasted and Pygmy Nuthatches, Brown Creeper, Golden-crowned Kinglet, Townsend's Solitaire, Virginia's and Grace's Warblers, Western Tanager, and Pine Grosbeak. At night, listen for the single or double hollow hoots of Flammulated Owl. For another good spot, continue south on Ariz. 273 about 5 miles to a forest road on the west (near the Sheep Crossing Campground), leading to the trail up 11,590-foot **Mount Baldy.** While only the intrepid will hike all the way to the top, the trail, which follows the West Fork Little Colorado River, offers fine birding.

11 Quite naturally, high-country birds are also the attraction on and around **Humphreys Peak,** at 12,633 feet Arizona's tallest mountain and the high point on the rim of an ancient volcano now forming the San Francisco Mountains. From Flagstaff, drive northwest about

7 miles to well-marked Snow Bowl Road, which leads north to the popular ski area. From here, a chairlift operating in summer provides easy access to the slopes of 12,356-foot **Agassiz Peak,** and a hiking trail leads to the top of Humphreys. Along the road up and around the ski area you may find Flammulated Owl, Williamson's and Red-naped Sapsuckers, Dusky Flycatcher, Clark's Nutcracker, Mountain Chickadee, Hermit Thrush, Dark-eyed Junco, and many of the other species listed above for the White Mountains.

12 Although most birders think first of Arizona's deserts and mountains, some of its best rarities have come from along the Colorado River, especially from the area around Parker Dam and **Lake Havasu.** Fall and winter are usually the best times to bird this area. From Parker, drive north 19 miles on Ariz. 95 to the dam, checking the river on the west for ducks and other waterbirds. Barrow's Goldeneye is seen regularly in winter in the mile of the river below the dam, and gulls congregate at the dam itself. Follow Ariz. 95 north and scan the lake for loons (Common is most frequent, but Red-throated, Pacific, and Yellow-billed have been seen), grebes (Horned is sometimes found along with Eared, Western, and Clark's), geese, and ducks.

NEW MEXICO

13 Travelers on I-25 in northeastern New Mexico can find good birding just minutes from the interstate at **Maxwell National Wildlife Refuge,** noted for migrant waterfowl, winter raptors, and some interesting breeding species. From Maxwell, 25 miles south of Raton, drive north less than a mile on N. Mex. 445, turn west on N. Mex. 505, and drive 2.5 miles to the refuge entrance on the north.

The three main lakes here can host more than 90,000 waterfowl at the peak of fall migration. Among the most common are Snow and Canada Geese (look for Ross's as well), Gadwall, Mallard, Northern Pintail, Bufflehead, Common Goldeneye, Common Merganser, and Ruddy Duck. Most years, Canada Goose, Gadwall, Mallard, and Blue-winged and Cinnamon Teals remain to nest, along with Pied-billed, Eared, and Western Grebes; American Avocet; and Wilson's Phalarope. In migration and in winter, look for raptors including Bald Eagle and Rough-legged Hawk, along with occasional Ferruginous Hawk, Golden Eagle, and Prairie Falcon. Northern Harrier and Swainson's and Red-tailed Hawks nest in the area.

In summer, practice your observation skills on look-alike Cassin's and Western Kingbirds (check throat and tail patterns); the Eastern Kingbirds here are much easier to identify. You might see the long-legged little Burrowing Owl nesting; along with Vesper, Savannah, and Grasshopper Sparrows; Blue Grosbeak; Yellow-headed Blackbird; and in some years, Cassin's Sparrow and Dickcissel. In winter, American Tree Sparrow is common.

14 Many high-country birds extend their ranges south into New Mexico along the Rocky Mountains, and roads to ski areas near Santa Fe and Albuquerque provide easy access to montane habitat. If you're visiting Santa Fe, stop first at the **Randall Davey Audubon Center** at the end of Upper Canyon Road for advice and birding. Look here for Black-chinned and Broad-tailed Hummingbirds (both absent in winter), Steller's Jay (winter), Western Scrub-Jay, Black-billed Magpie, Juniper Titmouse, and Spotted and Canyon Towhees.

Proceed up Hyde Park Road, also called the **Santa Fe**

Lake and marsh at northeastern New Mexico's Maxwell National Wildlife Refuge

Scenic Byway (N. Mex. 475), toward the Santa Fe Ski Area. Stop at **Hyde Memorial State Park** to look for Steller's Jay, Mountain Chickadee, Red-breasted and Pygmy Nuthatches, Brown Creeper, and Western Tanager. As the road climbs, watch for a parking area at **Aspen Vista,** where an old road, now a hiking trail, makes for easy walking. Clark's Nutcrackers give their harsh *kra-a-a* call, and lucky birders might see a Blue Grouse here or higher. The road ends at a large parking lot at the ski area at 10,400 feet, where the **Windsor Trail** leads up to 12,622-foot Santa Fe Baldy through aspen, blue and Engelmann spruce, and white fir. Williamson's Sapsucker, Three-toed Woodpecker, Gray Jay, Ruby-crowned Kinglet, Townsend's Solitaire, Pine Grosbeak, Red Crossbill, and Pine Siskin are among the birds you might find as you explore this beautiful forest.

Sandia Crest, a popular birding location for mountain species northeast of Albuquerque

15 Look for many of these montane species on the way up to 10,678-foot **Sandia Crest,** just northeast of Albuquerque. Drive east about 15 miles on I-40, drive north on N. Mex. 14 for 6 miles, then turn northwest on N. Mex. 536, also known as the Sandia Crest Byway. As the highway winds up into the Sandia Mountains, several **Cibola National Forest** picnic areas and trails offer birding opportunities. Listen for the American Robin-like song of Black-headed Grosbeak in the oak-pine-juniper woods at Sulphur Canyon picnic area, as well as the fluting of Hermit Thrush. Other nesting species you'll find as you ascend include Band-tailed Pigeon, White-throated Swift, Red-naped Sapsucker, Dusky and Cordilleran Flycatchers, Steller's Jay, Common Raven, Virginia's and Grace's Warblers, and Dark-eyed Junco.

Back down in the lowlands (relatively speaking) of Albuquerque itself, the Rio Grande creates a narrow green oasis along the west side of the city. Set in a riparian forest of cottonwoods and willows (and introduced Russian olives), the **Rio Grande Nature Center State Park** offers fine birding just a few minutes from I-40. To reach it, take Rio Grande Boulevard north from I-40 for 1.5 miles and turn left on Candelaria Road. Typical breeding birds you'll find along the trails include Gambel's Quail, Western Screech-Owl, Black-chinned Hummingbird (Calliope, Broad-tailed, and Rufous appear at feeders in migration), Western Wood-Pewee, Black and Say's Phoebes, Ash-throated Flycatcher, Cliff Swallow, Black-capped Chickadee, Bewick's Wren, Chipping Sparrow, Blue Grosbeak, Bullock's Oriole, and Lesser Goldfinch.

A 3-acre pond by the center is home to Pied-billed Grebe, Great Blue Heron, Black-crowned Night-Heron, Wood Duck, and a variety of other waterbirds. The number of species found here swells in spring and fall, when the Rio Grande *bosque* (Spanish for "woodland") serves as a corridor for migratory birds; vagrant eastern species such as Tennessee, Black-throated Blue, and Hooded Warblers occasionally put in an appearance.

16 Visitors are welcome at the **Hawk Watch International Fall Migration Site** in the Manzano Mountains, where southbound migrant raptors provide excellent close views as they fly low over the watch site on Capilla Peak, about 35 miles southeast of Albuquerque. To reach it, drive west from N. Mex. 56 in the town of Manzano, following signs for Capilla Peak Campground. As you approach the fire tower near the campground, park and walk west on the **Gavilan Trail** about a half mile to the site. Most years, some 5,000 hawks pass this point in September and October, though 1998 saw more than 9,000 birds in passage. Peak migration comes in late September and early October, with Sharp-shinned, Cooper's, and Red-tailed Hawks and American Kestrel the most commonly sighted raptors. Other species seen regularly include Northern Harrier, Northern Goshawk, Swainson's Hawk, Golden Eagle, Merlin, and Peregrine (more than one hundred in 1998) and Prairie Falcons.

17 New Mexico's most famous birding spot lies along the Rio Grande about 90 miles or so south of

Albuquerque. The 57,000 acres of **Bosque del Apache National Wildlife Refuge** stretch along 9 miles of the river, and the varied habitats here—wetlands, riparian cottonwood-and-willow woods, cropland, and arid uplands—have over the years attracted more than 320 species. One special bird, though, has come to symbolize the refuge: Sandhill Crane, which winters at Bosque del Apache in spectacular flocks numbering in the thousands. The nearby town of Socorro holds its Festival of the Cranes each November, an event that has become one of the country's most popular birding festivals, with speakers, field trips, and workshops. *(Call 505-835-1828 for information.)*

Waterbirds of all sorts can be found on the refuge year-round. Huge flocks of Snow Geese (up to 40,000 or more) winter here, along with Ross's (up to 14 percent of the white geese may be this species) and Canada Geese and occasional Greater White-fronted. Fifteen or more species of ducks can be found, often totaling more than 50,000 individuals. Five species of grebes can appear in migration: Pied-billed, Eared, Western, and Clark's, and rarely Horned. American White Pelican, Neotropic and Double-crested Cormorants, bitterns, herons, egrets, White-faced Ibis, Virginia Rail, Sora, Common Moorhen, and American Coot either nest or appear regularly. Spring, late summer, and fall see good numbers of shorebirds; Black-necked Stilt and American Avocet breed.

Twenty or more Bald Eagles make the refuge their winter home (though one winter saw 60 appearing in a single day), and a few Golden Eagles are usually around throughout the year. Both Chihuahuan and Common Ravens nest in the area, but it takes careful study to tell these two apart, unless a helpful gust of wind reveals the white bases of the former's neck feathers—and even then, the distinction is subtle. Bosque del Apache is also a fine place for visitors to get acquainted with typical southwestern desert birds such as Gambel's Quail, Greater Roadrunner, Lesser and Common Nighthawks, Common Poorwill, Black-chinned Hummingbird, Ladder-backed Woodpecker, Ash-throated Flycatcher, Verdin, Bushtit, Curve-billed Thrasher, Black-throated Sparrow, and Pyrrhuloxia, the crested finch that will remind Easterners of a female Northern Cardinal. Auto

tour routes and several observation platforms allow viewing of varied habitats within the refuge.

Sandhill Cranes at Bosque del Apache National Wildlife Refuge near Socorro

18 Farther south, dams on the Rio Grande create Elephant Butte and Caballo Reservoirs—and, not coincidentally, excellent birding for loons, grebes, diving ducks, gulls, and terns, mostly from fall through spring. To reach one favored viewpoint over **Elephant Butte,** New Mexico's largest lake, take the Elephant Butte exit from I-25, 14 miles north of Truth or Consequences, and drive east 8 miles on a very rough road to the lake. Turn north to North Monticello Point, part of **Elephant Butte State Park.** Look here

NEW MEXICO   **169**

Elephant Butte Reservoir, north of Truth or Consequences, one of the state's best water bird sites

in winter for Common Loon, Horned Grebe, sometimes thousands of Western and Clark's Grebes, and Bald Eagle, as well as assorted ducks. Rarities seen here have ranged from Brown Pelican to Sabine's Gull. The road paralleling the Rio Grande for 5 miles northeast of Truth or Consequences, N. Mex. 51, also traverses some excellent birding habitat and leads to the main area of the park, which offers several lookouts of the lower lake.

The Caballo exit from I-25 provides access to fine birding sites. Drive north and immediately east to reach **Caballo Dam** and **Caballo Lake State Park.** The dam offers good viewing of the lake and Rio Grande for winter waterbirds and Bald Eagles. This spot has been the state's best for gulls, and American White Pelican and Neotropic Cormorant (resident here) are seen often. Clark's Grebe breeds here. The park area below the dam can have interesting land birds in migration and winter. Western Screech-Owl, Verdin, Cactus and Rock Wrens, Phainopepla, and Rufous-crowned Sparrow are present year-round in the dam and park area.

N. Mex. 187 south from I-25 leads to **Percha Dam State Park,** a favorite of local birders. Here the best remaining riparian vegetation in the lower Rio Grande Valley attracts an excellent variety of migrants and wintering songbirds. Eastern and western strays show up here regularly. Residents include Gambel's Quail, Ladder-backed Woodpecker, Verdin, Cactus Wren (uncommon), Curve-billed and Crissal Thrashers, and Lucy's Warbler (late March to September).

19 In southeastern New Mexico, just northeast of Roswell, **Bitter Lake National Wildlife Refuge** is known as the state's best site for shorebirds. One natural lake and several man-made impoundments vary in levels throughout the year, attracting thousands of geese and ducks in fall migration, as well as flocks of Sandhill Cranes sometimes numbering in the tens of thousands in November. Grebes, American White Pelican, Neotropic and Double-crested Cormorants, waders (including occasional rarities such as Little Blue and Tricolored Herons and Reddish Egret), gulls, and terns frequent these wetlands seasonally. An 8.5-mile auto-tour route passes several of the refuge lakes and an observation platform at Bitter Lake.

Greater Roadrunner

Its generic name, *Geococcyx,* means "ground cuckoo," and that's just what the Greater Roadrunner is: a large cuckoo that flies only rarely and for short distances, preferring to stay on terra firma. Common throughout much of the Southwest, the roadrunner often stops and seems to inspect humans who are watching it, expressively raising and lowering its bushy crest. Roadrunners' legs are thick and strong, and these birds use their fabled speed to catch snakes, lizards, insects, small birds, and rodents.

Spring, late summer, and fall are the peak times for shorebird variety. Species range from common migrants such as Greater and Lesser Yellowlegs and Western and Least Sandpipers to a long list of rarities such as Whimbrel, Hudsonian Godwit, and Ruddy Turnstone. Semipalmated, White-rumped (late spring), Baird's, and Stilt Sandpipers all are regular migrants here. Snowy Plover, Black-necked Stilt, and American Avocet nest on the refuge, which is also New Mexico's only regular breeding site for Least Tern. Grasslands provide habitat for a good variety of winter sparrows, and Chestnut-collared Longspur is a common migrant and winter resident.

20 Carlsbad Caverns National Park offers nature lovers treats in addition to its underground wonders: At dusk, nearly 500,000 Mexican free-tailed bats leave the cave entrance to hunt insects, and the cave mouth is also home to the largest colony of Cave Swallows in the United States, present from March to October.

From the main park entrance, drive 6 miles south on US 62/180 and turn east on County Road 418 to reach **Rattlesnake Springs.** This disjunct section of the park is famed as one of the state's best "vagrant traps," or sites that attract rare strays; more than 300 species have been seen in this small area. The springs have a long history of use by Native Americans and early settlers, and today create an oasis in the desert that nearly always rewards a birding visit. Notable nesting birds include Yellow-billed Cuckoo, Vermilion Flycatcher, Bell's Vireo, Yellow-breasted Chat, Summer Tanager, Northern Cardinal, Pyrrhuloxia, Indigo and Painted Buntings, and Orchard and Hooded Orioles. In winter, eastern species found with some regularity include Eastern Phoebe, Eastern Bluebird, and Brown Thrasher.

21 In southwestern New Mexico, Silver City is the gateway to excellent birding areas. Some of the nesting species found in the **Gila National Forest** north of town include Flammulated and Spotted Owls; Acorn Woodpecker; Greater Pewee; Cordilleran Flycatcher; Plumbeous, Hutton's, and Warbling Vireos; Steller's, Mexican, and Pinyon Jays; Mountain Chickadee; Bridled and Juniper Titmice; Red-breasted and Pygmy Nuthatches; Ruby-crowned Kinglet; Western Bluebird; Hermit Thrush; Olive, Virginia's, Black-throated Gray, Grace's, and Red-faced Warblers; Painted Redstart; Hepatic and Western Tanagers; Dark-eyed Junco; and Red Crossbill.

For a sampling of these appealing species, take Little Walnut Road north from US 180 in Silver City 4 miles to the **Little Walnut Picnic Area,** at 6,600 feet in the national forest. After birding here, return to Silver City and take N. Mex. 15 north 13 miles, climbing to the Cherry Creek Campground and, a bit farther, the McMillan Campground. Two miles farther, a side road leads up 9,001-foot **Signal Peak;** driving part of this road can also be productive.

Return to Silver City and take US 180 northwest 25 miles; turn southwest toward Bill Evans Lake. In 3.5 miles, go right at a Y on a gravel road that ends in 2.5 miles at the national forest's **Gila Bird Habitat,** a riparian area along the Gila River with an excellent array of nesting species. Look here for Common Black-Hawk; Wild Turkey; Montezuma Quail (scarce, but possible even along the road); Yellow-billed Cuckoo; Elf Owl; Willow, Vermilion, and

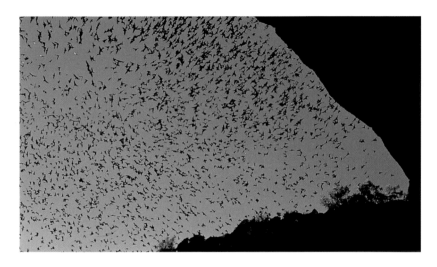

Brown-crested Flycatchers; Bridled and Juniper Titmice; Lucy's Warbler; Yellow-breasted Chat; Summer Tanager; Abert's Towhee; Northern Cardinal; and Pyrrhuloxia. You may see Common Merganser in the river, and check the skies for an occasional Zone-tailed Hawk (nests nearby) "masquerading" as a Turkey Vulture. The first Gray Hawk was seen near here in 1998, and there are hopes that as the habitat develops this species may begin breeding in the area.

Mexican free-tailed bats at the mouth of Carlsbad Caverns, where Cave Swallows also nest

Return to US 180 and continue northwest 4 miles to Cliff. Take N. Mex. 211 east a short distance and turn north on N. Mex. 293 (Box Canyon Road). Continue on this paved, then gravel road about 7 miles to the Nature Conservancy's **Gila Riparian Preserve.** Here, at the confluence of Mogollon Creek and the Gila River, you'll have another chance at finding many of the same species listed above for Gila Bird Habitat.

WESTERN TEXAS

22 One of the most remote parks in the lower 48 states, **Big Bend National Park** nonetheless places high on the list of the country's best, and best liked, birding destinations. This huge (800,000-acre) park, located where the Rio Grande makes a "big bend" north on its mostly southeastern way to the Gulf of Mexico, rewards travelers with dramatic mountain and desert scenery in addition to a fine list of special birds. Most of the park is Chihuahuan Desert, where Scaled Quail, Verdin, Cactus Wren, Black-tailed Gnatcatcher, Black-throated Sparrow, and Pyrrhuloxia are among the typical birds in a landscape of creosote bush, lechuguilla, ocotillo, yucca, and cactus. But varied habitats are found in riparian areas along the Rio Grande and in the Chisos Mountains, rising to 7,835 feet in the center of the park and thickly forested in oak, maple, juniper, and Arizona cypress. Most birders prefer to visit from late April through early June, when breeders are present and singing.

Entering the park from the north along a long desert highway (make sure your car is well serviced before traveling to Big Bend), you might see a Lesser Nighthawk flying low, or a colorful Scott's Oriole flashing by. After stopping at the visitor center at Panther Junction, drive east to **Rio Grande Village** and explore the picnic areas, campground, and nature trail. You'll probably be greeted by a Greater Roadrunner as you arrive. Watch the sky here for Gray Hawk or, if you're lucky, Common Black-Hawk. Check the cottonwoods and shrubs for White-winged and Inca Doves, Golden-fronted and Ladder-backed Woodpeckers, Black Phoebe, Vermilion and Ash-throated Flycatchers, Bell's Vireo, Crissal Thrasher (scarce), Summer Tanager, Painted Bunting, and Orchard and Hooded Orioles. Elf Owl usually nests somewhere in the area, so ask a

park naturalist about reliable locations for this little bird.

Your next stop should be the **Chisos Mountains Basin,** where there's a lodge, restaurant, and campground, and from which trails lead into the high country. On the way up, watch for blooming century plants, tall green spikes with masses of yellow flowers. In and near the basin, it's possible to see four or five species of hummer at one plant, including Blue-throated, Magnificent (occasionally comes down from higher areas), Lucifer (one of the park's specialties), Black-chinned, and Broad-tailed; Rufous arrives after breeding in late summer. Around the campground or

The Chisos Mountains rising above Chihuahuan Desert vegetation at Big Bend National Park, south of Alpine on the **Window Trail,** look for Black-capped Vireo (scarce, but nests along the Window Trail), Rock and Bewick's Wrens, Hepatic Tanager, Spotted and Canyon Towhees, Rufous-crowned and Black-chinned Sparrows, Black-headed Grosbeak, Varied Bunting (on the Window Trail), and Lesser Goldfinch.

Though it's a strenuous hike, the climb up to **Boot Spring** is one of America's classic birding quests. The object is Big

Bend's signature species, the Colima Warbler, a bird that nests nowhere else in the United States but these Chisos Mountains. If you have time and energy, leave early in the morning and climb to Laguna Meadow, continuing on the **Colima Trail** to Boot Canyon and returning down the **Pinnacles Trail.** It's a round-trip of 9.5 fairly hard miles, but you'll see fabulous scenery and a great list of birds, including, from mid-April through June, almost certainly a Colima. Other species to watch for: Zone-tailed Hawk (possible almost anywhere in the park), Band-tailed Pigeon, White-throated Swift, Magnificent Hummingbird, Acorn Woodpecker, Cordilleran Flycatcher, Hutton's Vireo, Mexican Jay, and

White-winged Dove perched on ocotillo, Big Bend National Park

Bushtit. Those who can't make it all the way to Boot Canyon can usually find Colima Warblers lower on the Pinnacles Trail or in **Laguna Meadow,** though a hike of 3 miles or so (one way) is necessary to reach the birds' habitat. Flammulated Owl nests in the high Chisos, but a permit to camp overnight, and luck, are necessary to find one.

Other fine birding sites in the park include **Blue Creek Canyon,** good for Gray Vireo, Canyon Wren, Phainopepla, Rufous-crowned Sparrow, and Varied Bunting; walk up the canyon from the old ranch house for a mile or more. Check also the **Sam Nail Ranch** (a desert oasis where anything might show up) and the **Cottonwood Campground** (look for Hooded Oriole here and, in the scrub nearby, Lucy's Warbler).

23 A hundred miles north of Big Bend, the **Davis Mountains** offer beautiful scenery and more than a little frustration, since very few areas here are publicly accessible. As you approach **Davis Mountains State Park** from Fort Davis along Tex. 118, watch for Common Black-Hawk, which nests along Limpia Creek. The park is known as a good spot to find the elusive Montezuma Quail, which is not so elusive when it comes to feeders in the campground. Other species to look for in the park, or along Tex. 118 as it climbs to the northwest, include Zone-tailed Hawk, Golden Eagle, Prairie Falcon, Greater Roadrunner, White-throated Swift, Acorn Woodpecker, Say's Phoebe, Western Scrub-Jay, Rock and Canyon Wrens, and Western Bluebird. Stop at the **Madera Canyon Picnic Area** for a chance at species such as Band-tailed Pigeon, Williamson's Sapsucker (winter), Gray Flycatcher, Plumbeous Vireo, Mountain Chickadee, Grace's Warbler, and Hepatic Tanager. Anna's Hummingbird is seen regularly in the Davis Mountains from late September through November.

24 Water is found in the desert at **Lake Balmorhea,** a private 573-acre impoundment between Balmorhea and Toyahvale. From fall through spring, a check might reveal Common Loon, grebes (including both Western and Clark's), and a variety of ducks, gulls, and terns; waders and shorebirds frequent the shores at times. As the only lake for many miles, Balmorhea has attracted some rare waterbirds over the years, from Yellow-billed Loon to Elegant Tern.

25 Texas' highest point is found near the New Mexican border in **Guadalupe Mountains National Park,** where Guadalupe Peak rises to 8,749 feet. Like Big Bend, the park features desert, mountain peaks, and the slopes between, and so hosts a broad range of species. Birders visit to see mountain species, including some that nest nowhere else in Texas. High-elevation birds include Band-tailed Pigeon; Flammulated, Spotted, and Northern Saw-whet Owls; Olive-sided and Cordilleran Flycatchers; Plumbeous and Warbling Vireos; Steller's Jay; Mountain Chickadee; Pygmy Nuthatch; Brown Creeper; House Wren; Hermit Thrush; Virginia's and Grace's Warblers; Western Tanager;

McKittrick Canyon, site of an excellent birding trail in Guadalupe Mountains National Park, east of El Paso

Dark-eyed Junco; and Pine Siskin. The steep and strenuous hike up to The Bowl will give you a chance at these birds, though the owls are, of course, not likely in daylight.

For low- and mid-level species, take the relatively easy hike up **McKittrick Canyon,** one of the most beautiful spots in the state. Along the way, watch for Black-chinned Hummingbird, Gray Vireo, Western Scrub-Jay, Juniper Titmouse, Green-tailed Towhee, Rufous-crowned Sparrow, and Black-headed Grosbeak. As you reach higher areas of ponderosa pine, look for Blue-throated Hummingbird, Grace's Warbler, and Hepatic Tanager.

26 **Muleshoe National Wildlife Refuge,** 20 miles south of the town of the same name, has long been known as an important wintering ground for Sandhill Cranes, as well as home to migrant and wintering waterfowl and migrant shorebirds. Water level in refuge lakes depends on rainfall, and so bird numbers can vary greatly from year to year. At times, thousands of waterfowl are present, along with 10,000 or more Sandhill Cranes. In drought years numbers can be far lower, though at least some cranes can always be found from October through February. Nesting birds at Muleshoe include such southwestern species as Scaled Quail, Greater Roadrunner, Ladder-backed Woodpecker, Ash-throated and Scissor-tailed Flycatchers, Curve-billed Thrasher, and Cassin's Sparrow. Look for Burrowing Owl at the prairie-dog town near refuge headquarters, and for nesting Snowy Plover and American Avocet along lake edges. In winter, you might find Ferruginous or Rough-legged Hawks or Golden Eagle soaring overhead.

27 The tabletop-flat High Plains of the Texas Panhandle terminate dramatically along the Caprock Escarpment, where the terrain falls hundreds of feet in rugged canyons to the Rolling Plains region. In **Palo Duro Canyon State Park,** just southeast of Amarillo, it may be hard to look for birds, so strikingly beautiful is the scenery around you. Look and listen in spring and summer, though, and you'll find gorgeous Painted Buntings singing from shrubs all over the park. Walk trails or explore campgrounds and picnic areas in spring and summer for Mississippi Kite; Wild Turkey; Scaled Quail; Greater Roadrunner; Golden-fronted and Ladder-backed Woodpeckers; Say's Phoebe; Ash-throated Flycatcher; Western Scrub-Jay; Bushtit; Rock, Canyon, and Bewick's Wrens; Rufous-crowned and Lark Sparrows; Blue Grosbeak; and Bullock's Oriole. The **Lighthouse Trail,** 6 miles round-trip, can produce good birds in stunning surroundings.

Zone-tailed Hawk

With its mostly black coloration, long wings held in a shallow V, and habit of soaring lazily, the Zone-tailed Hawk looks amazingly like a Turkey Vulture in flight. This similarity is believed to aid the Zone-tailed in hunting, since small rodents and birds may allow it to approach closely, mistaking it for the nonthreatening, carrion-eating vulture. When you're in the Zone-tailed's range of southern Arizona to the Rio Grande Valley of Texas, check Turkey Vultures carefully to make sure you don't miss its much less common mimic.

28 The **Hill Country** west of Austin and San Antonio may be the prettiest part of Texas, a ruggedly picturesque landscape drained by clear, bluff-lined rivers. Among birders the Hill Country is best known as the nesting-season home of the endangered Black-capped Vireo and Golden-cheeked Warbler. The strikingly patterned vireo breeds from northern Mexico and Texas' Big Bend east and north into Oklahoma, but the warbler nests only in central Texas, where estimates of its population range from 8,000 to 15,000 pairs.

The Hill Country also represents the approximate eastern limit of regular occurrence of several western birds, among them Scaled Quail; Common Poorwill; Golden-fronted and Ladder-backed Woodpeckers; Black and Say's Phoebes; Vermilion and Ash-throated Flycatchers; Western Scrub-Jay; Verdin; Bushtit; Cactus, Rock, and Canyon Wrens; Long-billed and Curve-billed Thrashers; Canyon Towhee; Black-throated Sparrow; Pyrrhuloxia; Scott's Oriole; and Lesser Goldfinch. In addition, Least Grebe and Green Kingfisher, Mexican specialties of southern Texas, occur rarely but regularly north into the Hill Country.

Golden-cheeked Warbler, which looks a bit like its close relative the Black-throated Green Warbler, requires a specific breeding habitat of mature oak-juniper woods. (The birds always incorporate strips of juniper bark in their nests.) Residential and ranching development has been a leading factor in its decline. One result of the effort to protect the warbler and the Black-capped Vireo has been the establishment of **Balcones Canyonlands National Wildlife Refuge,** made up of several tracts of land in the hills northwest of Austin. Still under development and with limited public access, the refuge has recently opened a few nature trails and viewing areas. A vireo site is found on RR (Ranch Road) 1869 about 8 miles west of Liberty Hill. Continue west to RR 1174 and drive south 2.3 miles to a nature trail where the warbler can be found. Call the refuge before visiting for up-to-date information. Not only are the vireo and warbler found in the refuge, it's also the easternmost breeding area in the United States for Vermilion Flycatcher, Bushtit, Canyon Towhee, and Black-throated Sparrow.

You'll have far better luck finding both Black-capped Vireo and Golden-cheeked Warbler if you learn their songs before searching. The warbler's song consists of four or five notes with the buzzy quality of its relatives the Black-throated Green and Townsend's Warblers. The vireo's song is a squeaky series of two- or three-note phrases, shorter than that of Bell's Vireo, which may be found in similar scrubby habitat. Male Golden-cheekeds begin to sing in mid-March when they arrive from their wintering grounds; they leave the Hill Country by the end of July. The vireo arrives in late March, lingering into September before heading south again, although it's difficult to find in late summer.

Golden-cheeked Warbler also nests in **Emma Long Metropolitan Park** just west of Austin (*take Tex. 2222 NW from Tex. 360 and turn W on City Park Rd.*). **Turkey Creek Trail** is the best site for the warbler.

A favorite Austin location for shorebirds and waterfowl is **Hornsby Bend Biosolids Management Facility** (*on FM 973, just N of Tex. 71*). The ponds here are good for waders and ducks, and when pond conditions are right, shorebirding can be excellent. Black-bellied Whistling-Ducks nest here. Check the woods near the Colorado River for migrants in season.

Golden-cheeked Warbler, an endangered specialty of the Texas Hill Country

29 Thirty miles west of Austin, **Pedernales Falls State Park** is an excellent spot to find Golden-cheeked Warbler. Birds are often seen and heard along the quarter-mile **Hill Country Nature Trail,** which is also a good place to learn some of the common plants of the area. Other breeding species in the park include Greater Roadrunner, Black-chinned Hummingbird, Golden-fronted and Ladder-backed Woodpeckers, Vermilion and Ash-throated Fly-catchers, Western Scrub-Jay, Verdin, Bushtit, Rock and Canyon Wrens, and Rufous-crowned Sparrow. Green Kingfishers are sometimes seen along the Pedernales River.

30 Farther south, **Lost Maples State Natural Area** near Vanderpool was named for its population of bigtooth maples, growing in sheltered canyons here at the extreme eastern edge of their range. The park is home to several rare, endemic, or unusual species, from plants to fish to amphibians, but birders visit to see Green Kingfisher (uncommon

Sabinal River bluffs at Lost Maples State Natural Area, near Vanderpool

and irregular), Black-capped Vireo, and Golden-cheeked Warbler, all of which nest here. Check with rangers for spots where these birds have been seen. In looking for the kingfisher, keep in mind how tiny it is compared to the familiar Belted Kingfisher. It often perches quietly on small branches low over the water. Many times it's seen only as a virtual blur flying up or down the Sabinal River, sometimes uttering a squeaky little *tick* call note. Lost Maples is also good for many of the same western species listed for Pedernales Falls. Typical of the Hill Country's blend of east and west, both Ash-throated and Great Crested Flycatchers nest here, along with Eastern Wood-Pewee, Yellow-throated Vireo, Painted Bunting, Scott's Oriole, and Lesser Goldfinch.

Southwest
Information

? Visitor Center/Information   **⑤** Fee Charged   **🍴** Food

🚻 Rest Rooms   **🚶** Nature Trails   **🚗** Driving Tours   **♿** Wheelchair Accessible

Be advised that facilities may be seasonal and limited. We suggest calling or writing ahead for specific information. Note that addresses may be for administrative offices; see text or call for directions to sites.

Rare Bird Alerts

Arizona:
Phoenix *602-832-8745*
Tucson *520-798-1005*

New Mexico:
Statewide *505-323-9323*

Texas:
Statewide *713-369-9673*
Abilene *915-691-8981*
Austin *512-926-8751*
San Antonio *210-308-6788*

ARIZONA

Coronado National Forest *(Page 153)*
Douglas Ranger District
3081 North Leslie
  Canyon Road
Douglas, AZ 85607
520-364-3468

? **🍴** **🚻** **🚶**

District office for Chiricahua and Cave Creek Canyon areas

San Pedro Riparian National Conservation Area *(Page 155)*
Bureau of Land
  Management
1763 Paseo San Luis
Sierra Vista, AZ 85635
520-458-3559

? **⑤** **🚻** **🚶** **♿**

Ramsey Canyon Preserve *(Page 156)*
The Nature Conservancy
27 Ramsey Canyon Road
Hereford, AZ 85615
520-378-2785

? **🚻** **🚶** **♿**

Also offers a bed-and-breakfast and naturalist-led field trips

Fort Huachuca *(Page 156)*
Public Affairs Office
(ATZS-PA)
Fort Huachuca, AZ 85613
520-533-7083

🚻 **🚶** **♿**

Patagonia-Sonoita Creek Preserve *(Page 157)*
The Nature Conservancy
300 East University
  Boulevard
Tucson, AZ 85705
520-622-3861

Patagonia Lake State Park *(Page 158)*
400 Lake Patagonia Road
Patagonia, AZ 85624
520-287-6965

⑤ **🚻** **🚶** **♿**

Birding boat tours on Sat. a.m., weather permitting

Madera Canyon Recreation Area
(Page 158)
Nogales Ranger Station
303 Old Tucson Road
Nogales, AZ 85621
520-281-2296

? **⑤** **🚻** **🚶** **♿**

Arizona-Sonora Desert Museum *(Page 160)*
2021 North Kinney Road
Tucson, AZ 85743
520-883-2702

? **⑤** **🚻** **🚶** **♿**

Saguaro National Park *(Page 160)*
Western District
3693 South Old
  Spanish Trail
Tucson, AZ 85730
520-733-5158

? **🚻** **🚶** **🚗** **♿**

Coronado National Forest *(Page 160)*
Santa Catalina
  Ranger District
5700 North Sabino
  Canyon Road
Tucson, AZ 85750
520-749-8700

? **⑤** **🚻** **🚗** **♿**

District office for Mt. Lemmon site

Boyce Thompson Southwestern Arboretum
(Page 161)
37615 Highway 60
Superior, AZ 85273
520-689-2811

🅿️Ⓢ🍴🚻🏃♿

Apache-Sitgreaves National Forest
(Page 161)
309 South Mountain Avenue
Springerville, AZ 85938
520-333-4301

🚻🏃

Closed Dec.-April

NEW MEXICO

Maxwell National Wildlife Refuge
(Page 164)
P.O. Box 276
Maxwell, NM 87728
505-375-2331

🅿️🚻

Randall Davey Audubon Center *(Page 165)*
1800 Upper Canyon Road
Santa Fe, NM 87501
505-983-4609

🅿️Ⓢ🚻🏃♿

Hyde Memorial State Park *(Page 165)*
740 Hyde Park Road
Santa Fe, NM 87501
505-983-7175

🅿️Ⓢ🚻🏃〰️♿

Cibola National Forest
(Page 166)
Sandia Ranger District
11776 N. Mex. 337
Tijeras, NM 87059
505-281-3304

Ⓢ🍴🚻🏃♿

Rio Grande Nature Center State Park
(Page 167)
2901 Candelaria Road NW
Albuquerque, NM 87107
505-344-7240

🅿️Ⓢ🚻🏃♿

Hawk Watch International Fall Migration Site
(Page 167)
1420 Carlisle, Suite 206
Albuquerque, NM 87110
505-255-7622

🏃

Also known as the Manzano Hawk Watch Site

Bosque del Apache National Wildlife Refuge
(Page 168)
P.O. Box 1246
Socorro, NM 87801
505-835-1828

🅿️Ⓢ🚻🏃〰️♿

Elephant Butte State Park *(Page 169)*
P.O. Box 13
Elephant Butte, NM 87935
505-744-5421

🅿️Ⓢ🚻🏃〰️♿

8-mile dirt road to North Monticello Point is extremely rough; four-wheel-drive vehicles recommended

Caballo Lake State Park
(Page 170)
P.O. Box 32
Caballo, NM 87931
505-743-3942

🅿️Ⓢ🚻🏃♿

Bitter Lake National Wildlife Refuge
(Page 171)
4065 Bitter Lake Road
Roswell, NM 88202
505-622-6755

🚻🏃〰️♿

Carlsbad Caverns National Park *(Page 172)*
3225 National Parks
    Highway
Carlsbad, NM 88220
505-785-2232

🅿️Ⓢ🍴🚻🏃〰️♿

Gila National Forest
(Page 172)
3005 Camino del Bosque
Silver City, NM 88061
505-388-8201

Gila Riparian Preserve
(Page 173)
The Nature Conservancy
212 East Marcy Street
    Suite 200
Santa Fe, NM 87501
505-988-3867

WESTERN TEXAS

Big Bend National Park *(Page 174)*
1 Panther Junction
P.O. Box 129
Big Bend, TX 79834
915-477-2251

🚻 ⑤ 🍴 🚻 🐎 ♿

Call regarding boat tours.

Davis Mountains State Park *(Page 177)*
P.O. Box 1458
Fort Davis, TX 79734
915-426-3337

🚻 ⑤ 🍴 🚻 🐎 ♿

Guadalupe Mountains National Park *(Page 177)*
HC 60, Box 400
Salt Flat, TX 79647
915-828-3251

🚻 🚻 🐎 ♿

Muleshoe National Wildlife Refuge
(Page 178)
P.O. Box 549
Muleshoe, TX 79347
806-946-3341

🚻 🚻 🐎 ♿

Palo Duro Canyon State Park *(Page 179)*
Rural Route 2, Box 285
Canyon, TX 79015
806-488-2227

🚻 ⑤ 🍴 🚻 🐎 ♿

Balcones Canyonlands National Wildlife Refuge
(Page 180)
10711 B, Suite 201
Austin, TX 78758
512-339-9432

🍴 🐎 ♿

Emma Long Metropolitan Park
(Page 181)
1706 City Park Road
Austin, TX 78730
512-346-1831

🚻 ⑤ 🍴 🚻 🐎 ♿

Hornsby Bend Biosolids Management Facility
(Page 181)
2210 South FM 973
Austin, TX 78725
512-929-1000

🚻 🚻 🐎

Pedernales Falls State Park *(Page 181)*
Rural Route 1, Box 450
Johnson City, TX 78636
830-868-7304

🚻 ⑤ 🚻 🐎

Lost Maples State Natural Area *(Page 181)*
HC 01, Box 156
Vanderpool, TX 78885
830-966-3413

🚻 ⑤ 🚻 🐎 🐟 ♿

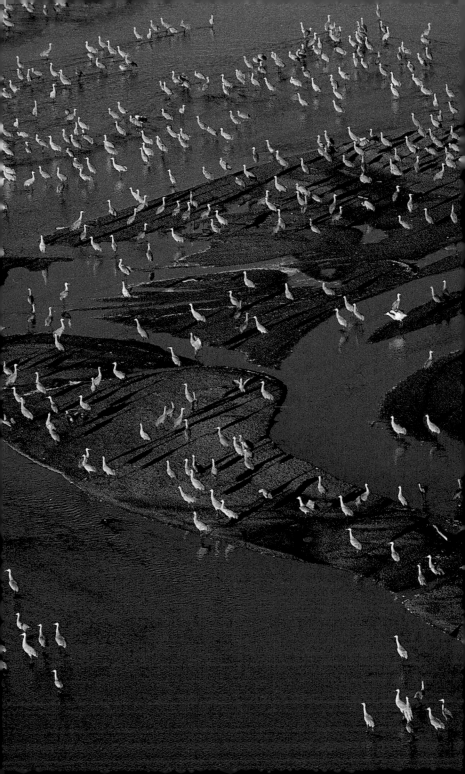

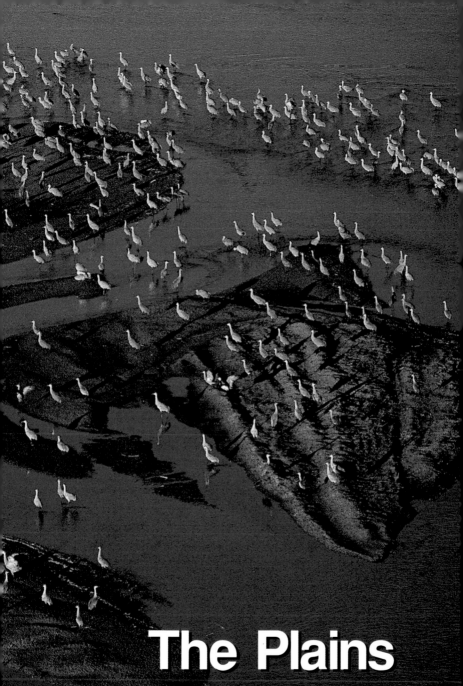

The Plains

L ooking at this strip of states in America's mid-section, a birder is bound to think: prairie. Along with that thought come visions of "dancing" prairie-chickens, displaying Scissor-tailed Flycatchers, and Chestnut-collared Longspurs and Bobolinks in song flight.

While many adaptable grassland species are still common, prairie in its various forms—tallgrass, short grass, and mixed grass—is one of our most imperiled habitats. Usually flat or gently rolling, with no trees to clear, it has in large part been plowed up for cropland or much altered by cattle grazing, and remaining natural tracts are precious, indeed.

In North Dakota, the grassland of Lostwood National Wildlife Refuge has long been a favorite birding destination, since it's one of the best places in the country to find Sprague's Pipit and Baird's Sparrow, two scarce prairie residents whose numbers have declined with the destruction of their habitat. Lesser Prairie-Chicken, another dwindling species, still dances at leks in Cimarron National Grassland in southwestern Kansas. Its relative, the Greater Prairie-Chicken, is much more widespread and can be seen at numerous sites throughout the region, including Sheyenne National Grassland in North Dakota, Fort Pierre National Grassland in South Dakota, and Burchard Lake Wildlife Management Area in Nebraska.

These Plains states feature more than just open space, of course. Much of their appeal comes from the "East

Preceding Pages: Sandhill Cranes on the Platte River, Nebraska
Above: Sharp-tailed Grouse
Below: Baird's Sparrow, Lostwood National Wildlife Refuge, North Dakota

meets West" aspect of their bird life. On the West, North Dakota's Theodore Roosevelt National Park, South Dakota's Black Hills, Nebraska's Pine Ridge, and Oklahoma's Black Mesa host birds with Rocky Mountain affinities. Eastern species find deciduous-forest habitat at places such as Little River National Wildlife Refuge in Oklahoma; Weston Bend Bottoms in Kansas's Fort Leavenworth; Fontenelle Forest Nature Center near Omaha, Nebraska; and Newton Hills State Park in South Dakota.

There are superb wetlands here, too. Quivira National Wildlife Refuge in Kansas and Nebraska's Rainwater Basin are two of the best, famed for migrant waterfowl and shorebirds, but also home to an enticing list of nesting marsh birds. Oklahoma's Hackberry Flat Wildlife Management Area, expanded and with an improved water supply, promises to develop into one of the Midwest's great wetland birding sites.

And any list of America's most thrilling birding phenomena would have to include the gathering of Sandhill Cranes on Nebraska's Platte River in spring migration. The sights and sounds of thousands of these impressive birds coming to roost on the river each evening has become a major regional tourist attraction, as well as one of the truly "must see" spectacles of North American natural history.

All in all, each of these five states offers far more diversity than residents of other parts of the country might realize, and each will reward exploration with a surprising variety of birds.

This chapter begins in an Oklahoma river bottomland and progresses northward to end in a North Dakota forest where Veeries and Northern Waterthrushes sing. ∎

Sprague's Pipit

Special Birds of the Plains

Trumpeter Swan
Sharp-tailed
　Grouse
Greater Prairie-
　Chicken
Lesser Prairie-
　Chicken
Black Rail
Sandhill Crane
Whooping Crane
Snowy Plover
Piping Plover
Burrowing Owl
Scissor-tailed
　Flycatcher
Bell's Vireo
Black-capped
　Vireo
Chihuahuan
　Raven
Sprague's Pipit
Cassin's Sparrow
Baird's Sparrow
Le Conte's
　Sparrow
Nelson's Sharp-
　tailed Sparrow
Harris's Sparrow
McCown's
　Longspur
Smith's Longspur
Chestnut-collared
　Longspur
Painted Bunting

OKLAHOMA

1 Birders travel to the southeastern corner of Oklahoma to explore the excellent bottomland-hardwood habitat at the **Little River National Wildlife Refuge,** a bit of southern swamp set in the "Sooner State." The sloughs and river channels lined with bald cypresses, sweet gums, and oaks ring with the songs of migrant warblers and other species in spring. Northern Parula and Yellow-throated, Prothonotary, Kentucky, and Hooded Warblers nest here, but the most sought-after of the breeding warblers is Swainson's, an elusive swamp dweller that can be found by listening for its distinctive whistled song, often described as ending with a rising *tee-oh*. Great Blue Heron and Great Egret breed in colonies in the refuge, as does Anhinga, a local specialty that's present from spring through summer but not always easy to see. Other breeding species include Wood Duck, Mississippi Kite, Red-shouldered Hawk, Chuck-will's-widow, Yellow-throated Vireo, and Fish Crow. With lots of luck, you might even see an alligator while you're here.

Roads in the largely undeveloped refuge are primitive in places but usually passable; first-time visitors should check with the office in Broken Bow for a map and travel advice. To reach the refuge, drive south from Broken Bow 2 miles on US 70; turn east on Craig Road, drive 1 mile, and turn south. Then drive another mile, turn east, and where the road forks in 0.75 mile stay right to the refuge. You'll have to retrace your path on this dead-end road. As an alternative, you can also continue east on Craig Road 3.2 miles from US 70 and turn south onto a road that makes a loop of several miles south into the refuge and back to Craig Road, passing through good Swainson's Warbler habitat along the way.

- Waterfowl and Bald Eagles at Sequoyah National Wildlife Refuge
- Waders and shorebirds at Salt Plains National Wildlife Refuge
- Western species at Black Mesa

Information section p. 231

Footbridge over the Mountain Fork River, Beavers Bend Resort Park, near Broken Bow

2 Not far to the north, **Beavers Bend Resort Park** (*take US 259 for 7 miles N of Broken Bow, then E on US 259A*) occupies a beautiful and rugged setting on the Mountain Fork River just below Broken Bow Lake. The park is at its best in spring migration, when the mix of pine and hardwood forest attracts a good variety of songbirds. The **Dogwood Trail,** which loops along the river in the western part of the park, is a particularly nice area. Pileated Woodpecker, Yellow-throated and Pine Warblers, and American Redstart nest in the park, and in winter waterfowl and Bald Eagle can be found along the river. Brown-headed Nuthatch is seen occasionally, but it's more likely along the nature trail in the **McCurtain County Wilderness Area,** reached by turning east off US 259 about 14 miles north of the park.

3 **Sequoyah National Wildlife Refuge** attracts great flocks of wintering geese and ducks to wetlands and croplands on the shore of Robert S. Kerr Lake. Take the

Vian exit from I-40 and drive south on the well-signed road to the refuge headquarters. Wintering Bald Eagles are common, perched in trees or soaring over the water, and a few pairs nest around the lake and might be seen year-round. Double-crested Cormorant is abundant around the lake for much of the year. Though Sequoyah is known for waterfowl, including Oklahoma's largest concentration of Snow Geese, a birding trip here can be worthwhile anytime. Breeding birds include Red-headed Woodpecker, Scissor-tailed Flycatcher, Bell's and Warbling Vireos, Prothonotary Warbler, Lark Sparrow, Indigo and Painted Buntings, and Dickcissel—all can be found by driving the 6-mile auto tour route and walking refuge nature trails. In summer, Great Blue and Little Blue Herons and Great and Snowy Egrets are common in marshes and along the lake. In migration, look for American and Least Bitterns, rails, and Sedge and Marsh Wrens in marshy places.

Just to the southeast, the Arkansas River below the **Robert S. Kerr Lock and Dam** (*take US 59 S from I-40*) attracts good numbers of gulls (most will be Ring-billed) from late fall through early spring.

4 Birders visiting Tulsa should make their first stop at the **Oxley Nature Center** in Mohawk Park. From US 75 in the north part of the city, drive east on East 36th Street North about 3 miles and turn north into the park, continuing past the zoo and turning west. In a relatively small area here you'll find prairie, marsh, and forest, and a correspondingly diverse selection of birds. Nearby **Lake Yahola** (*from 36th St. N., 0.2 mile E of US 75, drive N on Harvard Ave., turn E on Mohawk Blvd.*) is a local favorite. It can have excellent numbers of grebes, waterfowl, and gulls in migration and winter, and many rarities have appeared over the years, from Surf Scoter to California and Lesser Black-backed Gulls.

Several fine trails wind through varied habitats around the nature center, and a boardwalk crosses a marsh where waders, rails, and other wetland birds may be seen. The grassland near the interpretive building can be excellent for migrant and wintering sparrows, especially Harris's and occasionally Le Conte's. In migration, be sure to visit the deciduous forest in the North Woods area for songbirds; the road to the parking lot here also provides another viewpoint of Lake Yahola.

5 The most popular birding sites in Oklahoma City are two lakes located just a few miles apart in the northwestern part of town. From I-44, drive west on Okla. 66 and in 4.4 miles turn south to circle **Lake Overholser,** known for migrant and wintering loons (both Red-throated and Pacific have been found along with Common), grebes (Western is seen often), ducks, and gulls. Birders should always check the local hotline (see Oklahoma Information, p. 231), especially in winter, since constant coverage means rarities are quickly reported. Least Bittern and rails are sometimes found in the marshy area at the north end of the lake, and Prothonotary Warbler breeds in nest boxes here near the western extreme of its range. The northern part of Overholser is fairly shallow, and when low water level exposes mudflats, the lake can have excellent shorebirding.

Returning to Okla. 66, drive west about 2.5 miles, then turn north on Sara Road. Follow this about 1.5 miles to its end at **Rose Lake,** a wetland where shorebirds may be present in migration. Several rarities, including White Ibis, Roseate Spoonbill, and Wood Stork, have appeared here over the years.

To reach **Lake Hefner,** take Okla. 3 northwest from Okla. 74. In 2.5 miles turn north on North Macarthur Boulevard. Drive a little more than a mile and turn east on Britton Road. Where Britton reaches Lakeshore Drive, turn south, drive a short distance, and take a gravel road east to a lake viewpoint local birders call **Prairie Dog Point.** This can be an excellent site for migrant shorebirds and wintering gulls. The first state records of Little and Lesser Black-backed Gulls came from here, though of course such sightings are not to be expected. Ring-billed is the abundant species; Herring is seen often; and Bonaparte's and Franklin's are common in migration. Return to Lakeshore Drive and follow it north and east along the dam at the north end of the lake. Hefner is deeper than Overholser, and so is more likely to have loons and diving ducks. Check the ponds at the northeast corner of the lake for waterfowl.

6 West of Lawton, **Wichita Mountains National Wildlife Refuge** is best known for offering visitors the chance to see bison, elk, and longhorn cattle in a striking setting of prairie and rugged granite hills. Birders find the refuge an inviting destination, as well. Eastern species such as Chuck-will's-widow, Eastern Phoebe, Carolina Wren, Eastern Bluebird, and Eastern Meadowlark nest near western birds such as Common Poorwill, Western Kingbird, and Bewick's Wren. Look for Rock and Canyon Wrens and Rufous-crowned Sparrow on the rocky slopes of Mount Scott. Other nesting birds include Mississippi Kite, Wild Turkey, Greater Roadrunner, Painted Bunting, and Lark and Grasshopper Sparrows. The endangered Black-capped Vireo has made a comeback in scrub-oak areas here since programs were begun to control brood-parasitic Brown-headed Cowbirds, which lay their eggs in other birds' nests. In spring and summer, ask refuge personnel about produc-

Granite boulders at Wichita Mountains National Wildlife Refuge, west of Lawton

OKLAHOMA 195

Least Tern nesting area at Salt Plains National Wildlife Refuge, north-central Oklahoma

tive spots for this species. In winter, take Okla. 115 south of Quanah Parker Lake, where you'll have a good chance of finding Chestnut-collared Longspur in the grassland.

7 Southwest Oklahoma's most important wetland is **Hackberry Flat Wildlife Management Area,** southeast of Frederick. From Okla. 5, take US 183 south 2 miles and turn east toward the municipal airport. In 3 miles, just past the airport, turn south and drive 4 miles. The area will be on the east; you can bird from county roads or park and walk dikes around the impoundments. (Roads can be a problem in wet weather.) The largest wetlands restoration project in Oklahoma's history is creating an expanse of marsh and open water where waders, waterfowl, shorebirds, gulls, and terns are found seasonally. Look for Sandhill Crane (sometimes in the thousands) from fall through spring, and for Ferruginous Hawk and Prairie Falcon in winter, when geese and ducks throng the area. Peregrine Falcon may appear in migration or winter. Upland grassy areas host winter sparrows and longspurs. Twenty-three species of shorebirds have been seen at Hackberry Flat in a single day in spring migration, when hundreds of Wilson's Phalaropes might be found, along with fair numbers of Hudsonian Godwits. Buff-breasted Sandpiper has occurred in fall. Nesting species include Pied-billed Grebe, King Rail, Black-necked Stilt, American Avocet, and Wilson's Phalarope.

8 You'll find good birding, as well as Oklahoma's most otherworldly landscape, at **Salt Plains National Wildlife Refuge** north of Jet. Bordering the Great Salt Plains Reservoir on the west is a vast expanse of gleaming white salt atop underlying mudflats, a strange and exotic sight in the midst of rolling agricultural land. Snowy Plover, American Avocet, and Least Tern nest on these salt flats, and can often be seen in spring and summer from the selenite crystal area in the southwest section of the refuge, east off US 64 3 miles south of Cherokee (*open April–mid-Oct.*).

The refuge headquarters can be reached by turning west from Okla. 38 about 14 miles north of Jet. Nearby you'll find the **Eagle Roost Nature Trail** and the refuge auto tour route, both offering fine birding opportunities. The trail runs alongside Sand Creek Bay, where a variety of waterbirds can be found seasonally. Thousands of American White Pelicans and Sandhill Cranes appear in migration (an occasional Whooping Crane shows up, too), and flocks of geese and ducks are present from fall through spring, along with dozens of Bald Eagles.

Shorebirding is often excellent around the edge of the bay, with migrants such as Greater and Lesser Yellowlegs; Willet; Semipalmated, Western, Least, White-rumped, Baird's, and Stilt Sandpipers; Long-billed Dowitcher; and Wilson's Phalarope common in spring and fall. Nesting birds you might find along the auto tour route include several species of herons and egrets, White-faced Ibis, Mississippi Kite, Swainson's Hawk, Wild Turkey, Red-headed Woodpecker, Western and Eastern Kingbirds, Scissor-tailed Flycatcher, Bell's and Warbling Vireos, and Painted Bunting. Be sure to walk to Casey Marsh Tower for another chance to see waterfowl and Sandhill Crane.

The rugged, arid slopes of Black Mesa Preserve, at the tip of the Oklahoma Panhandle

On the south side of Okla. 11, about 5 miles west of Okla. 38, walk along the short **Sandpiper Trail** (*open April–mid-Oct.*) to see migrant shorebirds along the Salt Fork of the Arkansas River. On the eastern side of the reservoir, explore the area around **Great Salt Plains State Park** and the dam for waterfowl and Bald Eagle from late fall through early spring.

9 Ranking near the top of Oklahoma's favorite birding spots, the **Black Mesa** country at the western extremity of the Panhandle is home to several species seldom or never found elsewhere in the state. As you drive west on Okla. 325 from Boise City, watch for Chihuahuan Raven in agricultural lands; Common Raven is usually found around Black Mesa, farther west, but these species can overlap in range, and they can be difficult to distinguish. Look also for Scaled Quail, Greater Roadrunner, Say's Phoebe, Ash-throated Flycatcher, Horned Lark, Curve-billed Thrasher, Cassin's (sings in spring from the top of shrubby vegetation) and Black-throated Sparrows, and Lark and Lazuli Buntings, and in winter for Ferruginous and Rough-legged Hawks and Sage Thrasher.

Take the west turn toward **Black Mesa State Park,** but where the road turns north toward the park about 4 miles from Okla. 325, go south about a half mile to a large prairie dog town where you'll find Burrowing Owl from spring

through fall. Then return north to the state park, where Lake Carl Etling, one of the few bodies of water in the area, can attract interesting waterbirds. In spring and summer, look for Cassin's Kingbird here among the more common Western Kingbirds.

From the state park, drive north to Okla. 325, turn east, and in 3 miles turn north on a county road to reach the Cimarron River in less than a mile. Check the cottonwoods along the river for migrants in spring and fall, when you might find Black-throated Gray, Townsend's, or MacGillivray's Warblers or Western Tanager (rare in fall). Ladder-backed Woodpecker is a common resident, and Bullock's Oriole and Lesser Goldfinch nest here. Return to Okla. 325 and continue west. Just before the tiny town of Kenton, turn north on a road marked "Colorado"; drive 5 miles to the parking lot for **Black Mesa Preserve.** Here a one-way hike of 4 miles leads up the slope of an ancient lava flow to the highest point in Oklahoma, 4,973 feet above sea level. Some of the birds nesting here or in the vicinity include Common Poorwill, Western Scrub-Jay, Pinyon Jay (can be hard to find), Golden Eagle, Prairie Falcon, Black-billed Magpie, Juniper Titmouse, Bushtit, Rock and Canyon Wrens, Rufous-crowned Sparrow, and Canyon Towhee. In winter, Black Mesa can host Steller's Jay (rare), Clark's Nutcracker (rare), Mountain Chickadee (uncommon), Mountain Bluebird, and Townsend's Solitaire.

KANSAS

10 Fort Leavenworth was founded in 1827 to protect trade on the Santa Fe Trail. Coincidentally, this famed military post has also protected one of the finest tracts of bottomland hardwoods in the Midwest. **Weston Bend Bottoms,** as birders call this area inside a bend of the Missouri River, attracts a superb variety of migrant songbirds in spring and fall and is also home to an interesting selection of nesting species. From US 73 and Seventh Street in north Leavenworth, drive north on Grant Avenue, stopping at the information office for a map. Then continue to the **Chief Joseph Loop,** which runs past Sherman airfield in the northeastern part of the fort. From this road you can walk into the bottoms along several poorly marked trails. In the center of the area are mature oaks, pecans, maples, hackberries, and other trees, while elsewhere you'll find second-growth, grassy areas, and wetlands offering a diversity of habitat.

Nesting birds include Pileated Woodpecker; Acadian Flycatcher; Wood Thrush; Northern Parula; Yellow, Yellow-throated, Cerulean (rare), and Prothonotary Warblers; American Redstart; Scarlet Tanager; and Rose-breasted Grosbeak. Sedge Wren occasionally nests in grassy marshes in late summer. Great Blue Herons and a few Great Egrets occupy a heronry here.

11 Northeast of Topeka, **Perry Lake** makes a fine year-round birding destination. From Perry on US 24, drive north on Ferguson Road 3 miles to the U.S. Army Corps of Engineers office, where you can pick up a lake map. From fall through spring, drive across the dam and visit **Thompsonville** and **Rock Creek Recreation Areas** on the west side of the lake to scan for loons, grebes, waterfowl, and Bald Eagle. Below the dam, check the spillway area for wintering gulls, and the nature trail through the marsh off Spillway Road for waders, waterfowl, and migrant rails. Continue north on Ferguson Road. Any of the recreation areas on the east side of the lake, such as **Slough Creek, Longview,** and **Old Military Trail,** can be good for migrant songbirds. Drive north 1.3 miles past the turn to the Slough Creek area and turn east off Ferguson Road, following the road as it curves south to an overlook on the Slough Creek arm of the lake. From this point the huge nest of a resident pair of Bald Eagles can be seen to the east.

To reach **Paradise Point,** turn west from Ferguson Road 1.8 miles north of Kans. 92; when water levels are down, waders and migrant shorebirds can be common here. Where Ferguson Road bends northeast about 5.5 miles north of Kans. 92, continue north into **Upper Ferguson Marsh;** you can walk along the dike westward here to see waders, waterfowl, rails, and possibly nesting Sedge Wren. To reach **Lassiter Marsh,** turn north off Kans. 16 for 1.3 miles west of Kans. 4. There's good birding for wetland species along the road through this wildlife area, or you can walk the trail through marsh where Prothonotary Warbler whistles in spring and summer and Least Bittern may nest.

12 Just a few miles from the Missouri state line in east-central Kansas, **Marais des Cygnes Wildlife Area** is known for spring songbird migration, interesting breeding species, winter waterfowl, and, when water levels are right, for migrant shorebirds. Stop at the headquarters on the west side of US 69, 0.4 mile north of Kans. 52, where maps are available at a kiosk. Then return south on US 69; 0.9 mile south of Kans. 52 turn west into the area, following the Marais des Cygnes River. The **Unit A** impoundment to the west will have geese and ducks from fall through spring, and can be good for shorebirds when mudflats are present.

Upland Sandpiper, a shorebird that prefers to nest in grasslands

Geese over Quivira National Wildlife Refuge, southeast of Great Bend

As you approach the settlement of Boicourt in about 3 miles, turn north just east of the railroad track. After this road bends west under the rail line you'll pass through woods that are excellent in spring migration. Look for typical deciduous-hardwood nesting species such as Pileated Woodpecker; Acadian Flycatcher; Yellow-throated Vireo; Wood Thrush; Yellow-throated, Black-and-white, Prothonotary, and Kentucky Warblers; Louisiana Waterthrush; and Scarlet Tanager. Soon you'll reach **Unit G** of the wildlife area. A road runs around the perimeter of this impoundment, which can have waders and waterfowl, as well as shorebirds when water levels are low. Here and anywhere in the area, look for resident Wood Duck, Red-shouldered Hawk, Barred Owl, and Red-headed Woodpecker, migrant American White Pelican and Osprey, and wintering Bald Eagle. If you have time, explore other units of the area; note that changing water levels can create habitat for varied waterbirds, and that grassy places can be good for Upland Sandpiper, Scissor-tailed Flycatcher, longspurs, and sparrows in season.

Drive north on US 69 about 6 miles beyond Kans. 52 and turn east to **La Cygne Lake and Wildlife Area,** where you can check the lake for wintering waterfowl. Just over 2 miles east of US 69, turn south on a county road that leads through grassland where you might find wintering Rough-legged Hawk, Prairie Falcon, Short-eared Owl, or Lapland Longspur, and migrant Sprague's Pipit or Smith's Longspur. Upland Sandpiper and Grasshopper Sparrow nest here, and Swainson's Hawk is often seen in migration. This is private land, so bird from the roadside.

13 **Quivira National Wildlife Refuge** (*open June-Oct.*), southeast of Great Bend, is the favorite birding destination of many Kansans. To reach it, drive 6 miles east of Stafford on US 50 and go north on Zenith Road for 8 miles. Waterbirds are the main attraction here—nesting, passing through, and wintering in remarkable numbers and variety. Refuge roads make it easy to observe tens of thousands of migrant waterfowl (including occasional Trumpeter and Tundra Swans), flocks of American White Pelicans and Sandhill Cranes, herons and egrets from spring through fall, and a superb array of migrant shorebirds. Small groups of Whooping Cranes may appear, passing through quickly from mid-March to mid-April on their northward journey, but often lingering in October and November on their way south to the Gulf Coast of Texas.

You should drive as many of Quivira's roads and scan as many of its marshes and impoundments as you have time for. Be sure to check **Little Salt Marsh** just north of refuge headquarters for waterbirds, and stop to walk the **Migrant's Mile** interpretive trail (a section of which is wheelchair accessible) about 7 miles north of headquarters for marsh birds. Quivira's highlight, though, is its 4-mile **Wildlife Drive,** which loops alongside Big Salt Marsh in the northern part of the refuge. Tens of thousands of Sandhill Cranes can appear here in fall, and this is where Whooping Cranes are most likely to appear. American and Least Bitterns, White-faced Ibis, King and Virginia Rails, Sora, American Avocet, Wilson's Phalarope, Forster's and Black Terns, and

Yellow-headed Blackbird are just a few of the nesting species you might spot, and Black Rail is seen or heard regularly in spring. Look on the flats north of Big Salt Marsh for nesting Snowy Plover and Least Tern.

There's more to Quivira than waterbirds. Breeding birds of grassland and cottonwood groves include Mississippi Kite, Northern Harrier, Swainson's Hawk, Ring-necked Pheasant, Upland Sandpiper, Western and Eastern Kingbirds, Scissor-tailed Flycatcher, Bell's Vireo, Dickcissel, and Eastern and Western Meadowlarks. Winter visitors can include Bald and Golden Eagles, Ferruginous and Rough-legged Hawks, Short-eared Owl, an occasional Northern Shrike, and Lapland and Chestnut-collared Longspurs.

14 Located just northeast of Great Bend, **Cheyenne Bottoms** comprises another important wetland area, a 41,000-acre natural basin renowned for waders, waterfowl, and shorebirds. Drive north of Great Bend 8 miles on US 281, turn east on NE 60th Road, and drive 2 miles to the state wildlife area headquarters. If this is your first visit, you might want to drive north 2 more miles on US 281 to the kiosk at NE 80th Road to pick up a brochure on an auto tour route through the adjoining Nature Conservancy property. Most of the birds mentioned for Quivira refuge can be found here, though the area has had water-management problems in recent years and is not as productive as it once was. Still, a drive through Cheyenne Bottoms in spring can turn up an excellent variety of shorebirds, including Hudsonian and Marbled Godwits, White-rumped and Baird's Sandpipers, and Wilson's and Red-necked Phalaropes. Grebes, waders, American White Pelican, geese, ducks, gulls, and terns will be present in varying numbers throughout the year, and will reward a visit anytime (though keep in mind that this is a popular hunting area in fall).

Following the auto tour route through the Nature Conservancy preserve northwest of the state wildlife area will take you past a thriving prairie dog town (*SE of the corner of N.E. 100th Rd. and N. 20th Ave.*) where Burrowing Owls are increasing in number, unlike the unhappy decline in so much of their range. Another "town" is located along Redwing Road, south of Kans. 4, 5.5 miles east of US 281.

15 Minutes north of I-70 (*take Wilson exit and drive N on Kans. 232*), **Wilson Lake** has a history of turning up rare waterbirds, including such oddities as Brown Pelican and Black Skimmer. Diving birds are a specialty here from fall through spring: Pacific Loon is fairly regular, and Yellow-billed Loon has been seen. Horned, Western, and Clark's Grebes are regular migrants, and at times thousands of Common Goldeneye gather on the water, along with good numbers of ducks such as Redhead, Lesser Scaup, and Bufflehead. American White Pelican and Franklin's Gull appear in large numbers in migration, and Bald Eagles frequent the shoreline.

Wilson State Park (*from I-70 take Kans. 232 N 5 miles, then go W*) is a good spot from which to scan the lake, as is **Minooka Park** a few miles west. Long-eared Owls roost in cedar trees in the state park and elsewhere around the lake in winter, when Mountain Bluebirds can also be found. Pick up a map at the Corps of Engineers office at the dam, on Kans. 232 about 3 miles north of the state park turnoff, and explore other lake access points. Riparian habitats along the Saline River west of the lake can be good for songbirds. The grasslands around the lake are home to a population of Greater Prairie-Chicken, but it usually takes luck to spot them along the roadsides. Watch for an occasional Rough-legged Hawk or Northern Shrike in the grassland in winter.

Marbled Godwit, a scarce migrant in midwestern wetlands that nests in a few north-central states

16 Located about 15 miles north of Scott City on US 83 and Kans. 95, **Lake Scott State Park** attracts interesting migrant land birds and waterbirds, serving as an oasis in the surrounding expanse of prairie. Migrant songbirds found in the park's cottonwood, hackberry, ash, and willow trees include species from both East and West. Among the breeding birds are Mississippi Kite, Say's Phoebe, Black-billed Magpie, Black-headed Grosbeak, and Lazuli Bunting. Lake Scott itself is fairly small, but consistently attracts a good assortment of loons, grebes, and ducks from fall through spring. Rock Wren is common on the

Wilson Lake, east of Russell, an excellent site for migrant and wintering waterbirds

canyon bluffs here, and some years winter finches such as Purple Finch, Red Crossbill, Pine Siskin, and Evening Grosbeak appear in large numbers. Wintering Long-eared Owls can be found in cedars on the west side of the lake, and the prairie around the lake is home to large numbers of wintering Lapland Longspur and occasional McCown's and Chestnut-collared.

17 The largest tract of publicly owned land in Kansas is the **Cimarron National Grassland,** in the southwestern corner of the state north of Elkhart. Nearly 350 species of birds have been seen in this area of sagebrush, prairie, and riparian vegetation bordering about 25 miles of the Cimarron River, including birds of southwestern affinity, winter visitors and migrants from the Rockies, and many wanderers from East and West. Stop at the ranger office on US 56 in Elkhart before beginning your visit. Buy a map and pick up a copy of the "Sea of Grass" auto tour booklet. In spring, you can also ask about visiting the leks, or courtship grounds, of the rare and declining Lesser Prairie-Chicken, a regional specialty. In migration and winter, local birders check trees at the Elkhart cemetery and the shelterbelt across the street (*on North St., 0.4 mile W of US 56*) and the grassland's **Tunnerville Work Center** (*2 miles N of town on Kans. 27*) for Red-naped Sapsucker, Western Scrub-Jay, Mountain Chickadee, Red-breasted and Pygmy Nuthatches, Townsend's Solitaire, Canyon Towhee, and other uncommon to rare visitors.

Continue north 5.5 miles on Kans. 27 to the **Cimarron River Picnic Area,** where cottonwoods grow along the streambed. Look here for resident Great Horned Owl, Red-headed and Ladder-backed Woodpeckers, and Northern Flicker (mostly red-shafted, but some showing characteristics of this and the yellow-shafted form). In spring and summer you'll find Western and Eastern Kingbirds, House Wren, and Bullock's Oriole. Just north of the Cimarron River, turn west off Kans. 27 and in a mile check the ponds on the south for waterbirds and migrants. Another mile west, visit the **Middle Spring Picnic Area** for riparian habitat that can have interesting migrants. Then continue west to **Point of Rocks,** a bluff where Rock Wren is present from spring through fall, and where you might find a Greater Roadrunner. In migration and winter look for possible Green-tailed and Canyon Towhees and Rufous-crowned Sparrow.

As you drive through the grassland, other birds to look for from spring through fall include Mountain Plover (rare; try along Kans. 51 west of Kans. 27), Mississippi Kite, Long-billed Curlew, Burrowing Owl (at prairie dog towns), and Cassin's and Lark Sparrows. Year-round, watch for Scaled Quail, Black-billed Magpie, Chihuahuan Raven (rare), Horned Lark, and Curve-billed Thrasher (mostly in summer and scarce; nests in clumps of cholla cactus). In winter, the grassland is home to Ferruginous and Rough-legged Hawks, Golden Eagle, Northern Shrike, and mixed flocks of longspurs, with Lapland abundant and McCown's and Chestnut-collared present in lesser numbers.

NEBRASKA

18 Nesting birds of eastern deciduous forest reward a visit to **Indian Cave State Park.** To reach it, take Nebr. S64E east from Nebr. 67 just north of Shubert. With ecological characteristics of the southeastern U.S. (southern flying squirrel and chinkapin oak are found here, for example), this extensive wooded area along the Missouri River is home in spring and summer to Woodcock; Whip-poor-will; Acadian Flycatcher; Yellow-throated Vireo; Wood Thrush; Northern Parula; Yellow-throated, Cerulean, Black-and-white, and Kentucky (in wooded ravines) Warblers; Summer and Scarlet Tanagers; and Rose-breasted Grosbeak. Barred Owl, Red-headed Woodpecker, and Carolina Wren are present all year, and Prothonotary Warbler, near the edge of its range here, has been seen on occasion. **Trail Number 9** in the eastern part of the park is a good all-around bird walk. As might be imagined, Indian Cave also makes an excellent destination in spring migration.

19 Much the same can be said of **Fontenelle Forest Nature Center,** a favorite of birders in the Omaha area. Take Chandler Road east from US 75 about 3 miles south of I-80; in 0.5 mile, turn south on Belleview Boulevard and drive 0.3 mile to visit this 1,400-acre preserve set on a bend in the Missouri River. The scream of Red-shouldered Hawk is heard here at times, along with the slurred whistle of Louisiana Waterthrush beside streams, and the *teacher teacher teacher* song of Ovenbird. Yellow-throated Warbler nests here, Prothonotary Warbler has bred, and Veery has been heard in summer, though nesting hasn't been confirmed. In addition to deciduous-forest birds, Fontenelle also hosts waders, waterfowl, and other waterbirds in its wetland areas. Look for Pied-billed Grebe, Green

Heron, Black-crowned Night-Heron, and Virginia Rail in ponds and marshes. Sedge Wren has nested on occasion. The center offers a variety of nature programs throughout the year, including several on birds, and miles of trails (including a handicapped-accessible boardwalk) make exploration easy.

20 If you're visiting the Lincoln area from fall through spring, a visit to **Branched Oak Lake** can turn up varied waterfowl, shorebirds, and gulls. From Nebr. 79 at Raymond, drive west about 3 miles to the lake; then turn north to cross the dam. Common Loon is a regular migrant, but Red-throated, Pacific, and Yellow-billed have been spotted over the years, along with an impressive list of winter gulls including rarities such as Laughing, Mew, Iceland, and Lesser Black-backed, and Black-legged Kittiwake. Thousands of Franklin's Gulls can be found in migration at times, often concentrated in the area near the marina on the northwestern part of the lake. When water levels are right on the shallower western side of the lake, Branched Oak can have excellent migrant shorebirds.

Sandhill Crane

Several of the world's 15 species of cranes are classified as endangered, among them Whooping Crane, which breeds in Canada and winters in Texas. Sandhill Crane, however, continues to maintain a population in the hundreds of thousands, nesting in Canada, the Midwest, and West. (Nonmigratory populations in the South have suffered declines, though, and the Mississippi race is endangered.) Large flocks are seen in spring migration along Nebraska's **Platte River** (see p. 210) and wintering in places such as the **Sulphur Springs Valley** in Arizona, **Bosque del Apache National Wildlife Refuge** (see p. 168) in New Mexico, and **Muleshoe National Wildlife Refuge** (see p. 178) in Texas.

21 Mid-March through May, you can see the amazing courtship "dance" of the Greater Prairie-Chicken at **Burchard Lake State Wildlife Management Area.** From the junction of Nebr. 99 and Nebr. 4 north of Burchard, drive east 2.8 miles on Nebr. 4 and turn south; drive 1.5 miles and turn west into the area. Circle around the north side of the lake to reach the blind overlooking the "booming ground" on the west side. Scout the area in advance to learn the route, since you must be in the blind before dawn to avoid disturbing the birds (peak activity first two weeks in April). Henslow's Sparrow has nested in the grassland here, where you'll also find Grasshopper and Song Sparrows and Dickcisssel.

Some of the nearly half-million Sandhill Cranes that stop to roost on the Platte River in spring migration

22 Each spring, Nebraska's **Platte River** is the site of one of America's most impressive wildlife spectacles. Close to a half-million Sandhill Cranes stop in migration to roost in the shallow river, most of them along the stretch from Grand Island to Lexington. The cranes usually arrive in February; the population peaks in March, and the birds are mostly gone by late April. Cranes leave the river each dawn to feed in nearby fields and marshes, and return to the river at dusk in small groups. To see these long-legged birds fly in, giving their loud trumpeting call, their numbers growing until thousands may be in view at one time, has been described by countless witnesses as an awe-inspiring vision. Occasionally an endangered Whooping Crane, or a small group, will pause here on migration from Canada to Texas, usually in April. During the day, Sandhills feed and rest within 5 miles of the river; driving county roads south of the Platte River between Grand Island and Kearney will bring views of scattered groups of cranes.

The Platte River cranes have become a significant tourist attraction, and visitors can obtain viewing information from several sources. The National Audubon Society's **Lillian Annette Rowe Sanctuary,** 10 miles east of Kearney, offers crane viewing from blinds (*308-468-5282. Fee; reservations required*) and general advice. Farther to the east near Grand Island, **Crane Meadows Nature Center** also provides viewing blinds and towers as well as wildlife displays and public programs (*308-382-1820, fee; reservations required*). Or call the U.S. Fish and Wildlife Service (*308-236-5015*) for

information on their free tours. The hike-bike trail bridge northeast of **Fort Kearny State Historical Park** is a good vantage point, and there are parking areas and viewing platforms on Platte River bridges south of Alda (*take the Alda exit from I-80 and drive S*) and Gibbon (*take the Gibbon exit and drive S*). Both the Kearney (*308-237-3101 or 800-652-9435*) and Grand Island (*308-382-4400 or 800-658-3178*) Visitors Bureaus can help with viewing advice and maps.

23 Located south of York and Kearney is a 4,200-square-mile expanse of wetlands known as the **Rainwater Basin,** making up one of Nebraska's premier birding areas. Though much altered by drainage and farming, this natural lowland still hosts staggering numbers of waterfowl in migration, along with a diverse array of migrant shorebirds and nesting marsh birds. At times nearly five million waterfowl may be present in the basin and along the Platte River, including huge numbers of Greater White-fronted and Snow Geese, Mallard, and Northern Pintail, to mention just the most numerous of the 25 species of waterfowl that might be seen. Small numbers of Ross's Geese are present in just about every large flock of Snows. More than two dozen species of shorebirds stop to feed in spring, late summer, and fall.

Though there are dozens of publicly owned wetland sites in the region, perhaps the most accessible and productive for birding is **Funk Waterfowl Production Area.** To reach it, drive north from US 6/34 in Funk for 2.5 miles on the road toward Odessa and turn east; in a little over a mile you'll reach a parking area with a kiosk showing other parking lots and trails along dikes. In addition to hosting migrant waterfowl, shorebirds, gulls, and terns, Funk is home to summering birds including Pied-billed and Eared Grebes, American White Pelican, several species of waders (including Least Bittern and Black-crowned and Yellow-crowned Night-Herons and occasional White-faced Ibis), Virginia Rail, Sora, Sedge Wren, Yellow-headed Blackbird, and Great-tailed Grackle. The same species might be found at **Harvard Waterfowl Production Area.** From the junction of US 6 and Nebr. 14 north of Clay Center, drive west 8 miles, turn north for 2 miles, turn east 1 mile, and north again for a mile. In winter, a drive through Rainwater Basin could turn up Rough-legged Hawk, Prairie Falcon, Short-eared Owl, Northern Shrike, Horned Lark, Harris's Sparrow or Lapland Longspur. Bald Eagles are common in winter and early spring, preying on the flocks of waterfowl.

24 One of the Midwest's great gull-watching opportunities occurs at **Lakes McConaughy** and **Ogallala** in winter and early spring, when Ogallala, below McConaughy's Kingsley Dam, may be the only open water for miles around. To reach the dam, leave I-80 at Ogallala, drive north on US 26, and in 3 miles turn east on Nebr. 61. Huge numbers of gulls winter here, including some uncommon or rare species (especially Thayer's and Glaucous) among the thousands of Ring-billed and Herring; smaller numbers of gulls are present almost year-round. Viewing is easy here from roads, **Lake Ogallala State Recreation Area,** and an observation station set up to allow viewing of the numerous Bald Eagles that are present in winter. Lake Ogallala is also famed for migrant and wintering waterfowl. Birds such as Trumpeter and Tundra Swans; Greater Scaup; Surf, White-winged, and Black Scoters; Oldsquaw; and Barrow's Goldeneye show up with varying degrees of regularity among more common species such as Common Merganser. On Lake Ogallala and especially Lake McConaughy, look for migrant loons, grebes, and American White Pelican in addition to waterfowl.

The Lake McConaughy and Lake Ogallala area isn't just a winter waterbird destination. Depending on water level, mudflats attractive to migrant shorebirds may be exposed, and the marshes below the dam are worth exploring for rails and other wetland birds. Driving county roads through grasslands north and east of the dam might turn up a Greater Prairie-Chicken. Ferruginous and Rough-legged Hawks, Mountain Bluebird, and Lapland Longspur might be present from fall into spring. Drive Nebr. 92 westward along the north side of Lake McConaughy and investigate lake access areas. Piping Plover and Least Tern nest on sandy beaches along the lake's northeastern shoreline. Stop at the **Omaha Beach Recreation Area,** toward the western end of the lake, 15 miles west of the junction of Nebr. 61 and Nebr. 92; grebes and waders nest in nearby marshes, which can be good for migrant shorebirds. The **Clear Creek Refuge** at the west end of Lake McConaughy hosts large numbers of migrant waterfowl, raptors, Sandhill Cranes, and shorebirds. From fall through early spring, check stands of junipers for Townsend's Solitaire, a regular here.

25 **Oliver State Recreation Area** *(8 miles W of Kimball on US 30)* has gained a reputation as an excellent spot for migrant songbirds. While waterbirds might be present on Lake Oliver in migration, and shorebirds when mudflats are exposed, it's mostly birds in the riparian vegetation around its shore that attract birders in spring and, especially, in fall. There's good access off US 30 to recreation sites on the lake's north and east sides. In the scrub and woodland, migrants such as Cassin's Kingbird, Cassin's Vireo, Sage Thrasher, Townsend's and MacGillivray's Warblers, and Western Tanager are among those sought.

26 Northwestern Nebraska's **Pine Ridge** region is in some ways like a bit of the Rocky Mountains extending to the edge of the High Plains. Here forests of ponderosa pine cover rugged sandstone hills, with eroded badland canyons where cottonwood, ash, and hackberry grow. Birds found here year-round include Golden Eagle, Prairie Falcon, Northern Saw-whet Owl, Pinyon Jay, Pygmy Nuthatch, the white-winged race of Dark-eyed Junco, Red Crossbill, and Pine Siskin, while among the nesting-season species are Common Poorwill, White-throated Swift,

Western Wood-Pewee, Cordilleran Flycatcher, Plumbeous Vireo, Say's Phoebe, Violet-green Swallow, Rock Wren, Mountain Bluebird, Yellow-rumped and Black-and-white Warblers, Ovenbird, Western Tanager, Black-headed Grosbeak, and Lazuli Bunting. In winter, Clark's Nutcracker and Townsend's Solitaire sometimes appear.

Exploring areas near US 20 will give you a good chance to see many of these species. From Harrison, drive north 5 miles to the **Gilbert Baker Wildlife Management Area** along Monroe Creek, where trails from parking areas lead through deciduous riparian vegetation into pinewoods. Though it's nearly all through private property, the road through **Sowbelly Canyon** has long been a favorite Pine Ridge birding route. Drive north of Harrison 0.5 mile and turn east; after about 2.5 miles the road passes through the canyon, where you can bird along the way. In about another 3 miles, turn south on Pants Butte Road and return to US 20. Or you can continue about 1.5 miles north past Pants Butte Road, turn east, and in about a mile turn south through West Hat Creek Canyon to return to US 20. From Chadron, 50 miles east of Harrison, go south 8 miles on US 385 to reach **Chadron State Park,** another good birding site. By walking the **Blackhills Overlook Trail** to Overlook Point, you'll have a chance to see Lewis's Woodpecker, a scarce species in these parts.

Mountain Bluebird, a beautiful thrush of western uplands

If you're in the area in late spring or summer, drive west on US 20 to the Wyoming state line. Take the road just east of the line to the south, through rolling grassland where you might find Ferruginous Hawk, Long-billed Curlew, Say's Phoebe, Rock Wren, Brewer's Sparrow, and McCown's and Chestnut-collared Longspurs. Where the road goes east in about 7 miles, continue south. Birders call this the Henry Road, since it runs south about 45 miles to Henry on US 26. On a bluff 18 miles north of Henry, Cliff Swallows build their mud nests. In winter, dozens of Gray-crowned Rosy-Finches sometimes roost in these swallow nests in the evening, with 200 or more having been seen at times.

SOUTH DAKOTA

27 The rugged uplands of what is now eastern South Dakota were called Coteau des Prairies by 19th-century French fur traders. These "prairie hills" were pushed up by glaciers in the last ice age, and today this forested region, an anomaly in the midst of rolling grassland, can be explored at **Sica Hollow State Park,** a favorite destination to find nesting birds of deciduous woodland. To reach it, drive west from Sisseton 11 miles, turn north, and drive 5 miles. Here in a forest of basswood, ash, oak, elm, and maple, look for Broad-winged Hawk, Ruby-throated Hummingbird (a rare nesting bird in this region), Yellow-bellied Sapsucker, Willow and Least Flycatchers, Yellow-throated Vireo, Veery, Black-and-white Warbler (a scarce breeder in the state), Scarlet Tanager, and Rose-breasted Grosbeak. Wood Thrush has been found nesting in the area, and might be looked for, too. The half-mile **Trail of the Spirits** is productive for birding and provides a good introduction to park flora.

- Eastern birds at Sica Hollow and Newton Hills State Parks
- Waterbirds at Sand Lake and Lacreek refuges
- Highland species in the Black Hills

Information section p. 232

28 On S. Dak. 15, 8 miles east of Wilmot, **Hartford Beach State Park** is home to some of these same eastern deciduous species, but it's best known as the most likely place in South Dakota to find Pileated Woodpecker, the crow-size woodpecker with the far-carrying "laughing" call. Whip-poor-will occasionally nests here, right on the edge of its range. Set on the shore of Big Stone Lake, Hartford Beach also offers viewing of migrant loons, grebes, and waterfowl.

29 From the intersection of US 12 and S. Dak. 1 near Waubay, take S. Dak. 1 north 7 miles and turn west into **Waubay National Wildlife Refuge,** where lakes and sloughs host a good variety of waterbirds. Less than a mile after entering the refuge, stop at the Spring Lake Overlook for a panoramic view of the area, and then continue to the headquarters. Here a half-mile trail through a wooded area that can be productive for migrant songbirds leads to Hillebrand's Lake and an observation tower. Among the nesting birds at Waubay are Pied-billed, Horned, Red-necked (a few pairs), Eared, and Western Grebes; Double-crested Cormorant; American Bittern; several species of ducks; Northern Harrier; Gray Partridge; Virginia Rail; Sora; Piping Plover (rare and irregular); Willet; Upland Sandpiper; Marbled Godwit; Wilson's Phalarope; Forster's and Black Terns; Western and Eastern Kingbirds; Horned Lark; Tree Swallow; Sedge and Marsh Wrens; Bobolink; and Yellow-headed Blackbird. American White Pelican is a common summering bird, and waders such as Great and Snowy Egrets can appear in summer and fall.

Ring-necked Pheasant

So familiar is the Ring-necked Pheasant over much of the northern and western U.S. (it's even the state bird of South Dakota) that many people don't realize it's not a native species. Originally from Asia, this game bird was introduced here in the mid-19th century and has thrived in agricultural areas and grassy places. When encountered, they often run away instead of flying. The male's *kok-cack* call is a well-known sound on the plains; rival males fight fiercely when one intrudes on another's territory.

30 Like Waubay, **Sand Lake National Wildlife Refuge,** just west of Houghton, provides a resting and feeding area for great flocks of waterfowl in spring and fall migration. Sand Lake can have hundreds of thousands of Snow Geese in early spring and thousands of Tundra Swans in late October, as well as abundant Canada Geese, smaller numbers of Greater White-fronted and Ross's (Sand Lake is the best place in the state for this species in fall) Geese, and more than 20 species of dabbling and diving ducks. All the birds listed for Waubay also nest at Sand Lake save Red-necked Grebe. In addition, heronries are home to Great Blue Heron; Great, Snowy, and Cattle Egrets; Black-crowned Night-Heron; and White-faced Ibis. Little Blue Heron is a rare breeder some years. Sand Lake is the most likely place to find nesting Clark's Grebe in South Dakota, though it's rare. Here, as at many places in the region, tens of thousands of

Franklin's Gulls sometimes congregate in fall before migrating south.

Take S. Dak. 10 west of Houghton for 4 miles, turning south on County Road 16 to reach the refuge headquarters and the start of the 15-mile auto tour route. In addition to wetlands, Sand Lake provides habitat for grassland birds such as Swainson's Hawk; Upland Sandpiper; Short-eared Owl; Clay-colored, Vesper, Grasshopper, and Swamp Sparrows; Chestnut-collared Longspur; and Bobolink. Watch for Bald Eagles roosting in tall cottonwoods or soaring overhead in fall and spring.

31 The huge **Oahe Dam,** on the Missouri River just upstream from Pierre, is one of the state's best places to find gulls from fall through early spring, especially when the outflow may be the only open water around. In migration Lake Oahe hosts loons, grebes, and waterfowl, and Bald Eagles gather around the lakeshore and especially along the river below the dam. Viewpoints are easily accessed by taking S. Dak. 1804 or S. Dak. 1806 north from US 14 at Pierre. You'll find U.S. Army Corps of Engineers recreation areas on the Missouri below the dam, offering views of the east and west tailraces, and on the lakeshore above. Commonly occurring gulls include Franklin's, Bonaparte's, Ring-billed, California, and Herring, while Glaucous is regular, and rarities such as Thayer's Gull and Black-legged Kittiwake have appeared.

32 Greater Prairie-Chicken is fairly common in the prairie of **Fort Pierre National Grassland** south of Pierre. Staffers set up blinds each spring at "booming grounds" from which you can see males perform their courtship display. April and early May are the peak times for activity at the leks; call the national grassland office for information and reservations (see South Dakota Information, p. 232). If luck is with you, you might see this large grouse anytime of year by driving gravel roads through the grassland accessed by US 83. With lots of luck, you might find a wintering Gyrfalcon, as well—though Rough-legged Hawk is far more likely. Ferruginous Hawk nests on the grassland.

Coniferous forest and rocky outcrops in the Black Hills of western South Dakota

33 Encompassing the highest point in the United States east of the Rocky Mountains, South Dakota's **Black Hills** offer the traveler a chance at a number of high-country birds in forests of aspen, ponderosa pine, and spruce. One of the most popular birding routes in the region is the **Spearfish Canyon Scenic Byway** (US 14A) in **Black Hills National Forest,** which runs south from Spearfish 20 miles to Cheyenne Crossing. This superb drive is very popular with nonbirders, too; traffic will be lighter on an early morning visit.

Some of the species to look for as you start up the canyon in late spring and summer include Ruffed Grouse, White-throated Swift (common around cliffs), Lewis's Wood-pecker (scarce), Red-naped Sapsucker (in aspen and mixed woodland), Western Wood-Pewee, Dusky and Cordilleran Flycatchers, Pinyon Jay, Violet-green Swallow, Canyon Wren, Mountain Bluebird, Veery, MacGillivray's Warbler, Western Tanager, Black-headed Grosbeak, Lazuli Bunting, and Cassin's Finch. American Dipper can be seen along Spearfish Creek, but it's most likely found at Roughlock Falls, reached by turning west on Forest Road 222 at Savoy, about 15 miles up the canyon.

As you ascend through the spruce and pinewoods of the Black Hills, some of the possibilities include Northern Saw-whet Owl, Black-backed Woodpecker (scarce), Plumbeous Vireo, Gray Jay, Red-breasted Nuthatch, Brown Creeper, Golden-crowned and Ruby-crowned Kinglets, Townsend's Solitaire, Swainson's Thrush, Yellow-rumped Warbler, Dark-eyed Junco (the white-winged race), Red Crossbill, and Pine Siskin.

Stop and explore recreation areas along the scenic byway, as well as along Forest Road 222 west of Savoy, such as Timon Campground at 5,600 feet. If you continue past Cheyenne Crossing, you can turn south to **Hanna Campground** (5,600 feet), a productive spot for many high-elevation species. Three-toed Woodpecker is a possibility here; it's easiest to find in spring when males are "drumming." To reach **Black Fox Campground,** another favorite birding site, drive west from Cheyenne Crossing on US 85 for 13 miles to O'Neill Pass, turn southeast on Forest Road 231, and drive 11 miles.

One more note about the Black Hills region: A population of Virginia's Warbler nests in Boles, Roby, and Redbird Canyons in the southwestern part of the national forest, reached by taking Forest Road 117 north from US 16 at the Wyoming state line. The canyons are located along the first 10 miles from US 16, but continuing north will take you along a beautiful drive good for many Black Hills birds, far less traveled than Spearfish Canyon.

34 To the south of Wall, **Badlands National Park** is a place of striking and stark beauty, where weirdly eroded sedimentary rocks rise up from arid grassland. If you can take your eyes off the landscape (and occasional

Golden Eagle, a familiar, but still always exciting, raptor

pronghorn and bison), simply driving park roads might turn
up nesting species such as Northern Harrier, Swainson's and
Ferruginous Hawks, Golden Eagle, Prairie Falcon, Sharp-
tailed Grouse, Upland Sandpiper, Long-billed Curlew,
White-throated Swift, Loggerhead Shrike, Black-billed
Magpie, Mountain Bluebird, and Lark Bunting. Exploring
roadsides and trails, you could find Say's Phoebe, Bell's
Vireo, Rock Wren, and Lark and Grasshopper Sparrows.

For varied birding, take a walk along the trails near the
Ben Reifel Visitor Center at the eastern end of the park.
The **Cliff Shelf Nature Trail,** steep but only a half-mile
loop, traverses an oasislike area of vegetation, while the
longer **Castle Trail** passes through mixed-grass prairie and
badlands formations. Be sure to take the time to drive the
Sage Creek Rim Road in the western part of the park to
Roberts Prairie Dog Town, where you might find Burrowing Owls.

35 A fine assortment of waterbirds is the primary attraction at **Lacreek National Wildlife Refuge,** southeast of Martin *(from Martin, take S. Dak. 73 S 4 miles, then*

drive E following signs to the refuge). Lacreek lies within the Sandhills region, a rolling grass-covered duneland area, most of which is found in northwestern Nebraska. Extensive marshland brings in thousands of waterfowl to rest and feed in spring and fall, along with flocks of Sandhill Cranes. When water levels expose mudflats, Lacreek can be excellent for migrant shorebirds.

Trumpeter Swans, descendants of birds introduced in the 1960s, nest at the refuge, and many Trumpeters that breed elsewhere return to winter here. Other nesting species include Eared and Western Grebes, American White Pelican, Double-crested Cormorant, American Bittern, Black-crowned Night-Heron, American Avocet, Forster's and Black Terns, and Marsh Wren. Swamp Sparrow breeds here, atypically for this part of the state, and Yellow-headed Blackbird nests alongside Red-winged Blackbirds in marshes. Although Western Meadowlark nests in every county in South Dakota, this is the only part of the state where Eastern Meadowlark breeds. Bell's Vireo is common in shrubby thickets, and Ring-necked Pheasant, Sharp-tailed Grouse, Upland Sandpiper, Short-eared Owl, Loggerhead Shrike, and Bobolink are among the grassland nesters. Lacreek has two prairie dog towns where Burrowing Owl is seen frequently.

36 In the Coteau des Prairies in the southeastern part of the state, 6 miles south of Canton, **Newton Hills State Park** is home to several notable birds of eastern deciduous forest. Park at the Trail Camp area in the northern part of the park and walk the horse trail along Sargeant Creek, or take the **Woodland Trail** farther south, to look in spring or summer for American Woodcock, Whip-poor-will, Ruby-throated Hummingbird, Red-bellied Woodpecker, Yellow-bellied Sapsucker, Yellow-throated Vireo, Blue-gray Gnatcatcher (a rare specialty of the area), Wood Thrush, American Redstart, and Scarlet Tanager, among many other regular or occasional nesting species. Carolina Wren and Prothonotary and Kentucky Warblers, all at the northwestern edges of their ranges, have appeared, and the oak, basswood, and elm woodland here is very good for migrant songbirds in spring and fall.

NORTH DAKOTA

37 In spring and fall, birders in Fargo head to the Red River, where they look for migrants, especially eastern warblers, in the cottonwoods and other riparian vegetation along the floodplain. To reach **Oak Grove Park,** a favorite spot, take US 81 north from I-94 for 2.3 miles and turn east on Sixth Avenue North, which leads to the park. (At times in spring, high water on the Red River may limit access.) Explore trails along the river for migrant flycatchers, vireos, thrushes, and warblers. A bike path runs north for several miles along or near the river, passing oxbow lakes and scrubby areas offering diverse birding. The area across from El Zagal golf course is often quite productive.

38 **Sheyenne National Grassland** encompasses an expanse of tallgrass prairie in the southeastern corner of the state where Grasshopper Sparrows buzz and Bobolinks perform their song flights in spring and summer. The bird most sought here is Greater Prairie-Chicken, a grassland grouse known for the male's courtship "dance," performed on traditional display grounds called leks to the accompaniment of low "booming" calls. You can witness this thrilling spring performance by contacting the grassland office in Lisbon for information (see North Dakota Information, p. 233). To avoid disturbing the birds, you should be at the site before dawn and remain until the birds disperse, which may be several hours later. Quite often, males congregate at leks in late afternoon, though the exhibition is never as intense as at dawn.

The deciduous woodland along the Sheyenne River in the southeastern part of the state provides good birding for migrants and nesting species. To visit the **Mirror Pool Wildlife Management Area,** a fine example of this habitat, drive south from the junction of N. Dak. 18 and N. Dak. 46 near Leonard for 4 miles. Then drive west 4 miles and south 1 mile. A primitive road leads southeast across a pasture to the area, but in wet weather it may be impassable and you'll have to walk in. Look here for nesting Wood Duck, American Woodcock, Pileated Woodpecker, Yellow-throated Vireo, Scarlet Tanager, Rose-breasted Grosbeak, and Baltimore Oriole. Such uncommon to rare species as Barred Owl, Whip-poor-will, Red-bellied Woodpecker, and Yellow-billed Cuckoo are sometimes found in the Sheyenne River woodland as well.

Bobolink

Each fall, Bobolinks that nest in grasslands across the northern U.S. and Canada gather in flocks and fly thousands of miles to winter in similar habitat in the pampas and rice fields of southern South America. The male Bobolink is known for its "backwards" plumage—with the atypical pattern of lighter colors above and dark below—but by autumn it has molted to brown, buff, and yellow tones that match the female's. The Bobolink's penchant for feeding in rice fields led to its folk name of ricebird.

39 Open water and extensive cattail marshes attract a varied list of waterbirds to **Long Lake National Wildlife Refuge Complex** (*from the Sterling exit on I-94, drive S 13 miles on US 83; just S of Moffit, turn E to reach the headquarters*). Along the entrance road you'll pass through marshland where American Bittern, several species of ducks, Virginia Rail, Sora, Sedge Wren, Common Yellowthroat, and Red-winged and Yellow-headed Blackbirds nest. At a junction, turn north to cross a dike where you can scan the lake. Nesting birds on the refuge include Eared, Western, and Clark's Grebes; White-faced Ibis (numbers vary depending on water level); Willet; Marbled Godwit; American Avocet; Wilson's Phalarope; Franklin's Gull; and Common and Black Terns. Piping Plover breeds here, as well, though lake levels affect its occurrence, and American White Pelican is common from spring through fall. You'll find excellent marsh birding along an old road, sometimes drivable and sometimes only walkable, that leads east from a stone house located a short distance southeast of the dike road.

Ask at the office about visiting leks of Sharp-tailed Grouse in spring; several dancing grounds are located in the area, and personnel will know the best areas for viewing. Away from the water, look for nesting Northern Harrier,

Little Missouri Overlook, in Theodore Roosevelt National Park, western North Dakota

Western and Eastern Kingbirds, Lark Bunting, Clay-colored and Nelson's Sharp-tailed (scarce) Sparrows, and Chestnut-collared Longspur. In migration, numbers of waterfowl and Sandhill Cranes stop at Long Lake. In fall, crane flocks can total 20,000, and Whooping Cranes are rare visitors on their way to and from Canada and Texas. In late summer, shorebirds congregate along the shoreline.

40 **Garrison Dam,** which impounds the Missouri River to create sprawling Lake Sakakawea, attracts great numbers of gulls to its tailrace waters. To reach the area, drive west from US 83 on N. Dak. 200 through Riverdale; cross the dam, and on the west side turn south (the road will be the first one past the road that leads back east along the face of the dam). In 0.7 mile, turn east, downhill toward the power station. Double-crested Cormorant, ducks, terns, and other waterbirds are present seasonally, but it's the chance for an uncommon or rare gull that brings birders here; the best time is October through December.

Return to N. Dak. 200, turn east, and immediately turn

south on the road that leads below the dam to the **Garrison Dam National Fish Hatchery.** Just south of the hatchery ponds, a trail leads along the old channel of the Missouri River through a marshy nature area worth checking for migrants. Bald Eagle nests in this area and is seen often, and Northern Goshawk has been seen in fall and winter with some regularity. Wood Duck, Belted Kingfisher, Red-headed Woodpecker, Yellow Warbler, and Yellow-breasted Chat are just a few of the nesting birds here.

41 Several special species nest in the **Big Gumbo** area, a sagebrush prairie landscape in the southwestern corner of North Dakota. At Marmarth, 0.7 mile west of the Little Missouri River, turn south from US 12 onto Camp Crook Road, which parallels the river for 30 miles to South Dakota. Bird along this route or on side roads, watching for Ferruginous Hawk, Golden Eagle, Sage Grouse, Long-billed Curlew, Loggerhead Shrike, Horned Lark, Brewer's Sparrow, Lark Bunting, and Chestnut-collared Longspur. A few McCown's might be found among the Chestnut-collareds just north of the South Dakota state line, and Sage Thrasher has been seen in summer, though it's rare.

42 The Little Missouri River winds through both of the main units of **Theodore Roosevelt National Park,** set in the badlands of western North Dakota and named for the president who was a pioneering conservationist and an enthusiastic bird-watcher. The park's South Unit stretches along I-94 near Medora, while the North Unit is located on US 85 about 50 miles north. Species such as Warbling and Red-eyed Vireos, White-breasted Nuthatch, American Redstart, Yellow-breasted Chat, Spotted Towhee, Black-headed Grosbeak, Lazuli Bunting, and Bullock's Oriole nest in the riparian zone along the river, at spots such as Cottonwood Campground in the South Unit and Juniper Campground in the North Unit.

As you drive park roads past eroded buttes and bluffs, through arid terrain and grassland, watch for Turkey Vulture; Swainson's and Ferruginous (rare) Hawks; Golden Eagle; Prairie Falcon; Sharp-tailed Grouse; Say's Phoebe (nests on rock ledges); Black-billed Magpie; Rock Wren

Marsh vegetation at Dead Dog Slough, in Lostwood National Wildlife Refuge

(on bluffs); Mountain Bluebird; and Clay-colored, Field, Vesper, and Lark Sparrows; and Bobolink. Brewer's Sparrow is found occasionally. Look for Burrowing Owl in the park's several prairie dog towns from spring through fall, and listen for an occasional Common Poorwill on spring and summer evenings—this species is at the eastern edge of its range and irregular here.

43 Many birders have been made very happy by a visit to **Lostwood National Wildlife Refuge,** on N. Dak. 8 some 20 miles north of Stanley. This is one of the best places anywhere to find Sprague's Pipit and Baird's Sparrow, two scarce, declining, and sought-after species of Great Plains grassland. The refuge manages part of its rolling prairie for these two little birds, and both are quite common here in late spring and summer. As you search the grassland for these target species, you'll likely come across Northern Harrier; Sharp-tailed Grouse (abundant here; the refuge offers a blind for viewing a courtship lek); Upland Sandpiper; Marbled Godwit; Clay-colored, Vesper, Savannah, Grasshopper, and Song Sparrows; and Bobolink. With more effort, or a little luck, you could find Le Conte's or Nelson's Sharp-tailed Sparrows, the latter in vegetation on the edges of sloughs.

Lostwood lies in the "prairie pothole" region of the upper

plains, which at times seems to resemble a drive-through aviary where every dip in the terrain is filled with a small pond hosting nesting ducks and other marsh birds. Look in Lostwood wetlands for breeding Horned and Eared Grebes, American Bittern (scarce), a long list of ducks, Virginia Rail, Sora, Piping Plover (on the shore of alkaline lakes, such as Upper Lostwood), American Avocet, Willet, Wilson's Phalarope, Black Tern, Sedge (uncommon) and Marsh Wrens, and Yellow-headed Blackbird. Other breeders include Long-eared and Short-eared Owls (both irregular in occurrence), Willow and Least Flycatchers (check aspen groves), Warbling Vireo (also in aspen), Black-billed Magpie, and Baltimore Oriole (Bullock's is rarely seen). Migrant waterfowl and shorebirds are abundant, as are great numbers of migrant Sandhill Cranes, peaking in early April and from late September to mid-October. All in all, Lostwood ought to rank near the top of regional birding destinations.

44 With headquarters off N. Dak. 14 just north of Upham, **J. Clark Salyer National Wildlife Refuge** hosts many of the same species noted for Lostwood, including an impressive list of breeding waterbirds on its marshy impoundments. A 22-mile auto tour route allows exploration of wetlands, riparian vegetation along the Souris River, and prairie. On the 5-mile **Grassland Trail,** you can find Sharp-tailed Grouse (lek viewing is offered at the refuge), several species of sparrows including Baird's and Le Conte's, and Chestnut-collared Longspur. Long-eared Owl has nested near the headquarters. Ruffed Grouse nests at Salyer, near the edge of its range in the state. In fall there can be more than 500,000 waterfowl here, with more than half that number Snow Geese. Like Lostwood, Salyer has flocks of migrant Sandhill Cranes in spring and fall. The refuge has established a 13-mile canoe trail along the Souris River, offering the chance to see waterbirds and riparian species from a different viewpoint.

Prairie Potholes

Scattered across the northern plains, thousands of marshy depressions called "prairie potholes" distinguish one of the most productive, yet abused, ecosystems in North America. These glacier-formed wetlands host a range of animals from insects to mammals, but they're most famous as home to a significant proportion of the continent's duck population. Mallard, Northern Pintail, Blue-winged Teal, Northern Shoveler, and Gadwall are just a few of the species that return to the prairies each spring to raise new broods. Often small and shallow, potholes are easily filled for cropland or other development. The cumulative loss of vast numbers of ponds has led to declines in waterfowl populations, but in recent years conservationists have increased efforts to preserve this important habitat. Lostwood National Wildlife Refuge in North Dakota is an excellent place to experience the wildlife of the pothole region.

45 To visit **Wakopa Wildlife Management Area,** drive north from Dunseith 9 miles on US 281, turn east on County Road 43, and drive 9 miles to a road that leads north into the area. The aspen, birch, oak, and elm woodland here in the Turtle Mountains is known for diverse nesting birds. As you drive the roads here or walk some of the extensive trail system, look for Broad-winged Hawk, Ruffed Grouse, Ruby-throated Hummingbird, Least and Great Crested Flycatchers, Yellow-throated and Warbling Vireos, Mountain Bluebird (uncommon), Veery, Gray Catbird, Cedar Waxwing, Chestnut-sided and Mourning Warblers, American Redstart, Ovenbird, Northern Waterthrush, Rose-breasted Grosbeak, and Baltimore Oriole. White-throated Sparrow, a species with a very restricted range in the state, might be found here; it's a regular breeder at the nearby **International Peace Garden** *(701-263-4390),* on US 281 at the Canadian border.

46 The region around **Devil's Lake,** North Dakota's largest natural lake, makes a fine birding destination, though changing water levels affect the area's potential. High water has covered areas that once were expansive and attractive mudflats; still, Devil's Lake is one of the best areas in the state for waders and shorebirds. Great, Snowy, and Cattle Egrets and Black-crowned Night-Heron breed, and the rare Little Blue Heron may nest. Red-necked, Eared, Western, and possibly Clark's Grebes breed, and in 1998 a pair of Bald Eagles nested here—the first successful nest in

the state away from the Missouri River in decades.

Bends of the Souris River at J. Clark Salyer National Wildlife Refuge, north of Upham

From the town of Devil's Lake, drive west on N. Dak. 19 and in 9 miles turn south to **Grahams Island State Park,** which can be good for songbirds in migration and offers lake viewing for waterbirds. Four miles south of N. Dak. 19 (before you reach the park), turn west on a road that dead-ends at the lake. Here you can look for waders, waterfowl, shorebirds, gulls, and terns. The other side of this bay can be reached by driving east from US 281 at Minnewaukan.

On the south side of Devil's Lake, **Sullys Hill National Game Preserve** has more waterbird viewing at Sweetwater Lake, and the hardwood forest on the glacial-moraine hills is home to a good variety of nesting birds, including Broad-winged Hawk (Red-shouldered has been seen here),

A pair of Red-necked Grebes, an uncommon breeding bird in the contiguous United States

Ruby-throated Hummingbird, Yellow-throated and War-bling Vireos, Black-and-white Warbler, American Red-start, Northern Waterthrush, Eastern Towhee, and Baltimore Oriole. To reach the preserve, drive south from Devil's Lake 13 miles to Fort Totten and turn east.

47 Eastern deciduous birds highlight a nesting-season visit to **Icelandic State Park,** 6 miles west of Cava-lier on N. Dak. 5. Within the park, the 200-acre **Gunlog-son Nature Preserve** on the Tongue River is a favorite. Look here for Ruffed Grouse, Wild Turkey, American Woodcock, Black-billed Cuckoo, Barred Owl (occasional), Ruby-throated Hummingbird, Pileated Woodpecker, Yellow-throated Vireo, Veery, Black-and-white and Mourn-ing Warblers, American Redstart, Northern Waterthrush, Scarlet Tanager, and Rose-breasted Grosbeak. This is an excellent spot for migrant songbirds in spring and fall, and it's one of the places birders hope to find Gray Jay and Northern Hawk Owl in winter, though these species are rare finds in the state.

The Plains
Information

? Visitor Center/Information   **$** Fee Charged   **¶** Food

⑪ Rest Rooms   **↟** Nature Trails   **⊑** Driving Tours   **♿** Wheelchair Accessible

Be advised that facilities may be seasonal and limited. We suggest calling or writing ahead for specific information. Note that addresses may be for administrative offices; see text or call for directions to sites.

Rare Bird Alerts

Oklahoma:
Statewide *918-669-6646*

Kansas:
Statewide *316-229-2777*
Kansas City *913-342-2473*
Wichita *316-681-2266*

Nebraska:
Statewide *402-292-5325*

South Dakota:
Statewide *605-773-6460*

North Dakota:
Statewide *701-250-4481*

OKLAHOMA

Little River National Wildlife Refuge
(Page 191)
P.O. Box 340
Broken Bow, OK 74728
580-584-6211

⊑

Beavers Bend Resort Park *(Page 192)*
P.O. Box 10
Broken Bow, OK 74728
580-494-6300

? ¶ ⑪ ↟

Sequoyah National Wildlife Refuge
(Page 192)
Route 1, Box 18A
Vian, OK 74962
918-773-5251

⑪ ↟ ⊑ ♿

Oxley Nature Center
(Page 193)
5701 East 36 Street North
Tulsa, OK 74115
918-669-6644

? ⑪ ↟ ♿

Wichita Mountains National Wildlife Refuge *(Page 195)*
Rural Route 1, Box 448
Indiahoma, OK 73552
580-429-3222

? ⑪ ↟ ⊑ ♿

Hackberry Flat Wildlife Management Area
(Page 196)
HC 32, Box 580
Lawton, OK 73501
580-335-5262

Salt Plains National Wildlife Refuge
(Page 197)
Rural Route 1, Box 76
Jet, OK 73749
580-626-4794

? ⑪ ↟ ⊑ ♿

Great Salt Plains State Park *(Page 198)*
Rural Route 1, Box 52
Mountain Park, OK 73559
580-569-2032

? ⑪ ↟

Black Mesa State Park
(Page 198)
HCR-1, Box 8
Kenton, OK 73946
580-426-2222

? ¶ ⑪ ↟ ⊑ ♿

Black Mesa Preserve
(Page 199)
The Nature Conservancy
23 West 4th Street
Tulsa, OK 74103
918-585-1117

↟

KANSAS

Perry Lake *(Page 200)*
U.S. Army Corps of
Engineers
10419 Perry Park Drive
Perry, KS 66073
785-597-5144

? ¶ ⑪ ↟ ♿

Marais des Cygnes Wildlife Area *(Page 201)*
Route 2, Box 186A
Pleasanton, KS 66075
913-352-8941

Contact also for La Cygne Lake and Wildlife Area

Quivira National Wildlife Refuge *(Page 203)*
Rural Route 3, Box 48A
Stafford, KS 67578
316-486-2393

❓ 🚹 🚶 ⇌ ♿

Open June–Oct.

Wilson State Park
(Page 205)
Rural Route 1, Box 181
Sylvan Grove, KS 67481
785-658-2465

❓ 💲 🚹 🚶 ♿

Lake Scott State Park
(Page 205)
520 West Scott Lake Drive
Scott City, KS 67871
316-872-2061

💲 🍴 🚹 🚶 ♿

Cimarron National Grassland *(Page 206)*
P.O. Box J
Elkhart, KS 67950
316-697-4621

❓ 🚹 🚶 ⇌ ♿

NEBRASKA

Indian Cave State Park
(Page 208)
Route 1, Box 30
Shubert, NE 68437
402-883-2575

💲 🚹 🚶 ⇌ ♿

Fontenelle Forest Nature Center *(Page 208)*
1111 North Belleview Blvd.
Belleview, NE 68005
402-731-3140

❓ 💲 🚹 🚶 ♿

Branched Oak Lake State Recreation Area
(Page 209)
Route 2, Box 61
Raymond, NE 68428
402-783-3400

💲 🍴 🚹 🚶 ♿

Burchard Lake State Wildlife Management Area *(Page 209)*
P.O. Box 30370
Lincoln, NE 68503
402-335-2534

Lillian Annette Rowe Sanctuary *(Page 210)*
44450 Elm Island Road
Gibbon, NE 68840
308-468-5282

❓ 🚹 🚶 ⇌ ♿

Crane Meadows Nature Center *(Page 210)*
9325 South Alda Road
Wood River, NE 68883
308-382-1820

❓ 💲 🚹 🚶 ♿

Fort Kearny State Historical Park *(Page 211)*
1020 V Road
Kearney, NE 68847
308-865-5305

❓ 💲 🚹 🚶 ⇌ ♿

Rainwater Basin
(Page 211)
Nebraska Game and Parks
1617 First Avenue
Kearney, NE 68847
308-865-5310

🚶 ⇌ ♿

Lakes McConaughy and Ogallala State Recreation Areas
(Page 212)
1500 Nebr. 61 North
Ogallala, NE 69153
308-284-3542

❓ 🚹 🚶 ⇌ ♿

Oliver State Recreation Area *(Page 213)*
P.O. Box 65
Gering, NE 69341
308-436-2383

💲 🚹

Gilbert Baker Wildlife Management Area
(Page 212)
471 Squaw Creek Road
Crawford, NE 69339
308-665-2924

🚹

Chadron State Park
(Page 214)
15951 Highway 385
Chadron, NE 69337
308-432-6167

💲 🍴 🚹 🚶 ⇌ ♿

SOUTH DAKOTA

Sica Hollow State Park
(Page 215)
11545 Northside Drive
Lake City, SD 57247
605-448-5701

💲 🚹 🚶 ♿

Hartford Beach State Park *(Page 215)*
Rural Route 1, Box 50
Corona, SD 57227
605-432-6374

💲 🍴 🚹 🚶 ♿

Waubay National Wildlife Refuge
(Page 215)
Rural Route 1, Box 39
Waubay, SD 57273
605-947-4521

❓ 🚹 🚶 ♿

Sand Lake National Wildlife Refuge
(Page 216)
39650 Sand Lake Drive
Columbia, SD 57433
605-885-6320

Oahe Dam *(Page 217)*
U.S. Army Corps of
   Engineers
28563 Powerhouse Road
Pierre, SD 57501
605-224-5862

Fort Pierre National Grassland *(Page 217)*
P.O. Box 417
Pierre, SD 57501
605-224-5517

Black Hills National Forest *(Page 218)*
Rural Route 2, Box 200
Custer, SD 57730
605-673-2251

Badlands National Park *(Page 219)*
P.O. Box 6
Interior, SD 57750
605-433-5361

Lacreek National Wildlife Refuge
(Page 220)
HC 5, Box 114
Martin, SD 57551
605-685-6508

Newton Hills State Park *(Page 221)*
28771 482nd Avenue
Canton, SD 57013
605-987-2263

NORTH DAKOTA

Oak Grove Park
(Page 222)
Fargo Park District
701 Main Avenue
Fargo, ND 58103
701-241-1350

Sheyenne National Grassland *(Page 222)*
P.O. Box 946
Lisbon, ND 58054
701-683-4342

Mirror Pool Wildlife Management Area
(Page 222)
North Dakota Game and
   Fish Department
3320 East Lakeside Road
Jamestown, ND 58401
701-252-4634

Long Lake National Wildlife Refuge Complex *(Page 223)*
12000 353 Street SE
Moffit, ND 58560
701-387-4397

Garrison Dam National Fish Hatchery *(Page 225)*
P.O. Box 530
Riverdale, ND 58565
701-654-7451

Theodore Roosevelt National Park *(Page 225)*
P.O. Box 7
Medora, ND 58645
701-623-4466

Lostwood National Wildlife Refuge
(Page 226)
8315 N. Dak. 8
Kenmare, ND 58746
701-848-2722

Auto tour route open May-Sept.

J. Clark Salyer National Wildlife Refuge *(Page 227)*
P.O. Box 66
Upham, ND 58789
701-768-2548

Wakopa Wildlife Management Area
(Page 228)
7928 45th Street NE
Devils Lake, ND 58301
701-662-3617

Grahams Island State Park *(Page 229)*
152 South Duncan Road
Devils Lake, ND 58301
701-766-4015

Sullys Hill National Game Preserve
(Page 229)
P.O. Box 908
Devils Lake, ND 58301
701-766-4272

Icelandic State Park
(Page 230)
13571 S. Dak. 5
Cavalier, ND 58220
701-265-4561

Regional Birding Guides

Great Birding Trips of the West, Joan Easton Lentz (Capra Press, 1989). Eight chapters, each devoted to a birding route from the Colorado Rockies to the California coast.

Northwest

A Guide to Bird Finding in Washington, Terence R. Wahl and Dennis R. Paulson (T.R. Wahl, 1991). Birding sites in nine regions covering the entire state.

The Birder's Guide to Oregon, Joseph E. Evanich, Jr. (Portland Audubon Society, 1990). Descriptions of birding sites in eight Oregon regions.

A Birder's Guide to Idaho, Dan Svingen and Kas Dumroese (eds.) (American Birding Association, 1997). Descriptions of more than 110 sites around the state.

The Birder's Guide to Montana, Terry McEneaney (Falcon Press, 1993). Coverage of 45 major sites in Montana.

Central Rockies

A Birder's Guide to Wyoming, Oliver K. Scott (American Birding Association, 1993). Nineteen chapters encompassing sites around the state.

Birds of Yellowstone, Terry McEneaney (Rinehart, 1988). Where to find the birds of Yellowstone National Park.

Finding the Birds of Jackson Hole, Bert Raynes and Darwin Wile (Darwin Wile, 1994). Birds of the Jackson Hole area, including Grand Teton National Park.

A Birder's Guide to Colorado, Harold R. Holt (American Birding Association, 1997). Loop drives and sites covering the entire state.

Birding Utah, D. E. McIvor (Falcon Press, 1998). Covers 112 sites in Utah.

California

A Birding Northern California, Jean Richmond (Mt. Diablo Audubon Society, 1985). Covers 72 sites, most within 100 miles of San Francisco Bay.

Birder's Guide to Northern California, LoLo and Jim Westrich (Gulf Publishing, 1991). Covers sites from the Oregon border south to Yosemite and Monterey Bay.

San Francisco Peninsula Birdwatching, Cliff Richer (ed.) (Sequoia Audubon Society, 1996). Sites on the peninsula and south through San Mateo County.

A Birder's Guide to Southern California, Brad Schram (American Birding Association, 1998). A very detailed guide to sites from Morro Bay and Death Valley southward.

Southwest

A Birder's Guide to Southeastern Arizona, Richard Cachor Taylor (American Birding Association, 1995). Detailed descriptions of destinations in this very popular region.

Birds in Southeastern Arizona, William A. Davis and S.M. Russell (Tucson Audubon Society, 1995). More than 90 sites listed by geographic area.

New Mexico Bird Finding Guide, Dale A. Zimmerman *et al.* (eds.) (New Mexico Ornithological Society, 1997). Covers sites around the state, divided into nine regions.

Birding Texas, Roland H. Wauer and Mark A. Elwonger (Falcon Press, 1998). Covers the entire state in 120 sites in ten regions.

A Birder's Guide to Texas, Edward A. Kutac (Gulf Publishing, 1989). More than 150 sites across Texas.

A Birder's Guide to the Rio Grande Valley, Mark Lockwood *et al.* (American Birding Association, 1999). From New Mexico to the Gulf of Mexico, including Big Bend National Park.

The Plains

A Guide to Bird Finding in Kansas and Western Missouri, John L. Zimmerman and Sebastian T. Patti (University Press of Kansas, 1988). Covers all of Kansas, plus Missouri east to Sedalia and Springfield.

Hawaii and Alaska

Enjoying Birds in Hawaii, H. Douglas Pratt (Mutual Publishing, 1993). Details about birding sites as well as travel information.

A Bird Finding Guide to Alaska, Nick Lethaby (Nick Lethaby, 1994). Information on 23 sites, with suggestions on finding specialties.

Index

Illustrations are *italic*
Maps are **boldface**
Due to limited space, birds
  indexed only to indicate
  descriptive text

Illustrations Credits

All the bird paintings are from the *National Geographic Society Field Guide to the Birds of North America, Third Edition* © 1999, reprinted with permission of the National Geographic Society.

Cover, Phillip Singer; 1, Norm Smith; 2-3, Bruce H. Morrison; 4, Bates Littlehales/NGS Image Collection; 4-5, Chris Johns, National Geographic Photographer; 8, David Weintraub; 10-11, Lee Rentz; 12, Steve Howe/Third Planet.

Northwest
14-15, Michael Quinton/NGS Image Collection; 20, Terry Donnelly; 22, Charles Gurche; 23, Lee Rentz; 24, Fredrick Sears; 26-27, Richard Cummins; 29, Rob Curtis/The Early Birder; 31, Steven Holt/Aigrette Photography; 33, Tim Thompson; 34-35, Rick Poley; 36, Bruce Jackson/Jon Gnass Photo Images; 39, Tim Thompson; 40, Steven Holt/Aigrette Photography; 42-43, William H. Mullins; 45, William H. Mullins; 46, William H. Mullins; 48, Cliff Beittel; 50-51, Michael Quinton/NGS Image Collection; 52, Chuck Haney; 53, Cliff Beittel; 56, Michael Wilhelm.

Central Rockies
60-61, Jeff Vanuga; 66, Jon Gnass/Jon Gnass Photo Images; 67, T.J. Ulrich/ VIREO; 68-69, Ren Navez; 70, Cliff Beittel; 72, John Elk III; 75, Stephen & Michele Vaughan; 78, Cathy & Gordon Illg; 79, Willard Clay; 80, Cathy & Gordon Illg; 83, Steve Price; 84-85, Michael Neubauer/ColePhoto; 86, Stephen & Michele Vaughan; 88, Wendy Shattil/Bob Rozinski; 89, Cathy & Gordon Illg; 91, John P. George; 92, Scott T. Smith; 93, Joe McDonald/Bruce Coleman, Inc. 95, John P. George; 96, Lance Beeny; 99, Maxine Cass; 100, Laurence Parent; 103, Scott T. Smith.

California
108-109, Richard Cummins; 110, Phillip C. Roullard; 115, George Wuerthner; 116, John & Karen Hollingsworth; 119, Chuck Mitchell; 120, Michael Sewell/Visual Pursuit; 121, John Elk III; 123, Bob Miller; 124, David Koeppel; 125, Phil Schermeister; 126-127, Chuck Place; 129, Sylvain Grandadam/Tony Stone Images; 132-133, Marc Solomon; 134, Jeff Mondragon; 135, George H.H. Huey; 137, David Koeppel; 138, Ellie Tyler; 141, Ronald G. Warfield; 142, Richard Herrmann.

Southwest
148-149, Cliff Beittel; 155, Laurence Parent; 156, Willard Clay; 157, Scott T. Smith; 159, Willard Clay; 160, Paula Borchardt; 162-163, George H.H. Huey; 165, Steven Holt/Aigrette Photography; 166, Laurence Parent;169, Michael Frye; 170, John Sawyer/Index Stock Photography; 173, Michael Nichols, National Geographic Photographer; 175, John & Susan Drew; 176, David J. Sams/Tony Stone Images; 178, Laurence Parent; 181, Mark W. Lockwood; 182, Michael Neubauer/ColePhoto.

The Plains
186-187, Tom & Pat Leeson; 188, Cliff Beittel; 192, John Elk III; 195, Frank Moster; 196, John & Karen Hollingsworth; 198-199, Laurence Parent; 201, Cliff Beittel; 202, Herbert L. Stormont/Unicorn Stock Photos; 205, Cliff Beittel; 206-207, Andre Jenny/Unicorn Stock Photos; 210-211, Scott T. Smith; 214, Cliff Beittel; 218, Laurence Parent; 219, William Bernard; 220, Michael Frye; 224, John Elk III; 226-227, Paul Rezendes; 229, James P. Blair/NGS Image Collection; 230, Bates Littlehales/NGS Image Collection.

Credits

Copyright © 1999 National Geographic Society

Published by
THE NATIONAL GEOGRAPHIC SOCIETY

John M. Fahey, Jr.
President and Chief Executive Officer

Gilbert M. Grosvenor
Chairman of the Board

Nina D. Hoffman
Senior Vice President

William R. Gray
Vice President and Director, Book Division

David Griffin
Design Director

Elizabeth L. Newhouse
Director of Travel Publishing

Barbara A. Noe
Assistant Editor

Caroline Hickey
Senior Researcher

Carl Mehler
Director of Maps

Staff for this Book

Mary Luders
Project Editor

Joan Wolbier
Art Director

Marilyn Mofford Gibbons
Illustrations Editor

Paul Lehman
Chief Consultant

Paulette L. Claus
Lise Sajewski
Editorial Consultants

Jenifer Blakemore,
Deavours Hall, Karen Ivory
Editorial Researchers

Jenifer Blakemore
Indexer

Keith R. Moore,
Sven M. Dolling, Thomas
L. Gray, Michelle H. Picard,
Gregory Ugiansky
Map Research and Production

Meredith C. Wilcox
Illustrations Assistant

Richard S. Wain
Production Project Manager

About the Author

Mel White's earliest birding memory is of a Western Tanager he saw on a family vacation to Arizona when he was six years old. Four decades later, he still recalls this meeting of boy and bird when he considers the pleasures of travel—the delight in the new, whether expected or un-, and the transforming moment when a vision that existed only in the imagination is replaced by the real thing in binoculars.

An Arkansas native and a former newspaper reporter and magazine editor, Mel White is now a freelance writer specializing in travel and nature. A contributing editor for *National Geographic Traveler*, he writes frequently for other National Geographic Society publications and is author of the American Birding Association's *A Birder's Guide to Arkansas* and a volume of the *Smithsonian Guides to Natural America* series. His assignments have taken him from New Zealand to Amazonia to the Swiss Alps—and he usually manages to find time for birdwatching no matter where he goes.

Composition for this book by the National Geographic Society Book Division. Printed and bound by R.R. Donnelley & Sons, Willard, Ohio. Color separations by North American Color, Portage, MI. Covers printed by Miken Inc., Cheektowaga, New York.

Library of Congress Cataloging-in-Publication Data

White Mel, 1950-
 National Geographic guide to birdwatching site. Western U.S. / by Mel White.
  p.   cm.
 Includes index.
 ISBN 0-7922-7450-4 (alk. paper)
 1. Bird watching—West (U.S.)—Guidebooks.   2. Birding sites—West (U.S.)—Guidebooks.   3. West (U.S.)—Guidebooks.   I. Title
II. Title: Birdwatching sites.
 QL683.W43W48 1999
 598'.07'23478—dc21   99-13552
                                                        CIP